# LATE NIGHT WITH TRUMP

Political humor has been a staple of late-night television for decades. The Trump White House, however, has received significantly greater attention than that of past presidents, such as Barack Obama, George W. Bush, and even Bill Clinton. In response to Trump's strident politics, late-night comics, including Stephen Colbert, Jimmy Kimmel, Trevor Noah and Jimmy Fallon, have sounded key policy notes, further blurring the boundary between news and satire. Weekly humorists, including John Oliver and Samantha Bee, extend the critique with in-depth probing of key issues, while *Saturday Night Live* continues to tap the progression from outrage to outrageousness.

Using unique content analysis techniques and qualitative discussions of political humor, Farnsworth and Lichter show how late-night political humor, and these seven programs in particular, have responded to the Trump presidency. Employing a dataset of more than 100,000 late night jokes going back decades, these noted media scholars discuss how the treatment of Trump differs from previous presidents, and how the Trump era is likely to shape the future of political humor. The authors also employ public opinion survey data to consider the growing role these late-night programs play in framing public opinion and priorities. This book will interest scholars, the curious public, and students of politics, communications and the media, and contemporary American culture.

**Stephen J. Farnsworth** is Professor of Political Science and International Affairs and Director of the Center for Leadership and Media Studies at the University of Mary Washington. He holds a PhD in Government from Georgetown and is the author or co-author of seven books on the presidency and the mass media, as well as dozens of articles on US and Virginia politics. He is a recipient of the State Council of Higher Education for Virginia's Outstanding Faculty Award and has served as a Canada–US Fulbright Research Chair at McGill University in Montreal and as a Fulbright Specialist at Methodist College in Kuala Lumpur, Malaysia.

**S. Robert Lichter** is Professor of Communication at George Mason University, where he directs the Center for Media and Public Affairs. He has authored or co-authored over a dozen books and numerous scholarly and popular articles and monographs on the media and politics. He holds a PhD in Government from Harvard and has served on the faculties of Yale, Columbia, Princeton, Georgetown and George Washington University. His most recent book is *Politics Is a Joke! How Comedians Are Remaking Political Life* (with Jody Baumgartner and Jonathon Morris).

This is a serious book about political humor—but it's also guaranteed to give you some hearty laughs. Steve Farnsworth and Bob Lichter have produced a thoroughly researched look at late-night comedy. We've come a long way since the gentle jokes of Johnny Carson. For good or ill, contemporary TV comics have a sharp, outsized role in shaping public perceptions of candidates and officeholders. This astute volume will have readers in stitches as they recall jokes and skits surrounding the 2016 election, and it is also an excellent primer as we head into 2020.

**Larry J. Sabato**, *University of Virginia*

Based on a massive content analysis of thousands of late-night political jokes from the past seven Presidential election cycles, Farnsworth and Lichter offer the most sweeping assessment of the evolution of late-night political humor that the field has seen to date. With national public opinion data alongside observations about the changing tone of late-night comedy under the Trump Presidency, *Late Night with Trump: Political Humor and the American Presidency* is an essential addition to the libraries of scholars and students of political communication and entertainment.

**Dannagal G. Young**, *University of Delaware*

There is little doubt that late-night television programming plays an important role in US politics, both as an opportunity for publicity for politicians, and as a source of humor and commentary about current politics. Drawing on an impressive body of data on the content of major late-night programs, Farnsworth and Lichter offer an important and fascinating account of the history, functions and impact of this television genre, with a focus on the recent Trump-fuelled peak in late-night political humor.

**Stuart Soroka**, *University of Michigan*

Late night humorists have become prominent political actors. In this timely and comprehensive work, Farnsworth and Lichter document how comics have emerged as a "second front" in the contentious relationship between politicians and the press and have exacerbated the culture of public ridicule. They demonstrate how changing news norms have facilitated the rise of political comedy and provide rich historical context that sets the stage for understanding late night humor focused on Donald Trump. The rich empirical analysis of both the content of late night comedy and its effects on the public adds rigor to the study and brings fresh insights to research in this field.

**Diana Owen**, *Georgetown University*

*Late Night with Trump* is a must-read. It's unmatched in its evidence and analysis and for what it reveals about Trump, our politics, and the blurred line between news and political humor. Farnsworth and Lichter have long been known for their rigorous and imaginative content analysis, and this book adds mightily to their richly deserved reputation.

**Thomas E. Patterson**, *Harvard University*

# LATE NIGHT WITH TRUMP

## Political Humor and the American Presidency

*Stephen J. Farnsworth and S. Robert Lichter*

NEW YORK AND LONDON

First published 2020
by Routledge
52 Vanderbilt Avenue, New York, NY 10017

and by Routledge
2 Park Square, Milton Park, Abingdon, Oxon OX14 4RN

*Routledge is an imprint of the Taylor & Francis Group, an informa business*



*Library of Congress Cataloging-in-Publication Data*
Names: Farnsworth, Stephen J., 1961- author. | Lichter, S. Robert, author.
Title: Late night with Trump : political humor and the American presidency / Stephen J. Farnsworth, S. Robert Lichter.
Description: New York : Routledge, 2019. | Includes bibliographical references and index.
Identifiers: LCCN 2019033142 (print) | LCCN 2019033143 (ebook) | ISBN 9781138370647 (hardback) | ISBN 9781138370654 (paperback) | ISBN 9780429427916 (ebook)
Subjects: LCSH: Television talk shows–Political aspects–United States. | Television comedies–United States–History and criticism. | Trump, Donald, 1946—Humor. | Presidents–United States–Humor. | Political satire, American–History and criticism. | United States–Politics and government–2017—Humor. | Television and politics–United States.
Classification: LCC PN1992.6 .F25 2019 (print) | LCC PN1992.6 (ebook) | DDC 302.23/45–dc23
LC record available at https://lccn.loc.gov/2019033142
LC ebook record available at https://lccn.loc.gov/2019033143

ISBN: 978-1-138-37064-7 (hbk)
ISBN: 978-1-138-37065-4 (pbk)
ISBN: 978-0-429-42791-6 (ebk)

Typeset in Bembo
by Taylor & Francis Books

SJF: This book is dedicated to all the Tanyas in my family.
SRL: This book is dedicated to all the Patricias in my family.

# CONTENTS

# ILLUSTRATIONS

## Tables

## Boxes

# ACKNOWLEDGMENTS

This project is the result of support generously offered from many sources. The first debt is to those who have made their surveys available to scholars, including the public opinion and news consumption surveys produced by the Pew Research Center. We are also very grateful for our previous research collaborations and many political conversations with Diana Owen, Stuart Soroka, Sergei A. Samoilenko, Jim Lengle, Roland Schatz and Jody Baumgartner. These scholars have done much to shape our thoughts about presidential portrayals in news and entertainment mass media over the years.

Special thanks are due to our research assistants, Jeremy Engel and Deanne Canieso, who join us as co-authors of Chapter 3, as well as Noah Gardner and Shaelyn Patzer, who join us as co-authors of Chapter 4. We also thank Aisha Shafi, Joshua Wartel, Kate Seltzer and Farah Latif for research assistance during earlier phases of this project.

Thanks to political communication colleagues who commented on various research papers over the last several years that are the building blocks of this book. Our arguments here were refined in light of the generous advice and gentle critiques offered at research panels at the 2017 and 2019 meetings of the American Political Science Association, the 2016 and 2018 APSA Pre-conferences on Political Communication, the 2018 meeting of the Northeastern Political Science Association, the 2018 meeting of the Virginia Association of Communication Arts and Sciences, and the 2017 and 2019 Conferences on Character Assassination at George Mason University.

Thanks as well to Jennifer Knerr and her team at Routledge for their prompt and professional treatment of this book manuscript and for their patience in our efforts to provide up-to-the-minute discussions of entertainment politics.

We thank the George Mason University and the University of Mary Washington, in particular UMW's Waple Fellowship program, for financial support of this project. Thanks are also due to the UMW's Center for Leadership and Media Studies, which also provided financial support for this project.

We also thank Methodist College Kuala Lumpur, Malaysia, and the Fulbright Specialist Program for creating a wonderful environment for putting the finishing touches on this manuscript and for many conversations about cultural politics in the US and internationally. Special thanks are due to Yoke Lai Moey, Kheng Leik Khor, Yi-Zhong Tan and Kellie Ong as well as the students in the American Government class that this book's first author co-taught for sharing their insights about the US and about political humor.

Thanks to Routledge for allowing us to use here some of the tables and arguments from our chapter, "Donald Trump and the Late Night Political Humor of Campaign 2016: All the Donald, All the Time," in *The Presidency and Social Media: Discourse, Disruption and Digital Democracy in the 2016 Presidential Election*, Dan Schill and John Allen Hendricks, eds.

Thanks to Lexington Books for allowing us to use here some of the tables and arguments from our chapter, "Partisan Trends in Late Night Humor," in *Still Good for a Laugh? Political Humor in a Changing Media Landscape*, Jody Baumgartner and Amy Becker, eds.

Stephen thanks his parents and Tanya DeKona for their support and generosity over the years.

Robert thanks Hong Yu Wang for her untiring support and assistance.

All conclusions in this work, as well as any errors and omissions, are our responsibility.

Stephen J. Farnsworth
S. Robert Lichter

# 1

# THE IMPORTANCE OF POLITICAL HUMOR

Political humor has long been a staple of late night television. Large parts of the media audience turn to the post-prime-time comics for entertainment and even for an alternative source of news (Baym 2005). As far back as Senator John F. Kennedy's appearance on *The Tonight Show* during the 1960 presidential election campaign, presidents and presidential candidates have sought to humanize their image and bolster their public standing by appearing on late night talk shows (Gould 1968; Lichter et al. 2015). They have done so to respond to satirical attacks, and to minimize future attacks, once the hosts began to incorporate increasing amounts of political material into their stand-up routines. The candidates have even redirected their campaign approaches in response to comedic barbs, such as when Al Gore tried to loosen up after being mocked as too stiff and overbearing in a *Saturday Night Live* skit about the first 2000 presidential debate (Jones 2010).

While a variety of presidents, presidential candidates and other political figures have faced the skewers of late night comics in recent decades, Donald Trump stands head and shoulders above the rest in terms of the amount of ridicule directed his way, first as a presidential candidate and then as president. Of course, he also makes a bad situation worse. By attacking on Twitter the late night comics who ridicule him, Trump draws even more attention to their attacks (Brice-Sadler 2018).

Partly owing to Trump's outsized personality and his frequently outrageous pronouncements, the late night hosts had an unprecedented amount of material to work with during the combative 2016 presidential campaign and then during Trump's time in the White House (Lichter et al. 2016; Farnsworth et al. 2017, 2018). The growing aggressiveness of late night comedians is also occurring in a media environment that expands the attention they receive. Market forces encourage the comics to do so when traditional news outlets connect with smaller and more partisan audiences, when growing numbers of news consumers want their media diet to be highly entertaining, and as the boundaries between news and satire have become increasingly blurred by journalists, news consumers and politicians alike.

This blurring of media roles can reach absurd lengths. During his heyday as host of *The Daily Show* on Comedy Central, survey respondents identified Jon Stewart as one of the most admired journalists in America, tying real-life network news anchors Tom Brokaw and Dan Rather in public admiration (Baumgartner and Morris, 2011). CBS reportedly even considered Stewart as a possible replacement anchor for the *CBS Evening News* (Eggerton 2005).

In this book, we use content analysis to study political humor in the age of Trump. The Center for Media and Public Affairs (CMPA) at George Mason University coded the jokes on late night programs that focus on the president and his administration, identifying the source, target and topic of every humorous political comment during the opening monologues of the leading late night shows during the 2016 campaign and the first year of the Trump presidency.

We apply this content analysis approach to four leading late night comedy programs offering commentary at least four nights a week: *The Daily Show* on Comedy Central, *The Late Show* on CBS, *The Tonight Show* on NBC, and *Jimmy Kimmel Live!* on ABC. We also employ more qualitatively oriented discussions of the most prominent once-a-week humorists: *Full Frontal with Samantha Bee* on TBS, *Last Week Tonight with John Oliver* on HBO, and of course *Saturday Night Live* on NBC. While far from a complete list of the late night programs we could examine, the comics selected provide a mix of broadcast and cable outlets and program formats. CMPA has coded late night comedy monologues for decades, and therefore we can employ data from previous analyses of presidential humor to provide a broader context for understanding the late night humorists' treatment of Trump.

## Humor as a Way to Cope with Life's Challenges (Including Politics)

Humor has always been with us. Jokes provide a way to lighten the burdens of the day as well as to address the challenges of collective human existence. As long as there have been human communities, there have been public desires to poke fun at their leaders. The Egyptians, the Greeks and the Romans of antiquity all provided ways of mocking authorities to ease the burdens of daily survival (Berger 1997; Combs and Nimmo 1996). "There is, in human beings, it would seem, a need to laugh at ourselves and this need takes many different forms—from plays and poems to cartoons, comic strips, and jokes," notes Arthur Asa Berger (2011: 237).

Humor is a key coping mechanism for a world run by others, people who claim or at least presume to be one's betters. Jokes and mockery seem to be common responses to the sometimes-unpleasant realities of the moment, whatever they might be. Even where the expression of critical humor could be dangerous, it has continued to occur in some fashion. Bitter political humor circulated underground in totalitarian societies like the Soviet Union, even as it thrived in freer societies (Combs and Nimmo 1996).

The Central Intelligence Agency recently released some Soviet-era political jokes demonstrating the universality of humor, even of the politically risky sort: "A man was jailed 15 years for calling Joseph Stalin a fathead. One year for sedition, 14 years for revealing a state secret" (quoted in Hopper 2018).

While humor appears to be something close to a universal human desire, undertaking satire could be dangerous if conducted out in the open in some times and places. Earlier Greek comedy, like that of Aristophanes, delighted in ridiculing the powerful, something permitted openly during the days of Greek self-rule. Later, the military successes of Alexander the Great led to more centralized governmental control and a new set of leaders who took a dim view of political satire. As a result, subsequent generations of Greek writers focused their humor on domestic, not political, matters.

> There's comedy tonight so long as it doesn't threaten the imperial powers that be. Early in the history of civilization, it became very clear to those in authority that political comedy was dangerous, something that needed to be suppressed or displaced.
>
> *(Combs and Nimmo 1996: 5)*

The development of modern political institutions and increasing public literacy created a fertile environment for political satire and comedy. During the Renaissance, Machiavelli offered up plays that mocked the political authorities he examined in a more serious vein in works like *The Prince.* With apparent glee, Dante consigned many political leaders of his era to hell in his *Divine Comedy*. In England, Shakespeare mocked political figures for vanity and poor judgment in his plays (though of course he provided flattering portrayals of some other leaders). More than a century later, Jonathan Swift wrote with venom about the British government's failure to deal with famines in Ireland, satirically asserting that the Irish could solve the problem themselves by eating their children.

On this side of the Atlantic, the distant British monarchy and the restive nature of the colonials created a vibrant culture of political humor comparable to that found in Europe and one that if anything intensified as the years went by. The mocking gibes of Ben Franklin during the colonial era later gave way to the bitter humor of Mark Twain and H.L. Mencken in a subversive tradition that has existed throughout America's history (Combs and Nimmo 1996).

Since the nation's founding, US political humor has often focused on the virility or presumed lack thereof of politicians and leading figures in political discourse. Two centuries ago, humorists attacked President James Madison along these lines for his allegedly inept leadership during the War of 1812 – some commentators mocked him as Mrs. Madison's husband. Decades later another generation of humorists attacked Mark Twain for his opposition to US policies in the Spanish–American War, referring to him as an "aunt" (Winter 2011).

Like the jesters or "fools" of European royal courts, who had some license to "speak truth to power" at the royal court via a sharp comment, today's late night humorists occupy a space of "play" that protects them, at least to a degree. That space enables them to say taboo things that may be too critical or too controversial to be expressed safely by mainstream political actors without severe consequences (Gilbert 2004). The absurdity of the extreme exaggerations, in other words, provides a level of "comedic insulation" that minimizes the repercussions against humorists. They can always claim they were only kidding if the authorities (or the audience) view the joke as going too far (Palmer 1988).

Societies may relish the opportunity to cut their political leaders down to size, or at least enjoy others doing so in an entertaining way. A joke, even a sharp one, is a humorous way to try to reduce the arrogance and perhaps the creeping authoritarianism that is a potential risk in centralized, powerful, modern governments, even ones possessing democratic institutions and sentiments. In fact, the more arrogant the leader, the larger the target that leader represents.

But political humor is more than a defense against political figures who think too highly of themselves. Comedy also contains at its core an expression of optimism: the conviction that the future can be brighter than the past.

> A comic perspective fearlessly diagnoses the ridiculousness of politics, including but not endorsing the harm or pain; it is irreverent, even subversive, but not doctrinaire, since doctrine is just another part of the political comedy. … Comedy offers a hopeful and larger view of things: beyond every winter chill is a fertile new spring, where death is carried away and there are new human tangles for our comic pleasure.
>
> *(Combs and Nimmo 1996: 12)*

Indeed, in times of great suffering, like the aftermath of the horrific terrorist attacks of 2001, many Americans found comfort in the revival of humor following a period of deep mourning. When *Saturday Night Live* returned to the air a few weeks after the horrific 9/11 attacks, the program began with a solemn tribute to New York City's first responders, followed by permission to resume the jokes provided by none other than Mayor Rudy Giuliani, the heroic face of America's largest city in the weeks after the Twin Towers fell.

> Viewers who tuned in on September 29 to the first show that aired after the attacks found New York City mayor Rudolph Giuliani opening the night surrounded by city firefighters and police officers. After an earnest discussion of the attacks and the nature of heroism, followed by a musical performance by Paul Simon, SNL's executive producer Lorne Michaels joined Giuliani on

> stage, and the mayor affirmed the significance of SNL to New York City as "one of our great New York City institutions." After an awkward pause, Michaels asked Giuliani, "Can we be funny?" The audience laughed anxiously, perhaps in anticipation of a restored play frame. Giuliani responded to Michael's question with one of his own: "Why start now?" Seemingly relieved, the live audience laughed again, harder, at the political comedian and the comedic politician.
>
> *(Greene and Gournelos 2011: xii)*

If comedy sometimes seems to involve the construction of pain followed by time, the horrific deaths of 9/11 followed by the jokes of late September suggested to a shell-shocked country that the period of mourning would not last forever and normality would soon return to the traumatized nation.

The Iraq War, which began less than two years after the 2001 terrorist attacks, helped make what was old new again for political humor. Theaters revived traditional stories of political satire, including *Lysistrata* and *Hair*, during the Iraq War years, even though they harked back to earlier conflicts, like the Peloponnesian War of antiquity or the more recent war in Vietnam (Winter 2011). On the April 23, 2003 edition of *The Daily Show*, host Jon Stewart channeled the 1964 Cold War parody film *Dr. Strangelove*, explicitly comparing Deputy Defense Secretary Paul Wolfowitz, a hawkish voice in policy debates, to the ex-Nazi rocket scientist played by Peter Sellers. Stewart remarked Wolfowitz was "a wheelchair away from Dr. Strangelove" (quoted in Winter 2011: 170).

The relative powerlessness of most comedians offers some further insulation from retaliation, at least apart from periods of intense crisis. Comics' positions outside the power structure can make them less threatening and therefore more able to offer biting social criticism (Gilbert 2004). It is not as if comedians have votes in Congress, after all.

Consider, for example, Stephen Colbert's commentary about President George W. Bush at the 2006 White House Correspondents Dinner in Washington. Colbert spoke, not as himself, but as his cable news character, a parody of a Fox News conservative commentator.

> I stand by this man [President Bush]. I stand by this man because he stands for things. Not only does he stand for things, he stands on things. Things like aircraft carriers and rubble and recently flooded city squares. And that sends a strong message: that no matter what happens to America, she will always rebound—with the most powerfully staged photo ops in the world.
>
> *(quoted in Greene 2011: 119)*

Such a stinging rebuke would have seemed out of place immediately after 9/11 or during the combat phase of the Iraq War. By the time of this performance, however, Bush's approval ratings had fallen far below their peak. The Bush

Administration's mishandling of the aftermath of Hurricane Katrina in 2005 and the rising resistance to the continuing US-led occupation of Iraq that same year that had sapped the president's approval ratings had made him a less risky target for Colbert to mock (Farnsworth 2009, 2018). Even so, a number of Washington politicians and journalists condemned Colbert's remarks as too harsh for the setting. The pushback to the comedian, whose jokes that night attacked both presidential misjudgments and excessive journalistic deference to authority, offered another reminder (if we need one) that official Washington sometimes finds it tough to appreciate jokes made at its own expense. The fact that Washington reporters and politicians cannot abide jokes aimed at them makes the barbs all the funnier for those who live beyond the Washington Beltway.

As the Colbert example demonstrates, comics may sometimes have a lot of latitude, but at other times they do not. Contemporary political humor is aggressive, and modern comics enjoy some level of insulation against reprisal, to be sure. Even so, some critics observe that late night comedians, whose programs air on for-profit broadcast and cable networks, must be somewhat cautious, given the risk of offending advertisers or wary corporate executives (Greene and Gournelos 2011). Comedy is a business, after all.

Taking a show off the air for its political content is not an idle threat. Throughout the history of television, there have been such incidents of popular show cancellation. A famous example was the *Smothers Brothers Comedy Hour*, which offered countercultural messages and critical comments regarding government policies in the Vietnam War. The highly rated show battled network executives and censors during its contentious two seasons on CBS in the late 1960s, until the network brass decided the program was not worth the trouble (Bodroghkozy 1997).

The risk of cancellation for political reasons was not limited to the more cautious era of 1960s entertainment television. Phil Donahue lost his talk show on MSNBC because he opposed the Iraq War after 9/11 (Carter 2003). In mid-2002, ABC canceled *Politically Incorrect*, a late night talk show hosted by Bill Maher, after the host frustrated advertisers and the White House with his white-hot comments regarding the early US military responses to the 2001 terrorist attacks (Carter 2003).

> Living up to his show's title, Mr. Maher took issue with characterizations of the hijackers as cowards, arguing that "we have been the cowards, lobbing cruise missiles from 2,000 miles away." ABC's desire to bolster its late-night ratings and profits was also at the heart of its ultimately unsuccessful effort to woo David Letterman away from CBS two months ago.
>
> *(Carter 2003)*

Maher did eventually return to television, with a show called *Real Time*, which premiered on HBO roughly a year after the cancellation of his show on ABC

(Gurney 2011). Because HBO is a subscription-based cable channel with a smaller audience than the broadcast networks, it is willing to offer more controversial content than networks with larger audiences. This is an issue we will consider further when we examine another controversial HBO program, *Last Week Tonight.*

Such programming cancellations serve as reminders that for-profit media outlets are in the business of satisfying viewers, also known as customers. Television talk show hosts and comedians do not have a First Amendment right to have their programs broadcast on someone else's network, and these examples suggest that the level of criticism of government officials must remain within a range that allows the show to continue to attract a substantial audience.

## Three Forms of Humor

Humor often takes the form of one or more of three broad categories – incongruity, superiority and catharsis. Incongruity involves the connection between two seemingly unrelated matters or frames of interpretation that fit together once placed side by side. Superiority-oriented humor involves laughing at people or places seen as inferior to oneself. Catharsis humor involves the release of tension in a stressful environment, such as laughing at a faux pas (Davis 1993; Greene and Gournelos 2011; Martin 2007).

Incongruity humor – the distinction between what people expect and what is revealed – is probably the most common type of humor. "Jokes offer a good example of incongruity. The punch line of the joke is funny, incongruity theorists argue, because it offers an unexpected but acceptable resolution of the events described in a joke" (Berger 2011: 235).

Superiority humor has a long history. Aristotle observed that humorists can make men already "worse than average" look still worse, and Hobbes noted in *The Leviathan* that laughter sometimes comes from recognizing that another person is inferior to oneself (Berger 2011).

Catharsis humor may involve masked aggression, or the satisfaction of an instinct in the face of an obstacle (Berger 2011). According to Freud (2003[original 1905]), this type of humor can involve responses to lustful or hostile feelings or some other aspect of human sexuality.

This includes the significant amount of political humor that raises masculinity questions, as in dialogue voiced by *Dr. Strangelove* characters about retaining "precious bodily fluids" and the sexual demands expected of male nuclear war survivors living in female-filled bunkers following a nuclear missile exchange. (More recently, this humor manifests itself in jokes about the disconnect between the macho bluster and hawkish policies of Donald Trump and George W. Bush, even though both men found ways to avoid military service in Southeast Asia as young men during the Vietnam War.)

> We make humorous responses to tragedies because doing so has some kind of a therapeutic value for us, collectively speaking, even if the humorous

> texts are repugnant. It strikes me that using riddles to deal with tragedies is, psychoanalytically speaking, a kind of regression—to a period in our childhood when we were innocent and where the countless tragedies of the world did not mean anything to us. … "Sick humor" cycles that circulate after every tragedy and possibly help us to deal with the anxiety we face, ultimately, about our own deaths. Making light of 9/11 or other tragedies doesn't make them disappear, but does seem to help us get on with our daily lives.
>
> *(Berger 2011: 237–238)*

## Political Humor in a Contentious America

The rise of late night television talk shows as forums for political discourse roughly parallels a number of other trends in politics and political news. First, politics has become more divisive and partisan in recent decades, as the previous ability of political parties to serve as "big tents" for a variety of views gave way to more ideologically aligned and doctrinaire partisan organizations (Bond and Fleisher 2000). With the virtual disappearance of conservative Democrats and liberal Republicans, Democrats have come to represent the party of liberalism and Republicans the party of conservatism (Mann and Ornstein 2012). Voters have grown increasingly polarized during recent decades as well (Campbell 2016).

As political debate in the US moved towards more ideologically defined political parties, political discourse involving politicians broadened to include heretofore-ignored factors of that conversation. This era was marked by an increasing emphasis on private behavior and personal character, particularly when linked to sexual behavior (Sabato 1993). These factors became political wild cards, employed for maximum impact during the course of election campaigns (Lichter and Farnsworth, forthcoming; Sabato et al. 2000).

The news media communicated these changes to the public even as journalism itself was changing in its composition, its norms and its attention paid to behavior previously considered off limits for news stories. Increasingly, this produced coverage of personal scandals that journalists were often ambivalent about reporting, and which contributed to a long decline in public respect for both journalists and politicians (Cappella and Jamieson 1997; Patterson 1994, 2013). It did not help that purveyors of infotainment joined the mix with even less regard for privacy or decorum. Inevitably, old-fashioned journalists and the new breed of cable and social media ringmasters were painted with the same broad brush of public disapproval (Sanford 1999; Pew Research Center 2016a, 2016b, 2017).

This course of events and the broad cultural changes it brought were reflected in the normalizing of personal ridicule as a tool of political debate, public spectacle, and a means of discrediting opponents. Accusations of personal misbehavior, gaffes in which a garbled or inappropriate statement proved embarrassing, and even personal characteristics such as unattractive physical traits, lack of dexterity or less than stylish dress and grooming all became grist for the political mill (Sabato 1993; Wayne 2000).

In addition, political campaign ads became more negative, partly through the incorporation of personally embarrassing material (Geer 2006).

Meanwhile, both political parties began ramping up opposition research, which was intended to keep the stream of criticism flowing. Simultaneously, the widespread use of digital mobile devices made it possible for partisan voters to document statements and behavior on the campaign trail that once would have gone unnoticed or attracted only brief attention (Chadwick 2013; Stromer-Galley 2014). As a result, journalists began competing with entertainment venues for this embarrassing material. Mainstream journalists seeking "clickbait" content sometimes even referenced the late night comics in their news reports to attract and retain audiences increasingly looking beyond traditional media for information.

Tina Fey's imitation of Sarah Palin, the Republican 2008 vice presidential nominee, on *Saturday Night Live* represents a great example of the synergy between traditional news and entertainment media. In the wake of Palin's stumbling interview with Katie Couric of CBS News shortly after being named John McCain's running mate, Fey offered an over-the-top imitation of the Alaska governor that included both quotations from Palin's own public utterances and fictional comments that took her claims one step further toward the realm of absurdity and incoherence. That mocking became a key part of news reports on Palin, who was frequently portrayed during the campaign as ill-informed about policy and a poor choice for vice president (Greene and Gournelos 2011).

## *The Pivotal Politics of the 1980s and 1990s*

The widening reach of both political journalism and political partisanship were exemplified by three events clustered together in the late 1980s: the destruction of Senator Gary Hart's 1988 presidential campaign, the failure of Judge Robert Bork's 1987 nomination to the Supreme Court, and the nomination of Dan Quayle as the Republican Party's vice presidential candidate in 1988.

The first example demonstrated how much tamer political scandals of the past were compared to the current era. By mid-1987, Hart was the frontrunner for the 1988 Democratic presidential nomination. Given his strong but ultimately unsuccessful 1984 nomination campaign, Hart was well ahead of his potential rivals when rumors of his "womanizing" and an anonymous tip led the *Miami Herald* to stake out his Washington, DC townhouse. The paper's reporters documented an affair that the married Hart was having with a young woman named Donna Rice.

Hart denied the charges at first, but a picture appeared in the tabloid *National Enquirer* (and was reprinted in newspapers around the country) of Rice sitting in Hart's lap. Hart was wearing a t-shirt bearing the name of the yacht "Monkey Business." From that moment, he was followed by a scrum of reporters pressing him about his marital fidelity, a situation political scientist Larry Sabato (1993) popularized as a media "feeding frenzy."

Hart soon withdrew from the 1988 race, bitter that he endured a new standard of what was newsworthy. And he was right – numerous presidents, most notably John F. Kennedy, had carried on sexual affairs while in the White House, without any notice by the press at the time. But the floodgates had opened into a new era in which the personal had become political. In the years after Hart's fall, Sabato et al. (2000) catalogued dozens of cases in which political careers had been ruined by media investigations into private behavior, including cases of adultery that had occurred decades earlier. They concluded that many of these served no larger public purpose than titillating audiences. And titillate they did, as late night hosts increasingly turned their comedic attention to matters of human weakness among the nation's political leadership.

Although Hart's political collapse happened before late night comedy became heavily political, *The Tonight Show* host Johnny Carson helped shape public preferences about Hart, as well as Joe Biden, then a Democratic senator from Delaware whose first campaign for president in 1988 ran aground because of a plagiarism incident (Shales 1987a). As *Washington Post* television critic Tom Shales noted at the time, Carson made negative news coverage even worse for these candidates via his late night audience:

> It was over for Gary Hart when Gary Hart became a nightly fixture in the Carson monologue. The roar of the crowd was heard in the land, but not the kind of roar politicians like. ... "It's hard to be funnier than what's happening, sometimes," says Carson.
>
> *(Shales 1987a)*

Public discussion of marital infidelity was enough to sink a campaign in the 1980s, as Gary Hart learned in the run-up to the 1988 presidential election. Four years later, Bill Clinton demonstrated that marital misconduct soon ceased to be politically fatal to presidential candidates. By 2016, Donald Trump demonstrated a successful presidential candidate could brag of his serial marital infidelity and still win the votes of a large majority of Christian conservative voters.

Around the same time that the Hart sex scandal was unfolding in the run-up to the 1988 presidential campaign, an increasingly partisan political environment emerged in the wake of President Reagan's nomination of conservative judge Robert Bork to fill a vacancy on the Supreme Court. Fearful that Bork's decisions on the bench would help validate Reagan's conservative policies, liberal activist groups decided to broaden the nomination process into a national referendum on Bork's previous decisions and his general judicial philosophy.

On the floor of the Senate, Ted Kennedy (D-MA) predicted that Bork's confirmation would lead to the return of back-alley abortions, segregated lunch counters, and midnight raids by rogue police. A flood of mailings and political ads echoed these themes, including a TV spot narrated by actor Gregory Peck, which charged Bork with having "a strange idea of what justice is" (https://www.youtube.com/watch?v=NpFe10lkF3Y).

The subsequent wave of bad press doomed Bork's chances for success, and the Senate rejected his court nomination on a 58–42 vote, the widest margin ever (O'Brien 1988). This was the first time in memory that a Supreme Court nomination failed because of the application of no-holds-barred partisan politics, and the success of the anti-Bork forces inaugurated a new era of partisanship in the confirmations of presidential nominees. It also created a new verb, to "bork," which the *Oxford English Dictionary* defines as "[to] obstruct someone … by systematically defaming or vilifying them" (https://en.oxforddictionaries.com/definition/bork).

The Senate's reaction to Bork's record, as well as the public's reaction to the nominee's own public performance during his confirmation hearings, combined to undermine Bork's confirmation prospects (Shales 1987b). But the scandal offered opportunities for the late night comics to pile on as well. Johnny Carson, for example, offered this assessment during the Bork nomination process: "Bork isn't having a very good week. I saw him at a bar this afternoon sharing a margarita with Valerie Harper" (Shales 1987b). Harper, a well-known television star three decades ago, was famously fired from her own television series when she demanded a pay raise and greater control over the program (Shales 1987b).

While he did not have a verb named after him as Bork did, Judge Douglas Ginsburg, Reagan's subsequent nominee for that same Supreme Court vacancy, faced the same fate. Ginsburg withdraw his nomination after press accounts emerged that he had occasionally smoked marijuana as a Harvard Law School professor in the 1970s (O'Brien 1988). This disclosure led to some late night comedy, but nothing compared to the mockery that Bork and Hart endured.

Still more abuse was on its way. The following year, George H.W. Bush's surprise choice for vice presidential candidate, Senator Dan Quayle (R-IN), was widely perceived by journalists as a callow youth who was in over his head in national politics. After initial rumors of scandal in his past proved baseless, journalists settled for treating him as a figure of fun. His stammering replies to their questions and his apparent lack of gravitas turned him into the court jester of the Bush Administration (Liebovich 2001). Thus, allegations of stupidity joined those of sexual misconduct as fair game for critics.

By this time, media critics had begun to characterize political journalists as "character cops" who had arrogated to themselves the task of determining whether personal qualities and behavior disqualified politicians from high office (Sabato 1993). The factors behind this development included new technologies, heightened competition, alternative media sources and the increasing use of cutthroat campaign practices such as opposition research and attack ads (Geer 2006; Patterson 1994, 2013).

Any remaining reluctance of journalists to take on the character cop role disappeared following the appearance of presidential candidate Bill Clinton on the national political scene in 1992. Clinton appeared while trailing a string of potential scandals behind him, including public charges of adultery from former girlfriend Gennifer Flowers, questions about how he avoided military service during the Vietnam War, and charges that he had smoked marijuana in his youth (Liebovich 2001). Voters selected Clinton despite this list of demerits, which only grew longer after the new president arrived at the White House. Clinton's two terms in office featured a seemingly endless stream of scandal allegations, mostly dealing with sex but occasionally with the financial dealings of Bill and Hillary Clinton, as in the so-called Whitewater affair (Isikoff 2000). Hillary Clinton captured the raging partisanship of the period assertion with her assertion that "a vast right-wing conspiracy" was behind the many scandal charges. All this famously culminated in the President's 1998 admission, after months of denials, of an affair with Monica Lewinsky, a young White House intern (Campbell 2000).

For the late night comics, the Bill Clinton presidency was like eight years of Christmas every day, and it triggered new scandals directed as Republicans, as the subsequent efforts to drive Clinton from office backfired on the Republican majority in Congress. Amid charges of hypocrisy, journalists began to delve into the past peccadilloes of party leaders. *Hustler* publisher Larry Flynt joined the fray with a million dollar "bounty" on scandalous revelations about GOP lawmakers. The most prominent victim of this backlash – and of Clinton's aggressive efforts to spin the story in the direction of a partisan GOP witch hunt – was Rep. Bob Livingston (R-LA), who was in line to be House Speaker in 1998 but was driven from office after revelations of a past affair emerged (Farnsworth and Lichter 2006).

In light of these tawdry developments that affected both Democrats and Republicans, it is not surprising that scholars reported increases in negativity expressed by politicians, particularly during political campaigns, and in the coverage that political journalists gave to these events (Cappella and Jamieson 1997; Geer 2006; Patterson 1994). Nor was it surprising that the public's approval ratings of both partisan camps reached new lows (Mann and Ornstein 2012), even as each side blamed the other for the parlous state of political discourse (Sabato et al. 2000). While analysts may disagree on where the fault lies, it is clear that the decade from the late 1980s to the late 1990s saw the rise of a political culture of personal ridicule, endured – and indulged in – by politicians and journalists alike.

## The Evolving Norms and Changing Hosts of Political Humor

A parallel development to the changing political news landscape was the simultaneous emergence of political humor on late night television talk shows. In their early decades, talk shows and variety shows had mostly steered clear of political material, judging it more trouble than it was worth. This reflected the show business adage attributed to Broadway playwright George S. Kaufman that "satire is what closes on Saturday night" (quoted in Elliot 2014). The exception to this rule was NBC's *Saturday Night Live*, which began airing in 1975. The show's sketch comedy occasionally focused on political topics, most frequently in a faux newscast called "Weekend Update."

Foreshadowing the future tone of late night humor, however, comedian Chevy Chase found stardom by parodying President Gerald Ford's stumble when disembarking from Air Force One. Chase opened many shows by turning Ford's fall into a pratfall, knocking over or bumping into various objects, such as the Oval Office desk (Liebovich 2001). Unlike subsequent presidential imitators, Chase did not attempt to sound like or look like the president he was portraying, relying instead on over-the-top stumbling and physical comedy. Ironically, what became the popular image of Ford as a clumsy oaf belied the real Ford's athletic past – he was a Collegiate All-Star on a University of Michigan football team that twice went undefeated and won national titles.

While *SNL* regularly offered presidential impersonators and parodies of presidential debates during those years, these represented individual sketches on weekly shows here and there, a far cry from the regular drumbeat of political material that would be featured nightly in the monologues of late night talk show hosts in the years that followed.

## The Carson Era

The genre of late night talk became institutionalized under the direction of Johnny Carson. His *Tonight Show* on NBC dominated the ratings competition from 1962 until his retirement three decades later in 1992. Operating in an environment with little competition, Carson aimed for the great middle of the national audience, with monologues and guests that were for the most part comforting and inoffensive. As noted film director Billy Wilder put it, "He's the cream of middle-class elegance … He has captivated the American bourgeoisie without ever offending the highbrows, and he has never said anything that wasn't liberal or progressive" (quoted in Tynan 1978).

Carson included political material in his monologues, but usually in a way that would not offend most viewers. This meant making fun of politicians who were embroiled in scandals and those who committed gaffes, and then moving on. His apparent centrism and relatively light touch when it came to politics left it to his various competitors to tap into the underserved audience for more contentious or ideological material. These competitors included Merv Griffin and Dick Cavett, who brought in political material and controversial guests on the Vietnam War. His rivals, though, were always a sidelight to Carson and the relatively gentle humor he brought to political comedy. Carson lasted far longer on the air than did the more combative alternatives.

As *Washington Post* television critic Tom Shales wrote in a story reviewing Carson's first quarter century as a late night host:

> [Carson] balks and scoffs at intense interpretation of the monologue and its effect on public careers. "I never analyze it," he says. "I never analyze the

> show. Analyzing it would be a wasted exercise. I just go out and do it. Like George Burns said, 'If it gets a laugh, it's funny.'"
>
> Jack Paar's *Tonight Show*, which preceded Carson's, was as hot as Carson's is cool, a teapot for innumerable tempests. Once his monologue is over, Carson is not interested in topical guests or, really, in the latest controversies.
>
> *(Shales 1987a)*

Then along came Dan Quayle, whose rise to national prominence brought journalists and late night comics together in making fun of George H.W. Bush's vice president. To drive home their image of Quayle as an unprepared half-wit, journalists began to refer to TV talk show punch lines to illustrate their points. Thus, Quayle became the first nominee for national office in memory whom the press defined as a national joke (Farnsworth and Lichter 2006). Of course, Quayle did not help make his case for seriousness when he criticized *Murphy Brown*, a fictional TV character on a popular sitcom, for contributing to the moral decline of Americans by having a child on the show out of wedlock (Liebovich 2001).

When he retired in May 1992, Johnny Carson used his final monologue to thank Quayle for the comedic material, including the spat with a fictional TV character.

> But the events of this last week have helped me make a decision. I am going to join the cast of *Murphy Brown*, and become a surrogate father to that kid.
>
> During the run on the show there have been seven United States Presidents, and thankfully for comedy there have been eight Vice Presidents of the United States.
>
> Now I know I have made some jokes at the expense of Dan Quayle, but I really want to thank him tonight for making my final week so fruitful.
>
> *(quoted in Weinraub 1992)*

The politicians were noticing as well. Bush campaign manager Lee Atwater remarked that he monitored audience responses to *Tonight Show* monologues to see how politicians were playing in Peoria (Lichter et al. 2015: 207). Atwater's efforts were an early indication that humor was becoming a key part of the political milieu. Much of that evolution was thanks to Dan Quayle. A study of jokes on *The Tonight Show* and *The Late Show* from Inauguration Day in January 1989 through September 1991 found that Vice President Quayle topped all other political figures as the target of 417 jokes; President George H.W. Bush finished a distant second with 331 (Media Monitor 1991: 6).

The hapless vice president sought the presidency for himself years later, but his campaign quickly fizzled. Quayle simply could not emerge from behind the cloud of spending so much time as a key target of Carson's political humor.

### *The Leno–Letterman Years*

Carson may have enjoyed launching barbs at Quayle, Hart and other political figures, but his approach was mild compared to what would come next. The modern era of politicized monologues can probably be dated from 1992, when comedian Jay Leno replaced Johnny Carson as host of *The Tonight Show on NBC*. The following year David Letterman moved from NBC *Late Night* to *The Late Show* on CBS to compete directly with Leno. The competition to succeed Carson had been one of the most intense in the history of late night television, ending with Leno inheriting *The Tonight Show*. The unhappy loser was David Letterman, whose *Late Show* had long followed Carson's on NBC. Letterman then moved to CBS to compete directly with Leno. Both men stayed in these new posts for over two decades (apart from a brief effort by Leno in 2009–2010 to switch to a prime time show). Throughout their runs, they dominated late night talk show ratings against a changing cast of competitors, until Leno retired in 2014 and Letterman followed in 2015.

Together, they set the tone for late night humor, despite competition at various times from Conan O'Brien, Arsenio Hall, Bill Maher and others. The great exception to the conventional late night format, discussed in detail below, was the satirical "fake news" format developed by Jon Stewart on Comedy Central.

Leno was the closest match of his generation to Carson, relying on old-fashioned zingers and one-liners that would get a laugh in Middle America but not necessarily among urban hipsters. Even so, Leno did the most to re-direct the central themes of his routines towards politics. In 1993, when Leno and Letterman went head-to-head for the first time, Leno used nearly twice as much political material as his rival, by a margin of 1,535 to 883 jokes (Lichter et al. 2015). Leno's material was relatively low-key, and he was less likely than his rivals to be accused of partisanship.

Eventually, Republican politicians and conservative commentators began to adopt Leno as their favorite late night comedian. In fact, a *Breitbart* reporter labeled him "the last fair, balanced late night host" (Toto 2014). The politics of Hollywood being what they are, Leno found it necessary to protest publicly that he was in fact a dyed-in-the-wool liberal – a Michael Moore fan whose joke writers include no Republicans. Specifically, Leno said, "I'm not conservative. I've never voted that way in my life" (Franzen 2009). Compared to some of the current highly political late night entrants, from Stephen Colbert and Samantha Bee to John Oliver and Bill Maher, it's easy to see why conservatives would have looked to Leno for the old-fashioned middle of the road humor popularized by Johnny Carson.

By contrast, David Letterman was widely regarded as apolitical until late in his tenure. The transformation appears to have occurred in the wake of the tumultuous 2008 presidential election (Carter 2009). During that campaign, Republican nominee Senator John McCain made the mistake of canceling his *Late Show* appearance at the last minute. An outraged Letterman fought back through his monologues, with a profusion of ridicule that eventually brought the abashed candidate back on the show, where he delivered an abject apology, admitting to his inquisitor, "I screwed up." This incident produced Letterman's famous pronouncement, "the road to the White House runs right through me!" That may be hyperbole, but the exchange certainly illustrates the changing balance of power between politicians and comedians (Lichter et al. 2015).

Letterman's highly visible personal feuds with politicians may have contributed to the politicization of Letterman's monologues as his career progressed (Carter 2009). That observation is supported by CMPA data showing that Letterman's political joke totals jumped from 1,208 in 2007 to 3,187 in 2008 and 3,206 in 2009. By 2013, Letterman was using his "Stooge of the Night" routine to wage war against the Republican Congress for its opposition to gun control. The segments showed images of senators opposing tougher background checks in gun purchases with superimposed graphics showing how much money they had received from pro-gun groups.

## The Daily Show *Rises*

During this period of Leno versus Letterman, the only major change in the late night landscape came in 1999 on the cable network Comedy Central, where Jon Stewart turned *The Daily Show* into a satirical "fake news" program. Stewart's success eventually led to spinoff shows by cast members. Unlike the traditional stand-up comedians on most television talk shows, who relied heavily on one-liners, the Comedy Central comedians engaged in satire and were taken more seriously as popular commentators on politics and the news media. Stewart in particular gained a strong following among younger viewers and was rated in national surveys as one of the most trusted and admired journalists in America (Baumgartner and Morris 2011; Garber 2009; Pew Research Center 2007).

Thus, even as Leno and Letterman were dominating late night comedy on the broadcast network stage, the action was moving to the cable network Comedy Central. In 1999, Jon Stewart began to transform *The Daily Show* into a new format for political humor, which the host was proud to call "fake news." Put simply, Stewart brought satire to nightly late night talk. In addition, the show focused more narrowly on the world of politics and public affairs than any other television talk show. The nightly skewering of politicians and the journalists who covered them found a strong audience among younger viewers, in sharp contrast to the graying audience for Leno and Letterman on NBC and CBS respectively.

The redirection of *The Daily Show* and its new host benefited early on from some lucky timing. A continuing feature satirized the foibles of the candidates and the campaign news throughout the 2000 elections under the rubric "Indecision 2000." As it happened, the 2000 presidential election featured the greatest indecision in modern American politics, helping to build an audience for the show right up until the decision of who was going to be president was made, not by the voters but by the Supreme Court, on December 12, 2000.

Stewart also became personally involved in occasional political causes. For example, he helped push through the Senate a bill to provide health care for 9/11 early responders, by bludgeoning recalcitrant senators with a barrage of jokes, and by inviting some of the workers onto his show. More generally, as noted above, Stewart was widely regarded as a valued social and political critic and even a legitimate journalist. His work was a major factor in getting politicians and the public alike to take late night humor as a valuable source of information about politics.

Thus, partly through Stewart's innovations and influence, political humorists have become increasingly important sources of political criticism, even going so far as becoming shapers of news content and public opinion.

## Political Humor's Public Roles

Many of these humorists serve at least two critical public functions: first, they comment upon and reveal potential failings or hypocrisies of American society, especially those perpetrated by individuals in positions of political and/or economic power; second, and less overtly, they function as supplemental gatekeepers and framers in the agenda-setting work of the media (Gurney 2011: 3).

In 2005, *The Daily Show* produced a highly successful spinoff called *The Colbert Report*. Stephen Colbert, who had functioned as a fake news correspondent on *The Daily Show*, adopted the persona of a loud-mouthed right-wing pundit, at least partly modeled on such Fox News personalities as Bill O'Reilly and Glenn Beck.

Colbert became involved in real-world national politics by attempting to run a parody presidential campaign (running as both a Democrat and a Republican) and later by forming a super PAC, which raised over a million dollars. Some of the money was used to air spoof campaign ads. Colbert also teamed up with Stewart to stage a "Rally to Restore Sanity and/or Fear," which drew over two hundred thousand people to the National Mall in Washington, DC for the avowed cause of mobilizing reason and moderation against partisanship and extremism. Colbert also testified before a congressional subcommittee on the plight of migrant workers.

Journalists wrote about the actions and jokes of Stewart and Colbert as the two Comedy Central stars increasingly became public figures. But that doesn't mean the journalists always liked what they heard from the humorists, particularly when reporters themselves became the targets of the jokes, rather than elected officials. At one point in Stephen Colbert's remarks at the 2006 White House Correspondents Dinner, he faulted reporters for not being more aggressive in challenging the George W. Bush administration over its handling of Iraq and Katrina, among other issues (Carr 2007).

> Listen, let's review the rules. Here's how it works. The president makes decisions. He's the decider. The press secretary announces those decisions, and you people of the press type those decisions down. Make, announce, type. Just put 'em through spell-check and go home. Get to know your family again. Make love to your wife. Write that novel you got kicking around in your head. You know, the one about the intrepid Washington reporter with the courage to stand up to the administration. You know, fiction!
>
> *(quoted in Greene 2011: 132)*

The Washington journalists could not fire Colbert, but a year later the association invited a humorist with a very different style to this annual dinner of media and political luminaries. Rich Little, famous a generation earlier for his Ronald Reagan imitations, addressed the group, a nod to the less combative political humor of a previous era (Carr 2007). However, this guest from the past was at best a stopgap measure for those who were being burned by the new style of take-no-prisoners political humor that now dominated the late night comedy landscape. There could be no going back.

## *The New Late Night Landscape*

As Leno, Letterman, Stewart and Colbert were making their marks, more traditional and less visible hosts came and sometimes went, mostly without making a long-term mark politically with their monologues. They have included, among others, Arsenio Hall, forever remembered for helping revive the scandal-scarred presidential candidacy of Bill Clinton; Conan O'Brien, whose numerous late night slots included a brief and controversial stint as Jay Leno's would-be successor on *The Tonight Show*; and Seth Meyers, best known for his association with *Saturday Night Live* before he took over *The Late Show* in 2014.

One decidedly political voice belongs to Bill Maher, a television survivor who proudly wears his liberalism on his sleeve. As discussed above, his *Politically Incorrect* talk show on ABC more than lived up to its name when, in the wake of the 9/11 attacks, he defended the terrorists against charges of cowardice and lobbed it instead at the US military for "lobbing cruise missiles from 2,000 miles away. That's cowardly" (Bohlen 2001). The comment cost his show acrimony and advertisers, and it was canceled at the end of the season. The next season, however, Maher started a weekly talk show titled *Real Time with Bill Maher* on HBO. It has remained on HBO's evening schedule ever since.

Two other voices with broadcast network slots honored political material mostly in the breach, even as they became more prominent in recent years – Jimmy Kimmel and Jimmy Fallon. Until the past few years, Kimmel was known for his light material and focus on celebrities. Before the network late night comedy gig, he was a host on the *Man Show*, a raunchy cable offering designed to appeal to the worst instincts of hard-partying fraternity members (Garber 2018). Fallon, who worked at the "Weekend Update" anchor desk at *Saturday Night Live* earlier in his career, was a relative latecomer to the late night talk scene, taking over *Late Night* in 2009. Five years later, following Jay Leno's retirement, he graduated to *The Tonight Show*. If anything, Fallon's early lack of interest in monologues featuring political material exceeded that of Kimmel. Fallon specialized in creating a genial milieu with devices including music, dance, impersonations and games.

Finally, after two decades of late night talk show dominance by Jay Leno and David Letterman, and fifteen years after the emergence of Jon Stewart as a "fake news" host, there was a remarkable shuffling of the deck that in rapid succession produced new hosts of *The Tonight Show, Late Night* and *The Daily Show*. In addition, ABC moved up the starting time of *Jimmy Kimmel Live!* to allow Kimmel to compete directly with the flagship talk shows on CBS and NBC. In 2014, Leno retired and Jimmy Fallon took over *The Tonight Show*. In May 2015, Letterman retired and Stephen Colbert took over *Late Night*, while *The Colbert Report* ceased production. In August of the same year, Stewart retired, and South African comedian Trevor Noah took over *The Daily Show* a month later. With all these changes, three of the four leading talk shows had new hosts in place just in time for the 2016 presidential election to begin.

But it is not yet clear whether these personnel changes will produce corresponding long-term changes in the amount and focus of the political humor that they produce. In the sections below, we first examine the overall trends during presidential election years from 1992 through 2012 covered by the long-term CMPA data set. We then discuss similar data from the 2016 election based on a new study by CMPA. (This brief 2016 discussion will be a preview for Chapter 3, which discusses the campaign humor of 2016 in greater detail.)

## Amounts and Targets of Political Humor

The targets and topics of late night comedy were the subject of a long-term study by the Center for Media and Public Affairs (CMPA). Starting in 1992, CMPA examined over 100,000 jokes about politics and public affairs on several shows, including those hosted by Leno, Letterman, Stewart and Colbert. All coding was done by students who were trained by CMPA staff members. Coders had to attain a level of reliability of at least 80 percent agreement, and their coding continued to be spot checked throughout the analysis.

The study found that political material on late night television increased over time and reached its highest levels during presidential elections, when it eventually became a regular component of the campaign discourse. Accordingly, this final section of Chapter 1 focuses mainly on the targets of election year humor.

Table 1.1 shows the increase in political humor across the five election years from 1992 to 2008, using the combined totals of the NBC *Tonight Show* and the

**TABLE 1.1** Number of Political Jokes by Late Night Program

| | *Tonight Show* | *Late Show* | *Total* |
|---|---|---|---|
| 1992 | 1975 | 1117 | 3092 |
| 1996 | 2244 | 2055 | 4299 |
| 2000 | 2454 | 1406 | 3860 |
| 2004 | 2227 | 1480 | 3707 |
| 2008 | 3812 | 3187 | 6999 |

Source: CMPA

CBS *Late Show*, the only late night talk shows that aired throughout the period from 1992 to 2011. The totals more than doubled from 3,092 jokes in 1992 to 6,999 in 2008. The first big bump in jokes (from 1992 to 1996) corresponded to the first term of the Clinton presidency, while the second big increase corresponded to the problematic second term of George W. Bush, when Katrina, Iraq and other issues pumped up the volume of presidential humor.

The most popular targets were presidents and presidential candidates. As Table 1.2 shows, sitting presidents were the most frequently targeted individuals in seventeen out of the twenty-one years studied. Three exceptions were in 1996, 2008 and 2012, when Republican presidential nominees Bob Dole, John McCain and Mitt Romney exceeded the totals of the sitting presidents they sought to replace. In addition, in 2001 outgoing president Bill Clinton edged out his incoming successor George W. Bush. More generally, the presidential tickets of the two major parties combined to account for just under one-third (32 percent) of all political jokes in election years. Many of the remaining jokes were aimed at their defeated primary opponents.

The intensity of election campaigns, which dominate the news, and the need to come up with fresh material night after night feed into the tendency of comedians to accentuate a few personal characteristics of the contenders and relate the day's events to these qualities. The same is true of presidents, whose activities typically generate daily headlines. As the jokes feed on each other and echo characteristics often addressed more seriously in the news media, stereotypes emerge and are reinforced.

As noted above, Vice President Dan Quayle was the first major political figure whose public image developed through an interaction of bad press and late night jokes. The comedians portrayed him as an outright fool, e.g., "Reporters asked Dan Quayle what would be the solution to global warming and he replied, 'central air conditioning'" (Letterman, quoted in Lichter et al. 2015: 72). His relative youth was sometimes brought into play by jokes that treated him as not ready for adulthood, e.g., "Dan Quayle had a birthday this week. They had a huge party for him at Chuck E. Cheese" (Leno, quoted in Media Monitor 1991). While comedians surely welcomed Quayle as a highly valuable meal ticket, their

**TABLE 1.2** Most Targeted Individuals on Late Night Comedy

| | *Most Targeted* | *N (%)* | *Second Most* | *N (%)* |
|---|---|---|---|---|
| 1992 | George H.W. Bush | 612 (16.3%) | Bill Clinton | 421 (11.2%) |
| 1993 | Bill Clinton | 440 (16.3%) | Ross Perot | 75 (2.8%) |
| 1994 | Bill Clinton | 552 (16.2%) | Ted Kennedy | 85 (2.5%) |
| 1995 | Bill Clinton | 397 (13.3%) | O.J. Simpson | 220 (7.7%) |
| 1996 | Bob Dole | 839 (17.5%) | Bill Clinton | 657 (13.7%) |
| 1997 | Bill Clinton | 808 (27.0%) | O.J. Simpson | 260 (8.7%) |
| 1998 | Bill Clinton | 1717 (32.6%) | Monica Lewinsky | 303 (5.8%) |
| 1999 | Bill Clinton | 1317 (29.1%) | Monica Lewinsky | 342 (7.6%) |
| 2000 | George W. Bush | 905 (18.3%) | Bill Clinton | 803 (16.2%) |
| 2001 | Bill Clinton | 657 (19.2%) | George W. Bush | 546 (15.9%) |
| 2002 | George W. Bush | 314 (10.1%) | Bill Clinton | 193 (6.2%) |
| 2003 | George W. Bush | 406 (15.2%) | Bill Clinton | 241 (9.0%) |
| 2004 | George W. Bush | 1169 (22.3%) | John Kerry | 505 (9.6%) |
| 2005 | George W. Bush | 657 (20.4%) | Michael Jackson | 439 (13.6%) |
| 2006 | George W. Bush | 1213 (18.9%) | Dick Cheney | 430 (6.7%) |
| 2007 | George W. Bush | 784 (15.0%) | Paris Hilton | 256 (4.9%) |
| 2008 | John McCain | 1358 (10.2%) | George W. Bush | 1160 (8.7%) |
| 2009 | Barack Obama | 936 (8.5%) | George W. Bush | 466 (4.2%) |
| 2010 | Barack Obama | 728 (7.6%) | Sarah Palin | 298 (3.1%) |
| 2011 | Barack Obama | 270 (6.9%) | Herman Cain | 180 (4.6%) |
| 2012 | Mitt Romney | 1061 (16.5%) | Barack Obama | 401 (6.2%) |

Source: CMPA

*Tonight Show* (NBC) 1992-2012, *Late Show* (CBS) 1992-2012, *Arsenio* (Fox) 1992-1994, *Late Night* (NBC) 1993-2009, *Jon Stewart Show* (MTV) 1994, *Politically Incorrect* (ABC) 1997-2001, *Daily Show* (Comedy Central) 2003-2010, 2012, *Colbert Report* (Comedy Central) 2007–2010, 2012

jokes often dripped with disdain. As Leno put it, "People have said that every comedian's dream is to poke fun at Vice President Dan Quayle. I think it's every comedian's dream to poke fun at ex-vice president Quayle" (Lichter et al., 2015: 73).

However, any comedian who regarded Quayle as indispensable to his trade must have celebrated his successor as whipping boy in chief – Bill Clinton. Clinton arrived on the public stage wrapped in intimations of scandal, from which he never escaped for long. From Gennifer Flowers to Monica Lewinsky, fully half (50 percent) of all jokes about Clinton – over 3,000 in all – dealt with his sexual behavior. Examples: "With Bill Clinton as president, I finally understand why they celebrate President's Day with a mattress sale" (Leno, quoted in Lichter et al. 2015: 55); when Clinton visited a New York City high school, Leno commented, "He didn't want to give a speech. He just wanted to take advantage of some of those free condoms they're giving away" (Lichter et al. 2015: 149); and when he canceled a vacation to the Virgin Islands, Leno speculated, "Actually, the real reason, after Clinton left last year, no more virgins" (Lichter et al. 2015: 55). This vein of material normally proved so rich that, on a slow day for news that could be converted to political humor, Leno mused, "I wish Clinton would get another girlfriend. We need more jokes. Where is our president when I need him?" (Lichter et al. 2015: 56)

When George W. Bush replaced Clinton in the White House, the wellspring of presidential sexual humor abruptly dried up. Perhaps as a result, the late night comedians seemed to have trouble saying farewell to Clinton. As noted above, in 2001 there were more jokes about Clinton, who left office on January 20 of that year, than there were about his successor. If there is no presidential sexual humor, there is always former presidential sexual humor. (Bush's totals also dropped late in the year because comedians were loath to make fun of the president in the wake of the 9/11 terrorist attacks.)

Even so, Bush brought his own set of comical characteristics to the job. These included occasional malapropisms and physical awkwardness. But he mainly gave comedians a chance to dust off their "stupid guy" jokes left over from the Dan Quayle era. Even though Bush was a graduate of Yale University and Harvard Business School, 38 percent of all Bush jokes – over 2,300 – referenced his reputed lack of intelligence. Examples: when Bush fared poorly in the first presidential debate of the 2004 election, Letterman commented, "Experts are saying that if this was a game show, Bush would have gone home with a handshake and a quart of motor oil" (Lichter et al. 2015: 164).

Coverage of failed presidential candidates revealed similar patterns. For example, when Bob Dole ran for the president in 1996 at age 73, comedians quickly settled on his advancing years as the leitmotif of his candidacy. When Dole admitted that he dyed his hair to cover the gray, Leno commented, "It's like a Grecian formula kind of thing. Not the product you buy in the store. He actually got his from an ancient Grecian" (Lichter et al. 2015: 74). After Dole visited a kindergarten class, Leno remarked, "Dole stayed about fifteen minutes, then he had to leave because it was nap time – not for the kids" (Lichter et al. 2015: 155). All told, references to his age accounted for nearly two out of five Dole jokes (38 percent), while a secondary theme about his alleged moodiness accounted for an additional 12 percent of his jokes. For example, after Dole made a campaign stop in the Los Angeles area, Leno remarked, "He was not campaigning … Turns out Disneyland pays him to come here once a year to give scowling lessons to Grumpy" (Lichter et al. 2015: 74).

Such examples of stereotyping could be found for most of the major political figures over the past three decades. However, Barack Obama was at least a partial exception to this rule. As a candidate and as president, he was the target of fewer jokes than his predecessors were. Notably, reporters also covered Obama more positively than they treated his predecessors (Farnsworth and Lichter 2011b, 2012a). This relatively positive news made it more difficult for comedians to find personal characteristics around which to build a negative stereotype.

Accordingly, there was no single quality, or even set of qualities, that framed humor focusing on Obama. Indeed, many of the reputed "Obama jokes" turned out to be jokes about the reverence he received as a candidate and as a new president. For example, in his "fake news" report on Obama's trip to Israel, Jon Stewart reported that he "would be stopping in Bethlehem to visit the manger where he was born" (Lichter et al. 2015: 80). Obama's star eventually faded somewhat, and he followed his presidential predecessors in becoming the most joked-about individual from 2009 through 2011, albeit with lower joke totals than other recent presidents.

For the 21 years examined in Table 1.2 (1992–2012), presidents or presidential candidates ranked first every single year: seven years had George W. Bush at the top, and seven other years had Clinton ranked first. Obama, another two-term president, ranked first as the most joked-about figure in only three of his eight years as president. George H.W. Bush ranked first during his last year in office; the other top finishers were a trio of defeated Republican presidential candidates: Bob Dole, John McCain and Mitt Romney.

In addition to his seven first-place finishes, Clinton ranked second as the target of late night humor five times. George W. Bush had three second-place finishes, while O.J. Simpson, a football and film star who was acquitted of murder charges in a highly controversial trial, and Monica Lewinsky, America's most famous White House intern, ranked second in two different years.

Dan Quayle was not the only vice president targeted. Vice President Dick Cheney ranked second as a target of humor in 2006. While she was never vice president, 2008 Republican nominee, Alaska Governor and Fox News commentator Sarah Palin ranked second in humor in 2010. Presidential aspirant Herman Cain did not even become a major party nominee, but he ranked second as a joke target in 2011.

Thus, apart from the occasional scandal-scarred celebrity, late night humor has focused heavily on aspirants to and holders of national office. The case of Obama notwithstanding, the general experience of presidential candidates and presidents in office is clear from the examples cited above. When they make news, as they must, they are also providing material to late night comedians. The talk show hosts and their writers take the daily headlines they generate and make these the basis of jokes that ridicule some aspect of a politician's personality, politics, lifestyle or appearance.

Unlike their response to bad press, politicians cannot call for fairer or more accurate coverage from talk show hosts. After all, they are in the entertainment business, not the news business. Thus, complaining might just stimulate more of the same. The best politicians can do is to accept an invitation to go on a host's show and demonstrate that they can take a joke (Kolbert 1992; Morris 2009). But they are still prisoners of a new order in political communication, particularly campaign communication, in which talk show monologues are one component of a generally unfriendly media environment that includes both news and entertainment.

Table 1.3 shows the relative percentage of jokes made about the two major party nominees during election years from 1992 through 2016. (The 2016 data for Trump and Clinton stop shortly after Election Day, on November 11, 2016.) Trump's total of 78 percent of jokes, compared to 22 percent for Hillary Clinton, represents the most one-sided distribution of jokes between the two major party nominees in the entire quarter century. However, Trump was only one percentage point ahead of Mitt Romney's 77 percent share, compared to Barack Obama's 23 percent, in 2012. The third greatest disparity occurred in 2004, when George W. Bush endured 70 percent of all jokes, compared to 30 percent for John Kerry. The next biggest difference was the 64 percent of jokes aimed at John McCain, compared to 36 percent for Obama in 2008, followed by George W. Bush's 62 percent versus Al Gore's 38 percent in 2000. Not surprisingly, the two Bill Clinton elections had the smallest partisan differences: George H.W. Bush's 59 percent versus Clinton's 41 percent in 1992 and Bob Dole's 56 percent compared to Bill Clinton's 44 percent four years later.

Thus, the tilt in jokes about Trump is not so one-sided in historical context as it is relative to other contenders in the 2016 election. The most consistent division was partisan – Republican candidates always attracted substantially more jokes than their Democratic opponents did. Moreover, the gap became increasingly great over time, from less than a three-to-two margin in the earliest two elections to more than a three-to-one margin in the most recent two contests. Even Bill Clinton, whose behavior was like catnip to comedians, generated fewer

**TABLE 1.3** Proportion of Jokes about the Two Presidential Nominees (1992–2016)

| | *Republican* | | *Democrat* | | *Total Jokes* |
|---|---|---|---|---|---|
| 1992 | GHW Bush | 59% | B Clinton | 41% | 1033 |
| 1996 | Dole | 56% | B Clinton | 44% | 1496 |
| 2000 | GW Bush | 62% | Gore | 38% | 1451 |
| 2004 | GW Bush | 70% | Kerry | 30% | 1674 |
| 2008 | McCain | 64% | Obama | 36% | 2126 |
| 2012 | Romney | 77% | Obama | 23% | 1462 |
| 2016 | Trump | 78% | H Clinton | 22% | 2329 |

Source: CMPA

Note: Totals for 1992–2012 are based on entire calendar year in which election took place and use the same comedy outlets used for those years in Table 1.2. Totals for 2016 cover January 1 to November 11 and includes jokes from *Tonight Show* (NBC), *Late Show* (CBS), *Jimmy Kimmel Live!* (ABC), *Daily Show* (Comedy Central).

jokes than his GOP opponents did in both 1992 and 1996. And there is a limiting factor on Trump's contribution to the partisan trend. With the tilt already up to 77 percent toward the Republican in the previous election, there was simply not much room for an additional increase without the monologues becoming all Trump all the time (as sometimes seemed to be the case).

## What Comes Next?

In this opening chapter, we have focused on political humor at key moments during the first half-century of late night television comedy as well as the evolution of the presidency as a central figure of political satire and parody.

That discussion has set the stage for understanding the unique role that Donald Trump has played in the history of political humor. Chapter 2 examines the rise of Trump as a focus of attention for both news and entertainment media. Years before he became a presidential candidate, Trump was a rich source of humor, both within New York City and for the country as a whole. The pre-candidate Trump was a best-selling author and an intense seeker of publicity. He was a guest host on *Saturday Night Live*, the subject of a roast on Comedy Central and, most prominently, as host of *The Apprentice*, a popular reality television show, all before he became a national political figure.

Chapter 3 examines how Donald Trump dominated late night comedic discourse during every phase of the 2016 presidential election campaign, receiving far more attention than his Republican rivals during the nomination stage and far more than Hillary Clinton during the general election. The comedians offered political discourse that resembled mainstream election news coverage of presidential campaigns: very little policy-oriented commentary and a heavy focus on political strategy and personality.

In Chapter 4, we show how the late night comics directed a record number of jokes at President Trump during his first year in office. Trump's presidency also triggered a growing turn towards activism by the late night comics, as Jimmy Kimmel and others started using personal stories and policy discussions to try to shape public opinion regarding health care and other matters.

In Chapter 5, we examine public opinion surveys, conducted by the Pew Research Center and scholarly analyses that demonstrate how growing numbers of voters, particularly younger ones, are focusing more on political humor as they learn about politics, and as they establish their political interests and opinions. The chapter also examines some of the public views about the links between traditional news and the "comedy news" of late night humor.

Our final chapter turns to the future of political humor. What might the comedians do during the remainder of the Trump presidency and how might their treatment of Trump shape political humor as it addresses subsequent presidents?

# 2

# THE BLUSTERING BILLIONAIRE OF TALK SHOWS AND TWITTER

More than almost any other political or business figure of his generation, Donald Trump was a media creation – and a largely self-made one at that. From his first appearances on the New York City real estate and late night clubbing scenes four decades ago, Trump was the master of his own ceremonies. He aggressively courted media attention and celebrity status at every opportunity, doing so with finely tuned media instincts that even battle-tested public relations operatives would envy. Trump commented regularly on the prominent issues of the day, whether those concerns had much to do with him or not, such as the infamous Central Park jogger assault case.

When his business and personal interests were more directly involved, Trump used the media to advance his reputation. This included needling city officials who did not act as he wished and pushing for tax breaks that allowed him to create large real estate developments bearing the family name. All the while, he was building his business empire. He promoted Trump products at every opportunity, offering an image of excess that stretched from his palatial apartment and elite golf resorts to his luxury yacht and private jet. When he was unsatisfied with the level of attention reporters devoted to him, he even used an alias ("John Barron") to provide morsels of his own jet-setting lifestyle to the gossip-hungry New York tabloids. Reporters looked the other way as Trump pretended to be someone else as he told stories about himself (Fisher 2018; Hurt 1993).

From the start, though, Trump had set his sights on drawing his self-portrait on a canvas larger than Manhattan. He aggressively sought to build a national brand for himself via appearances on late night television and "shock jock" radio. He branded casinos, a university, steaks, wines, clothing and an airline shuttle. He bought a professional football team, feuded with other real estate moguls and regularly argued with *Forbes* magazine over how rich he really was. When all else failed, Trump used lawsuits to draw attention to his latest business ventures (or as a way to change the subject when things were not going well).

He and his co-authors wrote several best-selling books cataloguing his rise, his financial challenges and his revival – sporting his last name as the first word in the title (Trump with Leerhsen 1990; Trump with Bohner 1997; Trump with Schwartz 2004[originally 1987]). To increase book sales even further – and to increase the value of his personal brand – Trump publicly mused about running for president several times, years before his successful 2016 campaign (Hurt 1993).

Thus Trump established himself as famous for being famous – even before the Internet made that celebrity formula commonplace. In short, he went viral in the analog age, via the tabloids, glossy magazines, talk radio and talk television.

> As a real estate developer, Trump craved the respect of industry leaders, politicians and the *New York Times*, even as he attacked such institutions as elitist. Trump's attitude toward celebrities has followed the same pattern, a provocative mix of seeking their approval and attacking their privilege. Trump wanted to be New York's biggest builder, but even more than that, he wanted to be a grand American showman whose name was synonymous with a high-end, aspirational brand. He knew — both instinctively and through the tutelage of his mentor and lawyer, Roy Cohn — that a key way to build that brand was through celebrity, both his own and the reflected fame of Big Names.
>
> *(Fisher 2018).*

To be sure, Trump's obsessive media-seeking behavior was a win-win proposition. Trump wanted the attention and the media wanted readers and viewers. Trump always offered a compelling story, and he was ratings gold when it came to television. NBC wisely created *The Apprentice* and then *The Celebrity Apprentice* as vehicles to highlight one of the nation's most media-savvy entrepreneurs. Trump TV was an immense commercial success for the network (and for him), further building his reputation as a celebrity executive for those who already knew of him. For those who did not, these network television shows introduced Donald Trump to an even larger national audience of people who might spend money on his wine, his menswear collection and his steaks. They might even support his political ambitions someday.

News organizations were not the only media beneficiaries of Trump's presence in the national conversation. Such a relentless self-promoter represented a rich source of humor, both within New York City and for the country as a whole. His willingness to appear in so many media formats gave them the chance to sell his personal brand in one place after another. His bombastic temperament made him ripe for parody and mockery long before he became a presidential candidate. Over the past three decades, Trump has been a familiar enough figure to be invited to joke with the hosts on late night television talk shows. He took two celebrity star turns as a guest host of *Saturday Night Live,* where he was frequently lampooned by actors imitating him.

For those who know only of Trump's presidential-era feuds with late night comics, it may come as a surprise that years earlier he readily turned to those same outlets to help build his national brand. Trump, though, does not always dance with the one who brought him.

This chapter tells the story of Donald Trump's use of mass media – and mass media's use of Trump – to promote himself and the programs where he appeared or was a topic of conversation. His rise to the level of a viable presidential candidate in the years leading up to his run for president is a compelling story of how both news and entertainment media can make someone larger than life even as it sometimes cuts him down to size.

## Introducing Trump: Promoting the Celebrity and the Man of Business

In the 1970s, when Trump was first breaking into the New York City cultural world as a young man, he was mentored by Roy Cohn, a former aide to Senator Joseph McCarthy (R-WI) turned influential lawyer. Cohn introduced Trump to the likes of New York Yankees owner George Steinbrenner and Cindy Adams, one of Manhattan's leading writers of celebrity gossip (Fisher 2018). As Trump began to move about the city's rarified social circles, he even drew attention from the *New York Times*, which opened a 1976 feature story on him with these breathless sentences.

> He is tall, lean and blond, with dazzling white teeth, and he looks ever so much like Robert Redford. He rides around town in a chauffeured silver Cadillac with his initials, DJT, on the plates. He dates slinky fashion models, belongs to the most elegant clubs and, at only 30 years of age, estimates that he is worth "more than $200 million." Flair. It's one of Donald J. Trump's favorite words, and both he, his friends and his enemies use it when describing his way of life as well as his business style as New York's No. 1 real estate promoter of the middle 1970's. "If a man has flair," the energetic, outspoken Mr. Trump said the other day, "and is smart and somewhat conservative and has a taste for what people want, he's bound to be successful in New York."
>
> *(Klemesrud 1976)*

In addition to his growing celebrity status and his influential connections, Trump was telling a story Manhattan wanted to hear. His grand real estate visions for a revived, vigorous New York came at a time when the nearly bankrupt city appeared in public culture as an increasingly dystopian metropolis. *The Times*' puff piece on Trump appeared in the same year as the bleak film *Taxi Driver*, not to mention the notorious serial killer known as the "Son of Sam." At that low point of the city's despair, along came a brash developer with a big mouth and even bigger ideas for a city that was desperate for a rebirth. Trump's proposed renovation of properties near the Grand Central terminal and the redevelopment of the Penn Central yards on the city's west side spoke to an exceptional optimism for that time (Klemesrud 1976).

The go-go economy of the 1980s replaced the malaise of the 1970s, an emerging turbo-charged capitalism embodied by the fictional Wall Street financier Gordon Gekko in *Wall Street* (1987), whose motto was "greed is good." In real life, the rising young developer Donald Trump could have given Gekko a run for his money.

> By 1981, Trump was already the epitome of American business bravado. At 35 years old, he had cut historic multi-million dollar land deals, saved a blighted midtown Manhattan subway hub, and was in the process of erecting the black-framed glass behemoth of Trump Tower.
>
> *(Pagliary 2016)*

Trump and his gilded lifestyle highlighted popular television entertainment programs of the day, including *Entertainment Tonight*, where the brash business executive's life was featured alongside mega-celebrities like Cher, film star Robert Wagner and former president Gerald Ford (Kerr 1984). The developer named an airline after himself, the Trump Shuttle, as well as Trump Air, a helicopter service, and he slapped his name on many of his buildings (Hurt 1993).

Trump's national profile also expanded during these years via his ownership of the New Jersey Generals, part of the United States Football League (Eskenazi 1984). The USFL, which existed briefly as a rival to the NFL, received a significant amount of media attention thanks to the brash, media-savvy New York team owner who challenged the New York area NFL teams, the Giants and the Jets, to do battle (Eskenazi 1984; Geist 1984).

As Trump snatched NFL players for the USFL, many New York area celebrities, sports figures and politicians were at least as interested in being seen with Trump as Trump was in being seen with them – and he deeply desired the imprimatur of those with the greatest amounts of fame, fortune and power (Geist 1984).

> While executives of the other teams told the audience about problems of negotiation and arbitration, about dirty restrooms inside their arenas and street crime outside and about "attempting to move the Mets in the right direction," Donald Trump was electrifying the room with rat-a-tat-tat revelations, dropping names of star N.F.L. players and coaches he would sign in a matter of hours. He said further that he would "continue to create chaos" for the N.F.L. and, by the way, that he planned to build a domed stadium in New York.
>
> *(Geist 1984)*

Donald Trump seemed to enjoy the chaos he could engender in pro sports, as he went up against the established titans of the NFL. This love for disorder would also be a hallmark of the Trump presidential campaign and presidency that would take shape three decades later. One could observe the same reflection of the future in the hyperbole contained in his proposal for an expensive domed stadium in New York for a financially struggling football league. (More than three decades after Trump's boast, neither of the two New York area NFL teams play in a domed stadium.) When the renegade football league disbanded in 1985, Trump walked away with a financial loss estimated at $22 million (Hurt 1993).

Trump soon turned his attention to boxing, which fit in well with his existing investments in Atlantic City casinos. Despite his efforts, the media did not always allow Trump to change the subject as rapidly as he had hoped. The rival football league's failure foreshadowed Trump's subsequent involvement in sports. "Donald Trump, the New York real-estate developer who helped raise the average salary in the National Football League, is dedicated to the proposition that Atlantic City must not turn into the United States Football League of boxing," the *New York Times* noted with snark as it previewed a Mike Tyson heavyweight championship bout in New Jersey in 1987 (Anderson 1987).

After having put his name on so many properties, Trump then sought to branch out into television. The syndicated game show, *Trump Card*, filmed at Trump Castle in Atlantic City, gave contestants the opportunity to answer questions and thereby fill out an approximation of a bingo card (Carter 1989). When the show began airing in 1990, Trump said he was very optimistic: "I think it will be tremendously successful. We're trading on the glamour of the Trump Castle, the Trump Princess [his yacht] … The Trump name has never been hotter" (quoted in Van Luling 2017). Despite the substantial publicity and the great interest from television producers, however, the show only ran for one season.

The news was somewhat negative in Trump's real estate businesses as well. After he acquired a hotel and a rent-stabilized building at Central Park South, Trump engaged in a high-profile battle with the apartment building's tenants. He hired an aggressive law firm to pressure tenants to leave, peppering them with lease violation notices that pushed them into departing or facing extensive legal expenses to retain their apartments (Pagliary 2016). In their lawsuits, several tenants said that Trump had turned off their heat and water to force them out of their apartments, while Trump denied these harassment allegations (Pagliary 2016). In the end, Trump dropped his five-year effort to evict the tenants (James 1986).

Regardless of whether the news was good or bad, Trump served as his own public relations officer. For example, in a 1983 *New York Times* profile, Trump demonstrated his well-known aversion to modesty.

> "Not many sons have been able to escape their fathers," said Donald Trump, the president of the Trump Organization, by way of interpreting his accomplishments. Three of them, built since 1976, stand out amidst the

> crowded midtown landscape: the 68-story Trump Tower, with its six-story Atrium housing some of the world's most elegant stores; the 1,400-room Grand Hyatt Hotel, and Trump Plaza, a $125 million cooperative apartment. And more is on the way. "At 37, no one has done more than I in the last seven years," Mr. Trump asserted.
>
> *(Bender 1983).*

Trump's setbacks of the late 1980s did not deter him. He concentrated instead on his successes and his plans for a comeback. Despite the troubles with his professional football team, his quickly canceled game show and his debt-burdened casino and real estate holdings, Trump's self-promotion efforts were consistently aggressive. Trump the businessperson and New York City celebrity was prone to exaggeration regardless of circumstances, as he admitted in *Trump: The Art of the Deal*: "I play to people's fantasies. I call it truthful hyperbole. It's an innocent form of exaggeration—and a very effective form of promotion" (quoted in Swanson 2016).

Trump took risks, and he endured several bankruptcies of his businesses over the years, making him less a financial success story than he appeared to be in the media (Swanson 2016).

> By 1990, Trump had run up such enormous debts that ruin seemed all but inevitable. His annual interest payments on $2 billion in bank loans and more than $1 billion in bonds sold to finance the purchase of the casinos exceeded his cash flow. Forced to throw himself on the mercy of his banks, Trump bluffed and bargained his way out of the hole with a *sang-froid* that even his worst critics have acknowledged. In the end, he received a short-term infusion of capital and restructured the bank debt on more favorable terms; in exchange, he agreed to sell off his most egregiously nonperforming assets and to accept a monthly "allowance" of $450,000, which he proceeded to ignore. And then he started buying up property in the depressed market of the mid-90's.
>
> *(Traub 2004)*

In good times and in bad, Trump was very effective at presenting himself as successful and well connected – a person of consequence in a city filled with celebrities. He was part of the establishment, to be sure, but also something of a renegade who lived an immensely posh lifestyle but also exhibited a populist streak.

> Trump knew instinctively that he could enhance his own stature by being seen with celebrities, and he also knew he could do it by breaking the rules and bashing some of those same famous people. No other president has come to the White House as deeply schooled in the methods and madness of

> the American craft of celebrity. And no other president has used celebrities in quite the same way—both as inspiration to mold policies and as foils to entertain and satisfy his political base.
>
> *(Fisher 2018).*

Trump secured iconic Big Apple status on December 10, 1988, when he and his first wife Ivana Trump, as played by Phil Hartman and Jan Hooks, provided the *Saturday Night Live* opening: "Live from New York, it's Saturday Night!" In that opening segment, the two Trump characters gave each other large, gold and jewel-encrusted, highly ostentatious presents (Tropiano 2013). The same two performers impersonated the Trumps again during the show's February 17, 1990 episode, when the couple argued over the distribution of Trump's assets as they planned their divorce (Tropiano 2013).

## *Trump's Media Instincts: Converting Crisis into Opportunity*

One key strategy that also aided Donald Trump's rise to prominence in New York was his ability to see opportunities that would spring from injecting himself into ongoing news stories. In May 1989, a few days after New York City first learned of the horrific story of a white female jogger who was brutally attacked in Central Park, Trump took out ads in four of the city's daily newspapers arguing that the crime should lead to the reinstatement of the death penalty in New York State (Wilson 2002). The crime, which dominated the news of the city that spring, laid bare the city's often-simmering racial tensions.

> In the ad, Mr. Trump said Mayor Edward I. Koch had stated "that hate and rancor should be removed from our hearts," to which Mr. Trump replied: "I do not think so. I want to hate these muggers and murderers. They should be forced to suffer and, when they kill, they should be executed for their crimes." At the time, the attack victim was still in a coma. The ad does not name any defendant, instead referring collectively to "roving bands of wild criminals."
>
> *(Wilson 2002).*

Years later, DNA evidence cleared the teenagers, who originally confessed to the crime under dubious circumstances and went to jail for years for it. The new evidence identified instead a convicted murderer as the attacker (Wilson 2002). But Trump's efforts did feed into political pressure to restore capital punishment, and New York State passed a new death penalty law several years later (Halbfinger 1997).

Although it was over a lesser matter, Trump's instincts for injecting himself into a long-running news story also led to his involvement in the problematic public renovation project of Wollman Rink in Central Park. The city had kept the ice-skating rink closed for years and had already spent $13 million on problematic repairs when Trump offered in 1986 to rebuild the rink using his own money if he could lease it back to the city and operate it at a profit (Hurt 1993). Trump's offer served the double purpose of building his personal brand and making his rival, in this case New York City Mayor Ed Koch, look bad. The rink dispute was one of many times the two men sparred over the future direction of the nation's largest city (Freedman 1987). As the rink restoration was underway, Trump held news conference after news conference to take credit for incremental developments and to tout subsequent promotional activities (Geist 1986). In the end, Trump and Koch celebrated the rink's opening ahead of schedule and under budget in November 1986 at a gala event that included Olympian Peggy Fleming (Geist 1986).

## Trump's Expanding National Profile

In the 1990s and the decades that followed, Trump's desire for fame continued to take the form of media-oriented activities. There was the best-selling book, of course, which generated considerable national interest and attention. But the national marketing campaign was just getting started. He kicked off the 1990s with a *Playboy* cover photo and interview that he bragged about for a quarter-century, even after becoming a Republican presidential nominee in part through the support of conservative Christian voters.

> The racy *Playboy* magazine cover featuring the circa-1990 version of Donald Trump graced the billionaire's New York office for years — right next to awards from religious groups and clippings from other magazines that didn't feature naked pictorials.
>
> The cover and the extensive interview inside the March 1990 edition were a feather in Trump's cap, placing him in elite company with other political and entertainment luminaries spotlighted by the magazine.
>
> In the famous *Playboy* cover photo, Trump is wearing tuxedo pants, a cummerbund and a bow tie.
>
> But Playmate Brandi Brandt has donned his jacket — and nothing else.
>
> "I was one of the few men in the history of *Playboy* to be on the cover," he boasted to a *Washington Post* reporter taking a tour of his office during the 2016 presidential campaign.
>
> Trump embraced the association: During his bid for the presidency, he was known to autograph copies of the magazine, offering a quick scrawl during campaign stops.
>
> *(Wootson 2017).*

At the core of Trump's rebranding as a connoisseur of beautiful women was Marla Maples, the former beauty pageant contestant who first became the "other woman" and then wife number two. Trump lavished attention on her, in part because he thought having a beautiful young woman on his arm reflected well on him (Brozan 1992). The breakup of Trump's first marriage drew the attention of *Saturday Night Live* on February 24, 1990, where Dana Carvey's "Church Lady" character scolded Donald Trump, then played by Phil Hartman, and Marla Maples, played by Jan Hooks, for their sinful ways, referring to the couple as a "satanic sandwich" (Tropiano 2013).

The eventual nuptials offered another opportunity for Trump to bask in the media attention he so intensely craved. It also reminded everyone about how this one-time outer-borough boy had arrived at the pinnacle of the New York society scene without a blue-chip pedigree. And if he was bothered by a sniffy *New York Times* report on the festivities that portrayed him as a shameless arriviste, he never showed it.

> The middle-aged master builder finally decides to marry the actress-model mother of his infant child, a week after she unveils her new line of maternity clothes, in a ceremony at the grand hotel formerly managed by his former wife. The bride wears white, le tout New York is invited, and if an iota of social opprobrium attaches to the event, no one seems to notice.
>
> The Age of Innocence it's not.
>
> But when the bride is Marla Maples and the groom is Donald J. Trump, when the hotel is his (and his creditors') Plaza and the guest list features O. J. Simpson, Liza Minnelli, David N. Dinkins, Alfonse M. D'Amato and Howard Stern, blushing has long since ceased to be an issue for all but the roses on the five-tiered butter-cream cake.
>
> *(Purdum 1993)*

The wedding drew barbs from the popular culture as well as the establishment press. Late night host David Letterman joked that Trump "was relieved to be settling down to marriage, so he could start dating again" (quoted in Purdum 1993). Howard Stern, the radio shock jock who often bantered with Trump on his program and was a guest at the wedding, said on the day of Trump's nuptials: "It's probably in bad taste, but I give it four months" (quoted in Dullea 1993). In fact, the couple announced their decision to separate after less than four years of marriage (Weber 1997). About a year later, journalists reported that Trump was dating Melania Knauss, the Slovenian model who subsequently became Trump's third wife (Walder 1999).

Trump had more than marriages and girlfriends on his mind during these years. He also sought to restore his reputation with new commercial developments. In a news report entitled, "52-Story Comeback Is So Very Trump; Columbus Circle Tower Proclaims That Modesty Is an Overrated Virtue," the *New York Times* said in 1996 that Donald Trump and his business empire had recovered from hard times.

> Maybe he slipped under your radar over the last few years. Maybe you came to think of him as a real estate also-ran, or a chewed-over chunk of tabloid fodder.
>
> Look again. Up in the sky. It's Donald J. Trump. All 52 gold-tinted stories of him.
>
> The Trump International Hotel and Tower is open for business, looming over Columbus Circle and Central Park like a ghost of the Gulf and Western Building, which is precisely what it is. And with his new building, due for occupancy in the fall, Donald Trump seems to be busily renovating himself in much the same way: as himself – only more so.
>
> "This just represents the best point in my life," Mr. Trump said the other day, settling back in his stretch limousine. "I think it says that what I've been doing over the years has been right."
>
> If buildings could talk, this one would be shouting, "Forget about it!" Forget about the nagging Atlantic City casino debts, the loss of his plane and his yacht. Forget about the public collapse of his marriage and the soap-opera affair. Forget about the discrediting of the haute New York world that Mr. Trump once proudly embodied and aches to be part of again.
>
> *(Pogrebin 1996)*

Trump's willingness to appear on unrestrained entertainment programs like those hosted by Howard Stern, and his willingness to contribute to vulgar, demeaning commentary about women, would create problems for Trump as a presidential candidate. But in the years before the 2016 election, Trump felt quite comfortable talking like an aging frat boy, ranking women on their appearance and gleefully insulting those not up to his standards of physical perfection (Kaczynski and McDermott 2016).

> The most popular topic of conversation during these appearances, as is typical of Stern's program, was sex. In particular, Trump frequently discussed women he had sex with, wanted to have sex with, or wouldn't have sex with if given the opportunity. He also rated women on a 10-point scale. "A person who is very flat-chested is very hard to be a 10," he told Stern in one typical exchange.
>
> *(Kaczynski and McDermott 2016)*

Then came *The Apprentice*, which presented Trump even more forcefully before a national audience. The highly rated show was an excellent promotional vehicle for Donald Trump. It was a particularly effective way to reach people who knew little about New York or launching a business but knew an entertainer when they saw one. NBC shaped the show to make Trump the center of the action and the very model of a modern capitalist baron, shuttling around by helicopter and making hard business decisions every episode.

> Trump is god of "The Apprentice," its fate, its hero. And yet he often presides over this battle to the death with the leering malevolence of a Bond villain.

> He goes about either by black limo or black chopper, and he usually emerges from these war chariots with an ominous cuing of the strings. He materializes at the beginning of each episode to issue his entrepreneurial labor of Hercules. Then he often disappears until the very end, when he receives the contestants in a dark boardroom crossed with menacing shadows. And at the end of each episode, he administers the famous Blofeldian order of execution: "You're fired!" … Donald Trump is an egomaniacal, germophobic multi-multi-millionaire, and yet television viewers, and the folks who gather outside Trump Tower hoping for a glimpse, can't get enough of him.
>
> *(Traub 2004)*

One of the things that pleased Trump about the show was the opportunity it provided to receive requests from people who want to be on a show, a form of respect that others were required to provide. As one reporter noted, "Trump complained, halfheartedly and with characteristic exaggeration, about this new level of acclaim. ('If I walked on the streets with you right now we'd have a crowd of a thousand within seconds.') But he won't try to hide his euphoria about all the attention" (Segal 2004). The adulation, thanks to television, came at a good time for the mogul, when his casino business was sinking in debt, leading to a Chapter 11 bankruptcy filing (Segal 2004).

> Donald Trump, who does not believe in much, is a zealot in the cult of fame. It is, for him, the bottom line of all bottom lines. One day he was telling me about the major figures – "the biggest people, the most white-shoe people, people that you see at the art galleries" – who had called "begging" to appear on *The Apprentice*, even if they would deny ever watching the show. The whole thing filled him with gleeful scorn.
>
> *(Traub 2004)*

But Trump's financial problems during these years were not the focus of Middle America, which loved the drama provided by the show and its star and cared little about whether Trump deserved the expertise accorded to him on *The Apprentice*. As Eric Dezenhall, a Washington media crisis management firm executive, observed, "If your goal is to get people in the American heartland to watch your TV show, having outrageous hair and pink ties and using superlatives is a legitimate pathway to that goal. If your object is to earn the respect of other moguls, that's not the route" (quoted in Segal 2004).

## *Conan O'Brien Remembers Trump the Guest*

Longtime late night TV host Conan O'Brien frequently featured Donald Trump on his show (then on NBC), starting in 1997 and continuing through Trump's years on *The Apprentice* on that same network. O'Brien said one of Trump's early appearances did not go well, and he left the stage in a huff. O'Brien had asked how much money Trump had in his pockets at that moment, and Trump fished in his pockets and pulled out a condom (Doyle 2019). Trump vowed he would never be on the show again, O'Brien said, recounting that Trump told a producer as he stormed off the set: "That's the last time I'm gonna be on this f***ing show. He humiliated me in front of everybody" (quoted in Doyle 2019). He reconsidered and returned repeatedly to banter with Conan O'Brien in the years that followed.

For all the attention Trump sought via late night comedy, including several subsequent appearances on O'Brien's show, the business executive appeared a sharp contrast from many political leaders who could laugh at themselves at least part of the time (Doyle 2019). As O'Brien said:

> To really have a sense of humor, you have to be able to laugh at yourself. You have to be able to see the human condition as absurd. Our funny presidents have always been able to see the inherent absurdity of it all. John F. Kennedy served in the Navy and saw how f**ked up the Navy brass was and how badly things were done. His illnesses as a kid helped educate him that life was a crapshoot and inherently ridiculous. I think that gave him a great, witty sense of irony. Lincoln famously found himself to be hideous and was the first one to make fun of himself, our most self-deprecating president. I think all of that is anathema to Trump. Trump's superpower is constantly believing in the infallibility of Trump. Humility is a weakness to him. Having performed two different White House Correspondents' Dinners and seen Clinton and Obama sit there and laugh at themselves, I don't think Trump can do that.
>
> *(quoted in Doyle 2019)*

While he could never self-deprecate like Lincoln did – and who among us could? – Trump may have developed a better sense of humor as the years went by. He first hosted *Saturday Night Live* on April 3, 2004, when he observed in his opening monologue, "It's great to be here at *Saturday Night Live*, but I will be completely honest, it's even better for *Saturday Night Live* that I am here," a riff on his large ego (Inside Edition 2015). That *SNL* episode – one of two that Trump hosted – included an advertisement for a fictitious chicken restaurant, "Trump's House of Wings." It featured Trump, dressed in a yellow suit and tie, dancing with cast members dressed up as chickens (Inside Edition 2015). That fake ad generated some controversy, and *SNL* removed it from some of its archives – though for reasons that remain unclear to this day (Inside Edition 2015).

## Pivoting Towards Politics

In terms of his own brand of politics, Trump also offered a somewhat inconsistent narrative. In the years before the 2016 presidential election, he had given money to Democrats as well as Republicans, and he changed his party registration back and forth (Ceaser et al. 2017). Trump considered running for office off and on over the years and renewed his interest in politics during the Obama presidency, when he became a spokesperson for the "Birther" movement, which alleged without evidence that Obama was not born in the United States and therefore was ineligible to be president (Williamson et al. 2011).

The birther movement was hardly Trump's first entry into the political realm. Trump had cozied up to political figures – and sometimes sparred with them – from his first days as a young midtown developer. As he first began to make his way in the New York City of the 1970s and 1980s, he found it useful to interact with politicians, inviting them to his events and donating to their campaigns. As early as the 1980s Trump was talking about his interest in electoral politics. But even as he mingled among politicians, he did not present himself as one of them. He sometimes offered himself in sharp contrast, as the private-sector executive who could cut through the jungle of red tape and nasty political debate and actually get something done.

This self-framing of Trump as the man of action marked his years as a developer who chafed at the bureaucrats who stood in the way of his casino and hotel projects. He also rebelled against high-profile case studies of New York political gridlock, including two cases discussed above: the city's apparent inability to deter crime absent a death penalty and the mess of a repair to a highly visible ice skating rink in Central Park.

Trump first raised the possibility of being a presidential candidate in 1987, when he appeared to start laying the political groundwork by placing a series of advertisements expressing his political views in the *New York Times, Washington Post* and *Boston Globe*. To heighten the speculation, Trump then flew via helicopter to the pivotal first primary state of New Hampshire to talk politics with Portsmouth-area Rotarians (Hurt 1993). His theme that day, one he would use when campaigning decades later, was that other nations had "ripped off" the United States by not paying their fair share of collective defense costs (Hurt 1993). Subsequent news reports of his potential candidacy appeared in the *New York Times* and on ABC News' *20/20* and helped sell more copies of Trump's new book. In the end, he did not run for president, but talking about doing so clearly made him some money from book royalties (Hurt 1993).

The 1988 campaign was not the only time that Trump contemplated a presidential campaign. He and then-girlfriend Melania Knauss did a joint interview with Howard Stern in 1999, where Trump offered that he was exploring a presidential run in 2000 and bragged about his sex life with his model girlfriend (Walder 1999). While Trump was a well-known figure, he was not a popular one: a *New York Times*/CBS News poll conducted in advance of the 2000 campaign found that 70 percent of Americans viewed him negatively (Walder 1999).

Trump flirted with the idea of running as a Reform Party candidate for president in 2000, and he endured a few cantankerous meetings with state Reform Party committees before passing on that election as well (Nagourney 1999, 2000).

(The Reform Party started as a vehicle for Ross Perot, another business magnate turned presidential candidate.) Because the timing of those campaign appearances matched the release of another Trump book, some Reform Party activists had their doubts about Trump's commitment to the party and its policies (Nagourney 1999). Trump did emphasize the need to tighten immigration in those meetings, and he had a sit-down interview with Jay Leno on *The Tonight Show*, which honored his presence by playing "Hail to the Chief" as Trump's entrance music (Nagourney 1999).

After those would-be campaigns that went nowhere, Trump used *The Apprentice* to expand his brand as well as re-shape the public's views of him. While his first book sold 875,000 copies in hardcover, television provided an entirely different reach: 40 million people watched some part of the first-season finale of *The Apprentice* (Traub 2004). "The show was the top-rated new series and tied with *The West Wing* for attracting TV's most affluent prime time demographic. *The Apprentice* almost single-handedly rescued the lagging fortunes of NBC, the network that broadcast it" (Traub 2004).

## Trump, Obama and the Birther Rumor

When Barack Obama ran for president in 2008, and during Obama's tenure in office, Donald Trump, with the assistance of expanding and ever more influential social media outlets, spread the false rumor that Obama was not born in the United States and was therefore not eligible to be president (Chadwick 2013). Even after President Obama produced a birth certificate that proved he was born in Hawaii, Trump's false claims generated an enthusiastic response from Republican crowds and substantial attention from journalists (Abramowitz 2017).

In 2011, when Trump again flirted with the idea of becoming a presidential candidate, he surged in the polls and seemed to be a viable challenger to Obama (Brooks 2011). He tweeted more than 200 times about President Obama in advance of the 2012 election, constructing an argument about why he should not be re-elected – and repeated the by then-debunked birther claim. The fact that Trump's claims about Obama were false mattered little – what mattered far more was that the statements were useful for Trump.

Starting in April 2011, Trump provided a weekly commentary segment on *Fox and Friends*, where he offered his take on current political and business developments. He used his Fox News appearances to continue to promote the discredited claim that Obama was not born in the US, as well as offering his own political analysis and eventually improving his own electoral prospects (Bump 2019). If he ran for president in 2012, Trump said, his friend and political expert Roger Stone thought he would be a very strong candidate nominee (Bump 2019). In the end, Trump chose not to run in 2012, but the exploratory efforts that year foreshadowed the approach that he would take in 2016: that of a brassy leader who may play fast and loose with the truth but promises to shake up the system. As the conservative *New York Times* columnist David Brooks wrote:

> There has always been a fan base for the abrasive rich man. There has always been a market for books by people like George Steinbrenner, Ross Perot, Bill O'Reilly, Rush Limbaugh, Bobby Knight, Howard Stern and George Soros. There has always been a large clump of voters who believe that America could reverse its decline if only a straight-talking, obnoxious blowhard would take control. … Many people regard Trump as a joke and his popularity a disgrace. But he is actually riding a deep public fantasy: The hunger for the ultimate blowhard who can lead us through dark times.
>
> *(Brooks 2011)*

Since he was not a candidate in 2012, Trump remained a regular contributor to *Fox and Friends* until he declared for president in June 2015. That valuable media real estate provided several additional years of opportunities for the future presidential candidate to sell himself on the nation's leading conservative television outlet as the answer to Republican struggles to find a compelling, conservative presidential candidate (Bump 2019).

Trump specialized in a divisive approach, designed to undermine not just the Obama presidency but also the conventional orientations of traditional Republicans who had nominated the likes of Mitt Romney and John McCain. Trump's path to victory required increasing the anger of white working-class voters troubled by changing conditions in the US, and turning that anger to his own advantage. That formed a key part of his message on *Fox and Friends*, as well as in the presidential campaign to come.

## *Obama Gets Even: The White House Correspondents Dinner*

The White House Correspondents Dinner represents a rare public venue for a president to mock his critics in front of the country's most important political and cultural figures, as well as the national television audience tuning in to political Washington's premier social event. (Of course, he is mocked in turn by a professional comedian selected for that very purpose.) At the Correspondents Dinner in April 2011, President Obama had a rare opportunity to return fire against Donald Trump, who was in the audience that night as a guest of the *Washington Post*. The president proceeded to make the most of the moment.

> "Donald Trump is here tonight," the comedian in chief said, grinning. "Now, I know that he's taken some flak lately, but no one is prouder to put this birth certificate to rest than The Donald. Now he can get to focusing on the issues that matter. Like, did we fake the moon landing? What really happened at Roswell? And where are Biggie and Tupac?"
>
> It was almost painful to watch, the juxtaposition of the president, flexing his new post-birther comedy chops, and the real estate mogul-cum-politician,

grimacing at his table as Mr. Obama basked in his post-long-form-birth-certificate glow.

"All kidding aside, we all know about your credentials and experience," Mr. Obama said, as people in the room either chortled or grimaced nervously, all depending on their proximity to Mr. Trump.

In *Celebrity Apprentice*, Mr. Obama told Mr. Trump, teeth flashing, "the men's cooking team did not impress the judges from Omaha steaks, but you recognized that this was a lack of leadership, so you fired Gary Busey."

"These," Mr. Obama said, "are the kinds of decisions that would keep me up at night. Well-handled, sir. Well-handled."

*(Cooper 2011)*

Throughout this pummeling from the president, Trump sat stone-faced (Cooper 2011). While Trump did not choose to run for president in 2012, he would soon avenge his humiliation.

## Trump Gets Even: Anger and the Populist Challenge of 2016

While some believe that Trump brought unprecedented levels of populist anger to presidential politics, running for office has consistently been a contentious business. The level of citizen frustration with the government in Washington varies over the years as economic anxiety and political conditions change (Farnsworth 2003a, 2003b). But the anti–Wall Street fervor of populist leader and three-time Democratic presidential nominee William Jennings Bryan energized crowds more than a century ago. More recently, anger intensified during such times as the anti-communist "red scare" led by Senator Joseph McCarthy (R-WI) and the "massive resistance" to desegregating schools in the Jim Crow South. White working-class resentments fueled protests led by Alabama Gov. George Wallace in the 1960s, by independent business executive Ross Perot in the 1992 presidential campaign and by the Tea Party movement more recently (Adorno et al. 1950; Craig 1993, 1996; Farnsworth 2001, 2003a; Hibbing and Theiss-Morse 1995; Skocpol and Williamson 2012).

While these earlier movements had some political success, Trump prevailed where other populist efforts had not. His effective use of Twitter to attack the status quo resonated with many voters and helped him wrest the Republican nomination away from an experienced field of GOP governors and senators. He then defeated Democratic nominee Hillary Clinton, who had the bad luck to be an experienced political insider at a time when many voters yearned for an outsider who would shake up the system (Ceaser et al. 2017).

Trump was the culmination of more than two centuries of outsiderism: a silver-spoon populist (widely seen as a demagogue) who warned of rigged political processes, dangerous foreigners, slick lobbyists, greedy rich people, and

> snooty intellectual elites. He trafficked in insults and unfounded conspiracy theories, and some of his followers responded with a nasty zeal that crossed the line into bullying and violence.
>
> *(Ceaser et al. 2017: 9–10)*

Conservatives, particularly religious ones, were in a forgiving mood when it came to Trump. His departures from Republican orthodoxy on free trade and national security mattered little; nor did a personal lifestyle that hardly comported with Christian religious teachings. Before the 2016 campaign, even casual observers of Trump knew him for the ostentatious lifestyle he bragged about on television entertainment programs (Ceaser et al. 2017). At the time of his 2016 campaign, Trump was on his third marriage and for decades had enjoyed a lavish lifestyle that drew the attention of fame-worshippers everywhere but involved little attendance at religious services.

Trump's libertine history and gilded lifestyle made him an odd choice to be the voice of religious conservatives and angry white working-class populists, but many accepted him anyway (Ceaser et al. 2017). "Trump was the people's billionaire, offering unashamedly what the average American wanted, a Trump steak or a night at a casino, or showing the kind of luxury people could only yearn for, like a personal airplane" (Ceaser et al. 2017: ix).

Trump's aggressive character, demonstrated throughout his career as a developer and via his television appearances on Fox and elsewhere, generated extreme loyalty from some. Many angry voters embraced Trump's combative campaign, feeling that only he understood their feelings of being left behind in a rapidly changing economy and a rapidly diversifying nation. Some political scientists concluded that Trump particularly appealed to voters with authoritarian tendencies, generally defined as people who perceive the world in black and white terms, who seek a leader to restore order, who fear diversity, and who sometimes act aggressively toward those they consider outsiders (Adorno et al. 1950; Fromm 1941; Hetherington and Weiler 2009; MacWilliams 2016). Multivariate analysis of likely 2016 Republican primary voters revealed that an individual's authoritarian orientations and fear of a personal threat from terrorism predicted support for Trump rather than another Republican candidate (MacWilliams 2016).

> Throughout his campaign, Trump constantly used us-versus-them language to define the others who allegedly pose a threat to us and order. From Mexicans to Muslims, the others, as described by Trump, do not hold our values and are not like us. To Trump and the crowds who follow his lead, he alone recognizes the threat the others pose and he alone possesses the will to neutralize them. … Trump's messaging and strongman manner was a practical application of authoritarian theory to real politics – a clear, clarion call to American authoritarians that drove them to support his candidacy.
>
> *(MacWilliams 2016: 717)*

As he reflected on the large, emotional crowds standing before him at campaign rallies, Trump came to think he was bulletproof. As he famously said in January 2016: "I could stand in the middle of Fifth Avenue and shoot somebody. And I wouldn't lose any voters. OK. It's like incredible" (quoted in MacWilliams 2016: 720). Trump believed his supporters were very loyal, and he was right. He got into political troubles repeatedly and yet survived unscathed.

> He attracted millions of followers so devoted that they were unmoved by many unsavory revelations about their nominee. His backers enabled Trump to survive more scandals than any modern presidential candidate has ever faced, including Bill Clinton when he ran in 1992. Trump smartly concentrated on rural and exurban areas that were filled with voters who saw him as heroic.
>
> *(Sabato 2017: 4)*

To the late night comics, as we discuss in Chapter 3, Trump's larger-than-life persona, his elite lifestyle and his over-the-top rhetoric made him a gift of humor that kept on giving. The inhibited, reserved Hillary Clinton was not nearly as much fun to lampoon, though comedians of course found ways to mock her as well.

Channeling public anger was the key to Trump's ability to convert himself from gold-plated celebrity to populist tribune. As a celebrity long before he became a politician, he knew how to attract an audience and how to hold onto one. There was the famous opening speech referring to Mexico sending criminals and rapists across the border, and followed quickly by his campaign visit to the Laredo, Texas, border crossing, where he doubled down on divisive rhetoric. When this combative approach earned him the disapproval of many fellow Republicans, from then-campaign frontrunner Jeb Bush to US House Speaker Paul Ryan, Trump merely mocked their skittishness (Green 2017).

His rhetoric became increasingly apocalyptic as the 2016 general election unfolded (Green 2017). At an Arizona rally on October 29, 2016, Trump remarked, "A vote for Hillary is a vote to surrender our government to public corruption, graft and cronyism that threatens the survival of our constitutional system itself" (quoted in Green 2017: 8).

With the expansion of social media's reach and visibility, voters faced a growing challenge to obtain accurate information in a media environment populated by entrepreneurs promoting fake news for profit and Russian-backed hackers releasing misleading or false information about Hillary Clinton (Fisher et al. 2016). A study of online news content published in the *Columbia Journalism Review* found that the conservative website Breitbart News was at the center of a web of false information making its way across the Internet. This conservative disinformation campaign, led by Trump advisor Stephen Bannon, had no comparable program on the Democratic side (Benkler et al. 2017).

> Our own study of over 1.25 million stories published online between April 1, 2015 and Election Day shows that a right-wing media network anchored around Breitbart developed as a distinct and insulated media system, using social media as a backbone to transmit a hyper-partisan perspective to the world. This pro-Trump media sphere appears to have not only successfully set the agenda for the conservative media sphere, but also strongly influenced the broader media agenda, in particular coverage of Hillary Clinton.
>
> While concerns about political and media polarization online are long-standing, our study suggests that polarization was asymmetric. Pro-Clinton audiences were highly attentive to traditional media outlets, which continued to be the most prominent outlets across the public sphere, alongside more left-oriented online sites. But pro-Trump audiences paid the majority of their attention to polarized outlets that have developed recently, many of them only since the 2008 election season.
>
> *(Benkler et al. 2017)*

Facebook, which has more than a billion daily users, became another powerful vehicle for spreading disinformation.

> During the U.S. election, propagandists—some working for money, others for potentially state-sponsored lulz—used the service to turn fake stories into viral sensations, like the one about Pope Francis' endorsing Trump (he hadn't). And fake news was only part of a larger conundrum. With its huge reach, Facebook has begun to act as the great disseminator of the larger cloud of misinformation and half-truths swirling about the rest of media. It sucks up lies from cable news and Twitter, then precisely targets each lie to the partisan bubble most receptive to it.
>
> *(Manjoo 2017)*

Trump's savvy use of these factors demonstrates how he made the most of his media moment. He combined his public relations skills, particularly his ability to channel anger and to connect with public frustrations, with the rapidly changing media environment that seemed to give equal credence to baseless personal attacks and false statements on the one hand and to substantive policy debate and accurate information on the other. Earlier in the Internet age, candidate Trump might have been a sideshow, a cranky idiosyncratic character with a *bon mot* or two and a high media profile, particularly with the late night comics drawn to his larger-than-life persona. By 2016, though, the political ground had shifted a great deal. Rising populist anger, the high visibility of Fox News and new peer-to-peer communication opportunities helped make him a winner.

## Donald Trump, Public Policy and US Public Opinion

Finally, before we dig more deeply into how the late night comics treated Donald Trump, we need to consider the public's views of Trump as well as the electorate's policy priorities. In this chapter, and the ones that follow, we will consider the extent that late night mockery corresponded to public perceptions of presidential candidate and then President Trump We also consider how closely the policy-based humor corresponded to public perceptions and preferences toward the policy challenges the nation faced.

When Trump was running for president, he generated mixed public evaluations. As shown in Table 2.1, Democratic nominee Hillary Clinton bested him in many public evaluations during that campaign. In a September 2016 Gallup survey, Trump had a 40-point deficit on the question of whether he had the experience to be president. He also ran double-digit deficits behind Clinton on displaying good judgment in a crisis, managing the government effectively and personal likeability against an opponent cuttingly described by Barack Obama as "likeable enough." The public split roughly evenly on which candidate would be better at getting things done, which would be a stronger and more decisive leader, and which was more honest and trustworthy.

**TABLE 2.1** Comparing the Character of the Presidential Candidates, September 2016 (results in percentages)

*Q. Thinking about the following characteristics and qualities, please say whether you think each applies or doesn't apply to Hillary Clinton/Donald Trump. How about – [order of names randomized]?*

| | Applies to Clinton | Applies to Trump | Difference (Clinton – Trump) |
|---|---|---|---|
| Has the experience it takes to be president | 69 | 29 | +40 |
| Would display good judgment in a crisis | 54 | 39 | +15 |
| Can manage the government effectively | 54 | 41 | +13 |
| Is likable | 50 | 38 | +12 |
| Cares about the needs of people like you | 48 | 40 | +8 |
| Can get things done | 60 | 56 | +4 |
| Can bring about the changes country needs | 41 | 41 | 0 |
| Is a strong and decisive leader | 56 | 57 | –1 |
| Is honest and trustworthy | 33 | 35 | –2 |
| Stands up to special interest groups | 46 | 52 | –6 |
| Is healthy enough to be president | 60 | 77 | –17 |

Source: Newport 2016

Trump had a modest advantage over Clinton as being more likely to stand up to special interests. His only double-digit advantage was on being healthy enough to be president. Taken together, these poll numbers speak to the uphill nature of the Trump campaign during the fall of 2016 and the magnitude of the public doubts concerning the future president as the election drew closer (Newport 2016).

At the same time, these survey results suggest a variety of interesting avenues for political humor: Trump's perceived inexperience, his gruff demeanor, his honesty and his judgment all offered ready opportunities for jokes along these lines. For Clinton, Americans might be particularly receptive to questions about her honesty and her ties to campaign donors and special interests. As we shall see, some but not all of these public preferences matched up with the jokes aimed at the two contenders.

After Trump's election, questions of who he was and how he would do as president became far more salient. Fortunately, pollsters asked more detailed questions about public views of the new president focusing on why people said they liked or disliked Trump. In July 2017, for example, a Gallup survey compared a variety of public justifications for supporting or opposing the president. In this survey, 38 percent approved of Trump's presidency, while 56 percent disapproved (a margin that has been surprisingly consistent throughout Trump's term in office). As shown in Table 2.2, roughly two-thirds (65 percent) of those who disapproved cited his personal characteristics, while only one out of six (16 percent) mentioned issues or policies.

Similar surveys conducted during the first year of the Obama and Bush presidencies make clear how much Trump's character shapes his public evaluations. For Barack Obama and for George W. Bush, fewer people expressed disapproval at comparable points in their presidencies – 36 percent and 34 percent respectively. While nearly two-thirds of those objecting to Trump listed character matters, only 14 percent surveyed in 2009 mentioned Obama's character and only 17 percent surveyed in 2001 mentioned character issues involving Bush.

Of the Trump opponents who focused on matters of character, nearly half described the new president as not presidential, having a bad temperament or being arrogant or obnoxious. Smaller groups said that Trump did not know what he was doing, was looking out mainly for himself, or that he was misusing Twitter.

Those who objected to Trump for policy reasons focused on a range of issues, including foreign affairs, health care and policies that favor the rich. For those who expressed negative broad performance evaluations, most said Trump was doing a poor job or they opposed the choices he made in office.

As we shall see, these priority concerns among voters also shape humor narratives relating to the Trump presidency.

By contrast, Table 2.3 shows why Trump's supporters approved of his performance (as of mid-2017). A plurality (38 percent) mentioned general performance matters, saying that the new president was doing the best he could under difficult circumstances, that he was keeping his promises or that he was looking out for

**TABLE 2.2** Character Concerns and Trump Presidential Disapproval, July 2017

*Why do you disapprove of the way [Trump/Obama/Bush] is handling his job as president? (broad categories)*

| | Trump 2017 | Obama 2009 | Bush 2001 |
|---|---|---|---|
| Broad performance evaluations | 12% | 15% | 43% |
| Issues/Specific policies | 16% | 65% | 31% |
| Personality/Personal characteristics | 65% | 14% | 17% |

*Why do you disapprove of the way Trump is handling his job as president? (Detailed categories, percentage mentioning)*

| Character/Personality-related (net) | 65% |
|---|---|
| Not presidential/Bad temperament/Arrogant/Obnoxious | 29% |
| Inexperienced/Doesn't know what he is doing | 10% |
| Looking out for himself/Doesn't consider people's needs | 6% |
| Use of social media/Twitter | 6% |
| Untrustworthy | 6% |
| Racist/Sexist | 3% |
| Not knowledgeable | 3% |
| Wishy-washy | 2% |

| Issue/Policy-related (net) | 16% |
|---|---|
| Disagree with his policies (nonspecific) | 4% |
| Disapprove of his handling of foreign affairs | 4% |
| Disapprove of his health care policies | 3% |
| Favors the rich | 2% |
| Needs to unify the country | 1% |
| Disapprove of his environmental policies | 1% |
| Disapprove of his handling of the economy | 1% |

| Broad performance evaluations (net) | 12% |
|---|---|
| Disagree with what he is doing/Doing a poor job | 7% |
| Not fulfilling his campaign promises/All talk and no action | 3% |
| Trying to do too much | 1% |
| Doesn't have qualified advisers/staff | 1% |

Source: Newport 2017b

Responses are based on those surveyed who said they disapproved of the way the president is handling his job. For Trump, 56 percent disapproved. Not all response options are listed here.

**TABLE 2.3** Performance Evaluations Enhance Trump Presidential Approval, July 2017

*Why do you approve of the way [Trump/Obama/Bush] is handling his job as president? (broad categories)*

| | Trump 2017 | Obama 2009 | Bush 2001 |
|---|---|---|---|
| Broad performance evaluations | 38% | 41% | 50% |
| Issues/Specific policies | 33% | 40% | 9% |
| Personality/Personal characteristics | 24% | 15% | 24% |

*Why do you approve of the way Trump is handling his job as president? (detailed categories)*

| Broad performance evaluations (net) | 38% |
|---|---|
| Doing a good job/best he can under difficult circumstances | 12% |
| Keeping his promises | 11% |
| Does what is best for America | 10% |
| Better than Obama | 4% |
| Willing to give him a chance | 1% |

| Issue/Policy-related (net) | 33% |
|---|---|
| Creating job opportunities/Bringing jobs back to America | 6% |
| Agree with his policies/actions (nonspecific) | 5% |
| Active/Taking on many issues | 5% |
| Economy is getting better/Fixing the economy | 5% |
| Handling of immigration/terrorism | 4% |
| Trying new, different things/Changing things | 4% |
| Foreign policy | 2% |
| Conservative | 2% |

| Character/Personality-related (net) | 24% |
|---|---|
| Doesn't back down/Shows strong leadership | 9% |
| Not part of the Washington establishment/Not a politician | 7% |
| Transparent/Straightforward with the people | 3% |
| Honest/Has integrity | 3% |
| Intelligent/Smart | 1% |
| Like his handling of the media | 1% |

Source: Newport 2017b

Note: Responses are from those who said they approved of the way the president is handling his job. For Trump 38 percent approved. Not all response options are listed here.

America's best interests. One third of those who approved of Trump mentioned specific issue and policy concerns, particularly that he was bringing jobs back to the nation and that he was working on doing a better job with the economy, immigration or terrorism.

In sharp contrast from those who disapproved of Trump, supporters rarely mentioned character. Only 24 percent of those who thought Trump was doing a good job mentioned character issues, and the top two issues for those supporters were his strong, uncompromising leadership and the fact that he was not part of the Washington establishment.

Two years into Trump's presidency, Table 2.4 demonstrates that public evaluations of the president's character seemed quite similar to the concerns revealed during the campaign. Although he was no longer being compared to his vanquished rival, respondents continued to express doubts about Trump's honesty, his personality and his temperament, as well as whether he understood the problems of ordinary people.

Being president is a tough job, and presidents struggle to be successful in securing their policy preferences or even making progress towards solving long-running national policy challenges (Neustadt 1990). As shown in Table 2.5, Americans have many policy priorities. When Gallup asked Americans shortly after Donald Trump's inauguration what issues should be national priorities, large majorities identified a vast list of concerns. The top six were health care, federal spending, hunger/homelessness, crime/violence, the quality of the environment and the state of the economy. None of these top six issues qualified as a new matter of public concern, as past efforts to address these challenged proved insufficient. At least two-thirds of those surveyed considered each of them a priority, demonstrating how many matters the public expected a president to address. The long-running nature of such priorities offers citizens many reasons to

**TABLE 2.4** Evaluating Trump, January 2019 (results in percentages)

| *Q: Do you think Trump ___ or not?* | Yes | No |
|---|---|---|
| Is a strong leader | 48 | 51 |
| Is honest and trustworthy | 36 | 61 |
| Has the personality and temperament that it takes to serve effectively as president | 39 | 58 |
| Has brought needed change to Washington | 41 | 56 |
| Understands the problems of people like you | 33 | 65 |
| Is good at making political deals | 36 | 58 |

Source: Clement and Nakamura 2018

Note: *Washington Post* poll January 21–24, 2019, N = 1001.

**TABLE 2.5** Most Important Problems Facing the US, 2017 (results in percentages)

*Q: Next, I'm going to read a list of problems facing the country. For each one, please tell me if you personally worry about this problem a great deal, a fair amount, only a little or not at all? First, how much do you personally worry about – [randomized order, results in percentages]?*

| | Great deal | Fair amount |
|---|---|---|
| 1. The availability and affordability of health care | 57 | 25 |
| 2. Federal spending and the budget deficit | 49 | 27 |
| 3. Hunger and homelessness | 47 | 30 |
| 4. Crime and violence | 47 | 29 |
| 5. The quality of the environment | 47 | 30 |
| 6. The economy | 46 | 34 |
| 7. The Social Security system | 45 | 25 |
| 8. Drug use | 44 | 22 |
| 9. Race relations | 42 | 27 |
| 10. The possibility of future terrorist attacks in the U.S. | 40 | 26 |
| 11. Illegal immigration | 37 | 22 |

Source: Gallup national survey (March 2017 survey: N = 1018, MOE +/–4 points) quoted in Newport 2017a

sour on a president, and many opportunities for the late night comics to mock his perceived policy failures.

As we turn to Chapter 3, which focuses on the treatment of presidential candidates on late night comedy, and then to Chapter 4, which focuses on the comedic treatment of the Trump presidency, we shall see that personal foibles and policy missteps are the bread and butter of political humor. In this regard, Trump made sure humorists always found the buffet well stocked.

# 3

# CANDIDATE TRUMP AND CAMPAIGN COMEDY

*Co-authored with Jeremy Engel and Deanne Canieso*

Presidential campaigns are a time when even experienced politicians are at their most vulnerable. Senators and governors may enjoy exalted status because of their office and their reputations. But, once they seek the presidency, even the most experienced and even-tempered official must engage in the desperate plea for votes that is the fate of presidential candidates. These would-be presidents struggle to gain the notice and support of the sometimes-cranky and idiosyncratic voters in early primary and caucus states like Iowa, New Hampshire, South Carolina and Nevada. Unless they are leading contenders, candidates must also struggle to win the attention of reporters who are far more interested in scandals and gaffes than in policies or programs. While the frontrunners at the top of the pecking order may get the most media attention, they should expect the harshest media treatment of all (Farnsworth and Lichter 2011a).

The unpredictable and anxiety-filled maelstrom that Americans call a presidential campaign has long offered a rich buffet of material for late night comedians. As political humor became a staple of late night television talk shows, the comics increasingly aimed their fire at presidential campaign developments – if for no other reason than that there are more potential presidents to mock. Starting with Richard Nixon's appearance on *Laugh-In* during the 1968 presidential election, presidents and presidential candidates have tried to navigate both the opportunity and the peril contained in political humor. For the candidates, from the Nixon era to the present, these programs had at least the potential to humanize a politician's image and perhaps bolster one's standing by appearing on evening comedy programs (Gould 1968; Lichter et al. 2015). They could also be valuable vehicles for self-promotion. In 1992, the year these entertainment venues came into their own as sources of political news, Ross Perot launched his candidacy via appearances on *Larry King Live*, and Bill Clinton sought to win over younger voters by playing his saxophone on *Arsenio* (Davis and Owen 1998; Kolbert 1992).

The late night talk shows have remained prominent political venues ever since. As mentioned above, in 2008 a candidate who dared to cancel a TV talk show appearance (as Republican presidential nominee John McCain did to David Letterman) faced a barrage of criticism from the talk show host (Farnsworth and Lichter 2011a). After three weeks of comedic criticism, the chastened McCain went on *Late Night* to apologize profusely, thanking Letterman several times after the host said he would put the incident behind them. Letterman observed that the tables had turned in recent years: "The road to the White House runs through me," he joked (Lichter et al. 2015). As the saying goes, many a truth was said in jest.

The same might be said about the late night humor of 2016. Partly owing to Donald Trump's outsized personality and outrageous pronouncements, the talk show hosts had an unprecedented amount of material to work with, and the line between campaign news and campaign humor became increasingly blurred. In addition to the nightly talk shows, *Saturday Night Live* skits provided a weekly counterpoint to campaign events. Journalists in turn reported on what the comics were saying about the campaign, helping to increase their ratings. In addition, the new hosts and the long-running shows alike benefited from their ability to reach secondary audiences via YouTube and other social media, not to mention the websites and peer-to-peer communication that reposted much of the material from their skits and monologues.

In Chapter 2, we examined the rise to national prominence of Donald Trump, who became even more familiar because of the rich material he offered comics as well as his own extraordinary efforts of self-promotion. While Trump is the focus of this book, he was far from the only major source of humor during the 2016 presidential campaign. Taking a page from the cutting and often personality-oriented humor style of late night, Trump himself offered mocking asides about the personalities and physical appearances of his campaign rivals. These included attacks on Republican candidates Jeb Bush as "low-energy" and a "sad sack," Ted Cruz as "lying," "wacko" and a "loser," John Kasich as "pathetic" and "a total dud," Rand Paul as a "lightweight" who was "totally weird" and Marco Rubio as "little" and a "big loser" (Lee and Quealy 2019). Even though he never ran against him, Trump also reached into the Democratic nomination campaign to declare that Bernie Sanders was "crazy," "exhausted" and someone who "has totally sold out" (Lee and Quealy 2019).

Hillary Clinton, the 2016 Democratic presidential nominee (and the presumed front-runner throughout the nomination process) received particularly intense attacks from Donald Trump and his supporters. Trump mocked her as "crooked" at nearly every opportunity, prompting chants at his campaign rallies to "lock her up!" (Owen 2017) But he was just getting started, eventually also branding her as "too weak to lead," "a foreign policy disaster" and a "Wall Street puppet" (Lee and Quealy 2019). The comics may have been mocking Trump, but they sometimes echoed the narrative frames he created to undermine public support for his rivals.

## Late Night Campaign Humor

Some scholars believe that late night television talk shows, particularly *The Daily Show*, deserve to be considered as an alternative news source (Baym 2005). During his heyday as host of *The Daily Show* on Comedy Central, Jon Stewart was identified by a Pew Research Center poll as one of the most trusted journalists in America, comparable to NBC's Tom Brokaw or CNN's Anderson Cooper (Baumgartner and Morris 2011). As a result, presidential candidates have increasingly treated these talk shows as a means of reaching potential voters who have little interest in traditional political news but are exposed to campaign information via infotainment programming. During the 2008 campaign, for example, presidential candidates and their family members made 80 appearances on these shows (Lichter et al. 2015). While most of the attention was focused on the favorites for winning the nomination, these shows also offered opportunities for those further back in the pack, who otherwise received little to no media coverage.

Some critics of talk shows consider the hosts too soft on the candidates, particularly during interviews (Kinsley 1992). But research into the content of talk shows has found that they do a better job than journalists at focusing on substantive issues during presidential campaigns. By contrast, journalists placed greater emphasis on the campaign horse race and the candidates' strategies and tactics. A CMPA study of national TV talk shows during the 1992 campaign found that 74 percent of the political segments of talk shows focused on substantive matters (primarily policy issues and candidate qualifications). By contrast, campaign coverage on the ABC, CBS and NBC evening news programs that year ranged from only 26 percent to 34 percent substantive content (Farnsworth and Lichter 2011a).

Scholars have also identified partisan differences in the targets of late night jokes. Republican presidential nominees were joked about more often than their Democratic counterparts were during each of the six presidential election campaigns from 1992 through 2012 (Lichter et al. 2015). For example, during the 2012 election, 16 percent of all political jokes took aim at Mitt Romney, compared to only 6 percent that targeted Barack Obama (Lichter et al. 2015).

Late night political humor has gained in attention and influence as people reduce their consumption of traditional media, such as daily newspapers and evening news shows on the broadcast television networks. This trend has been particularly pronounced among younger adults, many of whom turn to soft news as a major source of political information (Baumgartner and Morris 2011; Mitchell et al. 2014). Politicians often try to minimize the negative impact, or even try to "work the refs" of political comedy, by appearing as guests on these shows (Lichter et al. 2015). By being willing to face grilling by the likes of

Noah and Colbert, candidates can both build up credibility with viewers and perhaps even receive a softer treatment now and then from the hosts themselves (Compton 2018).

How did these factors play out in the way late night comedians treated the 2016 election? To find out we first turn to the nominating phase. This includes 2,854 jokes the late night comics made about political figures during the last four months of 2015, before the start of the primaries, and the first four months of 2016. By the end of April, there was little doubt that the nominees would be Donald Trump and Hillary Clinton, despite increasingly desperate efforts by their remaining opponents to stem the tide. During this entire eight-month period, we tracked political jokes by Jimmy Fallon (*The Tonight Show* on NBC), Stephen Colbert (*The Late Show* on CBS), Jimmy Kimmel (*Jimmy Kimmel Live!* on ABC) and *The Daily Show*, the Comedy Central program with new host Trevor Noah. (We began tracking *The Daily Show* on September 28, when Noah formally took over from Jon Stewart.) The three broadcast network shows had the largest audiences of any late night talk shows broadcasting more than once a week, while *The Daily Show* has been especially popular with young adults. We tracked both the traditional joke formats, the "one-liners," and the more extensive lead-in humor more commonly employed on Comedy Central's *Daily Show*.

The second analysis looks more closely at the topics of late night humor directed at the two major party nominees, while extending the time period through the general election. Specifically, we examined the treatment of Donald Trump and Hillary Clinton across more than a year of campaign discourse, starting on September 1, 2015 and ending on November 11, 2016, a few days after Election Day on November 8. (This slight extension past Election Day to the end of the week allowed us to capture the comedians' initial reactions to Trump's unexpected victory on November 8.)

Thus, we were able to compare the two party nominees against the larger landscape of their own party's contenders, and then against each other after they secured their nominations. CMPA coded over 3,000 jokes about Clinton and Trump, analyzing each one for its policy, political, and/or personal content. (Many jokes covered more than one issue area.) College students trained by CMPA senior staff conducted the coding. Training continued until the coders attained at least 80 percent reliability ratings. Videos of all relevant materials were examined rather than transcripts or captions, which can miss visual punchlines.

These two interlinked studies represent an updating of the CMPA historical database, which includes more than 100,000 jokes by hosts on popular late night TV shows from 1992 through 2012. This material includes not only jokes about political figures but also those directed at government and social institutions, such as churches and the military, as well as jokes that addressed a social or economic problem, like inflation, gay rights or climate change. Due to limited resources, however, this study of 2016 political humor was limited to jokes directed at individual political figures.

## The Bumpy Road to the Nomination

During the eight-month presidential nomination period, presidential candidates dominated late night humor. As shown in Table 3.1, during the run-up to the state primary and caucus period from September 1 through December 31, 2015, the late night comics routinely devoted a majority of their political jokes to presidential candidates. Jimmy Fallon told the most candidate jokes (487 or 77 percent of his jokes), but Jimmy Kimmel told the greatest percentage of jokes devoted to political candidates (335 or 86 percent). Stephen Colbert devoted roughly two-thirds of his political jokes to the candidates during that four-month period. Similarly, Trevor Noah devoted roughly two-thirds of his jokes at political figures during the three months that he was part of the analysis.

**TABLE 3.1** Candidate Late Night Joke Analysis, Late 2015

| Total Candidate Jokes | | | | | | | | | | |
|---|---|---|---|---|---|---|---|---|---|---|
| | Sept. | % | Oct. | % | Nov. | % | Dec. | % | Total | % |
| Fallon | 166 | 69 | 99 | 72 | 142 | 88 | 81 | 84 | 487 | 77 |
| Colbert | 176 | 65 | 73 | 53 | 73 | 82 | 25 | 86 | 347 | 66 |
| Kimmel | 129 | 78 | 74 | 89 | 75 | 92 | 57 | 93 | 335 | 86 |
| Noah | 5 | * | 108 | 69 | 90 | 76 | 65 | 88 | 268 | 68 |
| **Total** | **476** | **66** | **353** | **69** | **380** | **85** | **228** | **88** | **1437** | **74** |

| Republican Candidate Focus | | | | | | | | | | |
|---|---|---|---|---|---|---|---|---|---|---|
| | Sept. | % | Oct. | % | Nov. | % | Dec. | % | Total | % |
| Fallon | 133 | 56 | 53 | 39 | 108 | 67 | 62 | 65 | 356 | 56 |
| Colbert | 108 | 40 | 56 | 41 | 61 | 69 | 21 | 72 | 246 | 47 |
| Kimmel | 123 | 75 | 52 | 63 | 60 | 74 | 55 | 90 | 290 | 74 |
| Noah | 4 | * | 61 | 39 | 74 | 63 | 64 | 86 | 203 | 51 |
| **Total** | **368** | **77** | **222** | **63** | **303** | **68** | **202** | **78** | **1,095** | **56** |

| Democratic Candidate Focus | | | | | | | | | | |
|---|---|---|---|---|---|---|---|---|---|---|
| | Sept. | % | Oct. | % | Nov. | % | Dec. | % | Total | % |
| Fallon | 33 | 14 | 46 | 34 | 32 | 20 | 19 | 21 | 130 | 21 |
| Colbert | 56 | 21 | 20 | 15 | 9 | 10 | 4 | * | 89 | 17 |
| Kimmel | 4 | * | 22 | 27 | 15 | 19 | 1 | * | 42 | 11 |
| Noah | 1 | * | 48 | 31 | 14 | 12 | 1 | * | 64 | 16 |
| **Total** | **94** | **20** | **136** | **39** | **70** | **42** | **25** | **10** | **325** | **17** |

Source: CMPA

Notes: Noah coverage began on September 28. Some political jokes relate to more than one candidate and cannot be classified as clearly directed towards one party or another. * Percentages not calculated when N < 10.

Of the 1,437 political jokes told during those four months, over three out of four (76 percent, or 1,095) were about Republican candidates, who were part of a larger field than the Democratic contenders. (The individual candidate findings are shown in Tables 3.3 and 3.4). Jimmy Kimmel had the highest proportion of jokes aimed at the Republican candidates (74 percent) and Trevor Noah the least (51 percent). The highest percentage of jokes directed at Democrats came from Fallon (21 percent) and the lowest from Kimmel (11 percent). The high water mark for Democratic jokes came in October, when Fallon directed one-third (34 percent) of his jokes at the Democratic field. No other month or individual comic in late 2015 devoted even one-quarter of the jokes to Democrats. (Because some political jokes focused on more than one candidate, and still others did not refer to any specific candidate, not all jokes targeted exclusively Republican or Democratic candidates.)

Table 3.2 shows the late night joke totals during the first four months of 2016, when the state-by-state campaigning took place in earnest. Once again candidate jokes dominated, with 78 percent of the political jokes focusing on the presidential field. The results were very similar for the four comics during these four months, with candidates being the subject of the jokes between 76 percent and 79 percent of the time.

Of the 1,417 political jokes offered during those four months, 1,036 (73 percent) were directed at the Republican field, a total that was almost identical to the previous four months. During this four-month period, Noah's show devoted 64 percent of all jokes to Republicans, the highest level, and Fallon's show had the lowest percentage, with 53 percent of the jokes targeting Republicans. No more than one-quarter of the jokes were directed at the entire Democratic presidential field, with a high of 25 percent by Fallon and a low of 13 percent on *The Daily Show*.

In the three remaining nomination phase tables, we look at the individual candidates whose actions and attributes generated the comedy. As shown in Table 3.3, Donald Trump ranked first in all four months of late 2015. In fact, in three of the four months he was the subject of twice as many jokes as the runner-up in the joke race. (The one exception was November, when Ben Carson was a relatively close runner-up.) Carson finished out of the top ten in September, but was third in October, second in November, and sixth in December, when his poll numbers had started to fade.

Carson's experience demonstrates that saying little on the campaign trail does not spare a candidate from ridicule. Consider a *Tonight Show* jab at Ben Carson, who was the subject of 142 jokes during that three-month period. Following one of Carson's understated debate performances, Jimmy Fallon opined, "Ben Carson's the first human to get 25 hours of sleep per day. I feel bad making fun of Carson, but it's not like he's gonna see it" (Lichter et al. 2015).

Among the Republican candidates, former Florida Governor Jeb Bush was consistently popular with humorists. He finished third in the joke rankings for September, sixth in October, and third in both November and December. Senator Ted Cruz (R-TX), who ended up being the chief remaining rival to Trump, did not even make the top 20 list of joke targets during September and

**TABLE 3.2** Candidate Late Night Joke Analysis, Early 2016

Total Candidate Jokes

| | Jan. | % | Feb. | % | March | % | Apr. | % | Total | % |
|---|---|---|---|---|---|---|---|---|---|---|
| Fallon | 118 | 77 | 116 | 88 | 106 | 72 | 97 | 78 | 437 | 78 |
| Colbert | 104 | 84 | 89 | 86 | 63 | 63 | 48 | 66 | 304 | 76 |
| Kimmel | 58 | 87 | 89 | 78 | 104 | 73 | 58 | 84 | 309 | 79 |
| Noah | 91 | 81 | 92 | 89 | 95 | 66 | 89 | 82 | 367 | 79 |
| **Total** | **371** | **82** | **386** | **85** | **368** | **69** | **292** | **78** | **1417** | **78** |

Republican Candidate Focus

| | Jan. | % | Feb. | % | March | % | Apr. | % | Total | % |
|---|---|---|---|---|---|---|---|---|---|---|
| Fallon | 83 | 54 | 84 | 64 | 75 | 51 | 51 | 41 | 293 | 53 |
| Colbert | 72 | 58 | 57 | 55 | 48 | 48 | 38 | 52 | 215 | 54 |
| Kimmel | 38 | 57 | 69 | 61 | 79 | 55 | 44 | 64 | 230 | 58 |
| Noah | 75 | 67 | 77 | 75 | 79 | 55 | 67 | 62 | 298 | 64 |
| **Total** | **268** | **59** | **287** | **64** | **281** | **53** | **200** | **53** | **1036** | **57** |

Democratic Candidate Focus

| | Jan. | % | Feb. | % | March | % | Apr. | % | Total | % |
|---|---|---|---|---|---|---|---|---|---|---|
| Fallon | 35 | 23 | 32 | 24 | 28 | 19 | 44 | 35 | 139 | 25 |
| Colbert | 31 | 25 | 19 | 18 | 13 | 13 | 8 | * | 71 | 18 |
| Kimmel | 17 | 25 | 16 | 14 | 20 | 14 | 8 | * | 61 | 16 |
| Noah | 15 | 14 | 12 | 12 | 15 | 10 | 19 | 18 | 62 | 13 |
| **Total** | **99** | **22** | **79** | **17** | **76** | **14** | **79** | **21** | **333** | **18** |

Source: CMPA

Notes: Some political jokes relate to more than one candidate and cannot be classified as clearly directed towards one party or another. Percentages not caluculated when N < 10.

October of 2015. When Cruz surged in the polls, he surged in the comic rankings. He ranked eighth in November but moved into second place in December 2015, as improved poll numbers triggered more comedic commentary.

As was the case in national news coverage before the start of the primaries and caucuses, Republicans received most of the attention. Although the Democrats did not face as much ridicule on late night during these four months, Hillary Clinton finished second in the humor sweepstakes in September and October and fifth in November and December. Vermont Senator Bernie Sanders, who emerged as her chief rival for the Democratic nomination, was consistently further back, ranking fifth in total jokes for September, fourth in October and November, and eighth in December. That pattern reflected Clinton's consistent advantages

**TABLE 3.3** Top Late Night Joke Targets, Late 2015

| *September* | | *October* | | *November* | | *December* | |
|---|---|---|---|---|---|---|---|
| Trump | 204 | Trump | 104 | Trump | 101 | Trump | 109 |
| H. Clinton | 61 | H. Clinton | 46 | Carson | 79 | Cruz | 23 |
| Jeb Bush | 50 | Carson | 40 | Jeb Bush | 49 | Jeb Bush | 21 |
| Obama | 46 | Sanders | 33 | Sanders | 32 | Christie | 13 |
| Sanders | 25 | Chafee | 31 | H. Clinton | 22 | H. Clinton | 13 |
| Boehner | 24 | Jeb Bush | 26 | Jindal | 18 | Carson | 12 |
| Walker | 20 | Biden | 25 | Obama | 17 | Obama | 10 |
| Christie | 18 | McCarthy | 20 | Cruz | 13 | Sanders | 7 |
| Paul | 14 | Christie | 13 | Huckabee | 12 | Kasich | 6 |
| Putin | 12 | Webb | 12 | O'Malley | 10 | Cheney | 4 |
| Carson | 11 | B. Clinton | 8 | Rubio | 7 | O'Malley | 4 |
| Fiorina | 11 | Gowdy | 7 | Christie | 5 | B. Clinton | 3 |
| Rick Perry | 11 | Rand Paul | 6 | Fiorina | 4 | Fiorina | 3 |
| Brady | 8 | Fiorina | 5 | Eisenhower | 4 | Graham | 3 |
| Gilmore | 8 | O'Malley | 5 | Kasich | 3 | Rubio | 2 |
| Graham | 8 | Putin | 5 | Lessig | 3 | M. Obama | 2 |
| Rubio | 6 | Obama | 4 | Putin | 3 | McConnell | 2 |
| Jindal | 5 | Amin | 4 | B. Clinton | 2 | | |
| Jinping | 5 | McCain | 4 | Both Clintons | 2 | | |
| Cheney | 4 | Rubio | 4 | Vitter | 2 | | |

Source: CMPA

Note: Targets have to be the subject of at least two jokes to be listed. In addition, only the top 20 targets per month are listed.

over Sanders in preprimary polling, suggesting both that she would be the nominee and that the Republican contest would likely be far more interesting.

Not all leading political joke targets were running for president in 2016. President Obama ranked fourth in the humor contest during September, and former House Speaker John Boehner (R-OH) ranked sixth that month. Russian President Vladimir Putin was the highest-ranking international political figure in September, ranking 12th, and he remained in the top 20 for the final three months of 2015. Obama was in the top 20 all four months of 2015 analyzed as well.

A few unusual names made the top 20 lists during the fall of 2015. New England Patriots quarterback Tom Brady, famous more for winning Super Bowls and for allegations of deflated footballs than for politics, endorsed Donald Trump and ended up being the source of eight jokes during September 2015. Uganda dictator Idi Amin, who died in 2003, was the source of four jokes during October.

Table 3.4 shows that Donald Trump also finished first in the joke rankings during all four months of the primary and caucus period from January through

**TABLE 3.4** Top Late Night Joke Targets, Early 2016

| *January* | | *February* | | *March* | | *April* | |
|---|---|---|---|---|---|---|---|
| Trump | 137 | Trump | 150 | Trump | 187 | Trump | 113 |
| Sanders | 67 | Sanders | 51 | Sanders | 44 | Cruz | 60 |
| Jeb Bush | 47 | Jeb Bush | 49 | Cruz | 38 | Sanders | 43 |
| B. Obama | 46 | H. Clinton | 36 | H. Clinton | 33 | H. Clinton | 29 |
| Cruz | 33 | Cruz | 30 | B. Obama | 26 | Kasich | 18 |
| H. Clinton | 17 | Rubio | 27 | Rubio | 26 | B. Obama | 13 |
| O'Malley | 17 | Carson | 25 | Carson | 21 | Fiorina | 7 |
| Christie | 16 | Christie | 11 | Romney | 20 | Priebus | 6 |
| Carson | 15 | B. Obama | 9 | Kasich | 17 | Hastert | 4 |
| Palin | 15 | Kasich | 7 | Christie | 7 | Ryan | 4 |
| Rubio | 8 | O'Malley | 6 | Jeb Bush | 6 | Jeb Bush | 2 |
| Fiorina | 6 | Paul | 5 | Garland | 5 | O'Malley | 2 |
| Paul | 6 | Gilmore | 4 | McConnell | 5 | Huckabee | 2 |
| Jindal | 5 | Fiorina | 3 | Trudeau | 4 | | |
| Ryan | 3 | G.W. Bush | 3 | Graham | 3 | | |
| B. Clinton | 2 | Romney | 3 | Ryan | 3 | | |
| Graham | 2 | Santorum | 3 | Palin | 3 | | |
| Haley | 2 | Biden | 2 | Lincoln | 2 | | |
| Putin | 2 | Pope Francis | 2 | Schwarze-negger | 2 | | |
| | | | | F. Castro | 2 | | |
| | | | | Biden | 2 | | |
| | | | | Kerry | 2 | | |
| | | | | Queen Elizabeth | 2 | | |
| | | | | R. Castro | 2 | | |

Source: CMPA

Note: Targets must have at least two jokes to be listed.

April 2016. Once again, Trump consistently finished well ahead of the second-place finisher every month. Thus, Trump was consistently and overwhelmingly the leading joke target in a crowded field throughout the preprimary and primary seasons. Notably, his margin was matched almost exactly by the overall joke totals of the two political parties. During the preprimary period in 2015, jokes about Republican candidates outpaced those about Democrats by a three to one margin (74 to 26 percent). During the primary/caucus period of January through April, the margin was the same – 74 percent Republican jokes compared to 26 percent for their Democratic counterparts. And as we shall see below, the general election saw more of the same – 74 percent of the jokes were about Trump compared to 26 percent that were aimed at Hillary Clinton. Therefore, in terms of partisan targets, the comedians were nothing if not consistent.

On the Democratic side, the primary season brought a heightened scrutiny of Bernie Sanders, who finished second in the joke tally during January, February and March, as he scored a number of early primary wins and gave the Clinton campaign more competition than had been expected. Sanders also finished third in April, behind only Trump and Cruz, who at that point was one of the few remaining Republican candidates for president who was still competing against Trump. Cruz also moved up the rankings during the latter period, with fifth-place finishes in January and February and a third-place finish in March. Jeb Bush finished third in January and February, but dropped out of the top 10 once his campaign fizzled.

Perhaps surprisingly, Hillary Clinton did not dominate the joke conversation on her way to becoming the Democratic nominee. She was sixth in January and fourth in February, March and April. President Obama, though term-limited, was the subject of more jokes than any Democrat running for president other than Sanders or Clinton. He ranked fourth in January, ninth in February, fifth in March and sixth in April. Moreover, all the major Democratic contenders other than Clinton and Sanders had dropped out of the race by February. These also-rans included former Virginia Senator Jim Webb, former Rhode Island Governor Lincoln Chafee, and former Maryland Governor Martin O'Malley.

As noted above, one did not have to be a candidate during 2016 to receive attention on late night. In early 2016 former Republican vice presidential nominee Sarah Palin, the 2008 running mate of John McCain and a vocal endorser of Donald Trump, cracked the top 10 in January, tied for 20th in February, and tied for 15th in March (though she was not the subject of a single joke during April 2016). Mitt Romney, the Republican Party's 2012 presidential nominee who became active in the "Never Trump" movement, ranked eighth as a humor subject in March, up from 16th in February.

Russian President Vladimir Putin ranked in the top 20 for the first four months of 2016, though in three of the months he tied for 20th with one joke each month. Besides Putin, several other foreign figures were the subject of humorous discussion on late night. For example, Pope Francis was the subject of two jokes during February, and newly elected Canadian Prime Minister Justin Trudeau was the subject of four jokes in March. Queen Elizabeth II of the United Kingdom was joked about twice in March.

In Table 3.5, we combine the monthly results to provide top 10 lists for late 2015 and early 2016. In both periods, Donald Trump was the target of the late night comedians' zingers aimed at politicians more than one time out of four. Hillary Clinton was second during late 2015 and fourth in early 2016. Bernie Sanders was second during early 2016, after ranking fifth during the final months of 2015. Ted Cruz was third during early 2016, a significant increase from his eighth-place finish during late 2015.

Nine of the top ten political figures targeted in late 2015 were candidates for president. The one exception was President Obama, who ranked sixth. Obama

**TABLE 3.5** Top Late Night Joke Targets, Top 10 Totals

| *Late 2015* | *Jokes* | *Percentage* |
|---|---|---|
| 1. Donald Trump | 518 | 26.7% |
| 2. Hillary Clinton | 199 | 10.2% |
| 3. Ben Carson | 142 | 7.3% |
| 4. Jeb Bush | 146 | 7.5% |
| 5. Bernie Sanders | 97 | 5.0% |
| 6. Barack Obama | 77 | 4.0% |
| 7. Chris Christie | 49 | 2.5% |
| 8. Ted Cruz | 35 | 1.8% |
| 9. Marco Rubio | 29 | 1.5% |
| 10. (tie) Carly Fiorina | 23 | 1.2% |
| 10. (tie) Bobby Jindal | 23 | 1.2% |

| *Early 2016* | *Jokes* | *Percentage* |
|---|---|---|
| 1. Donald Trump | 587 | 32.3% |
| 2. Bernie Sanders | 205 | 11.3% |
| 3. Ted Cruz | 161 | 8.9% |
| 4. Hillary Clinton | 115 | 6.3% |
| 5. Jeb Bush | 104 | 5.7% |
| 6. Barack Obama | 94 | 5.2% |
| 7. Ben Carson | 62 | 3.4% |
| 8. Marco Rubio | 61 | 3.4% |
| 9. John Kasich | 43 | 2.4% |
| 10. Chris Christie | 34 | 1.9% |

Source: CMPA

also ranked sixth in the early 2016 rankings, and once again was the only name on the top 10 list who was not a candidate for president during 2016.

## The Road to the White House

Table 3.6 shows a detailed comparison of the humor directed at the two major party nominees. Stephen Colbert told the most political jokes during the general election study period (from the start of the first major party convention on July 18 through November 11, a few days after the election). The pattern for three of the four late night comics examined was consistent: 81 percent of Colbert's jokes focused on Trump, as compared to 80 percent of Noah's and 78 percent of Kimmel's. Fallon's famous head-rubbing and otherwise congenial September interview with Trump faced criticism for not being more critical (Merry 2016), and the data show that Trump fared better on *The Tonight Show* than on the offerings of the other networks. Even on Fallon's show, Trump was still the subject of notably more ridicule than Clinton (64 percent versus 36 percent). As we noted above, the result was that Trump outpaced Clinton overall in the joke race by a three to one margin (74 percent versus 26 percent).

In addition to *whom* the comedians were joking about, we examined *what* they were joking about. Table 3.7 divides the jokes into three subject areas: policy content, non-substantive political content (such as political strategy and the horse race), and personal matters (such as the candidates' character and personality traits). We examined the jokes during three separate segments of the campaign: before the Iowa Caucus (September 1, 2015 through January 31, 2016), from the start of the nomination contests up to the start of the first nominating convention (February 1 through July 17, 2016) and from the start of the nomination conventions through the election and a few days beyond (July 18 through November 11, 2016). For both candidates during all three periods, personal matters dominated the humor: more than four out of every

**TABLE 3.6** General Election Joke Totals

| | *Trump* | *%* | *Clinton* | *%* | *Total* |
|---|---|---|---|---|---|
| Fallon | 180 | 64 | 101 | 36 | 281 |
| Colbert | 284 | 81 | 65 | 19 | 349 |
| Kimmel | 176 | 78 | 50 | 22 | 226 |
| Noah | 199 | 80 | 51 | 20 | 250 |
| **Total** | **836** | **76** | **267** | **24** | **1103** |

Source: CMPA

Note: Jokes were aired from the start of the first major party convention through the election, from July 18, 2016 to November 11 2016.

**TABLE 3.7** Topic Areas of Presidential Candidate Jokes

| Before the Iowa Caucus (September 1, 2015 through January 31, 2016) | | | | | | | |
|---|---|---|---|---|---|---|---|
| | All Jokes | Policy | % | Politics | % | Personal | % |
| Trump | 672 | 58 | 9 | 161 | 24 | 605 | 90 |
| Clinton | 161 | 9 | 6 | 66 | 41 | 150 | 93 |
| **Total** | **833** | **67** | **8** | **227** | **27** | **755** | **91** |
| From the Iowa Caucus to the Start of the Party Conventions (February 1, 2016 through July 17, 2016) | | | | | | | |
| | All Jokes | Policy | % | Politics | % | Personal | % |
| Trump | 844 | 114 | 14 | 359 | 43 | 802 | 95 |
| Clinton | 222 | 31 | 14 | 140 | 63 | 193 | 87 |
| **Total** | **1066** | **145** | **14** | **499** | **47** | **995** | **93** |
| Party Conventions through General Election (July 18, 2016 through November 11, 2016) | | | | | | | |
| | All Jokes | Policy | % | Politics | % | Personal | % |
| Trump | 836 | 156 | 19 | 547 | 65 | 662 | 79 |
| Clinton | 267 | 19 | 7 | 190 | 71 | 222 | 83 |
| **Total** | **1103** | **175** | **16** | **737** | **67** | **884** | **80** |
| Full Campaign Period (September 1, 2015 through November 11, 2016) | | | | | | | |
| | All Jokes | Policy | % | Politics | % | Personal | % |
| Trump | 2351 | 325 | 14 | 1059 | 45 | 2058 | 88 |
| Clinton | 657 | 59 | 9 | 396 | 60 | 565 | 86 |
| **Total** | **3008** | **384** | **13** | **1455** | **48** | **2623** | **87** |

Source: CMPA

Note: Percentages do not sum to 100 because jokes can refer to more than one topic area.

five jokes included some material regarding character, personality or other personal traits, including 88 percent of the jokes focusing on Trump and 86 percent of those focusing on Clinton. Many of those jokes also focused on political calculations and the horse race, particularly in the late summer and fall, when 65 percent of jokes relating to Trump and 71 percent of the jokes relating to Clinton included references to political calculations. Political matters were notably less prominent in the preseason campaign jokes, referenced in only 24 percent of Trump's jokes and 41 percent of Clinton's.

Few jokes offered policy content: not once during those three periods did the frequency of jokes that focused on policy exceed one out of five. This is not particularly surprising (Niven et al. 2003). One might expect the late night comics to focus on personalities – human foibles are often rich veins for humor – and perhaps never more so with the larger-than-life personalities offered on the ballot in 2016. Likewise, the heavy news media emphasis on political calculations offers joke writers a ready source of information from the daily news (Farnsworth and Lichter 2011a; Patterson 2016). Even so, greater policy content in the jokes would provide more information for the surprisingly large number of voters who are using the late night comedy shows as a source of campaign information (Baumgartner and Morris 2011).

## BOX 3.1 CLINTON VERSUS TRUMP JOKES, 2016

- [In reference to Clinton's "basket of deplorables" comment] Secretary Clinton, I know you're the candidate, but here's a tip. If you want to be president, don't call the American people names. Even if you're elected, no one wants to hear: "My fellow Americans, a quarter of our union are douchebags." And I think it's an unfair generalization. Do Trump rallies attract some people who say awful, racist things? Of course. But that's just the guy on stage. *Stephen Colbert, September 13, 2016*
- Get this: a new report found that Donald Trump wanted to fire waitresses at one of his golf courses because he didn't find them attractive enough. So it looks like Hillary's not the only candidate who's had problems with a server. *Jimmy Fallon, September 30, 2016*
- When Hillary and a black person walk down the street, half of America locks both doors. Yeah, they see a black guy, they go to cross the street, then they see Hillary on the other side and they go: "I'll just stay in the middle. I'll take my chances with the traffic." I'm telling you, people, Hillary Clinton is living the black experience. She's never been found guilty of committing a crime, and still, still, she has had to suffer through having an intimate relationship with law enforcement. *Trevor Noah, November 2, 2016*
- Trump had some problems with the truth [at the previous debate]. Apparently, Trump made more than 34 comments that were either lies or misstatements. Clinton was tagged with four. No surprise. Before the debate, *Politico* analyzed a week's worth of Trump speeches and found that "Trump averaged about one falsehood every three minutes and 15 seconds." Which is damning. Though, on the plus side, you can use Trump's lies to tell if your microwave popcorn is done. *Stephen Colbert, September 27, 2016*

The extent to which current events shape the trajectory of humor is shown in Box 3.1, the first of three boxes in this chapter offering some of the greatest hits of the late night presidential campaign humor in 2016. While these selected jokes cannot convey the complete range of topics that shaped post–prime time snark, they demonstrate how closely aligned the day's headlines and the topics of late night humor can be. (The jokes selected seemed to us to be something approaching an all-star lineup, that would have enough staying power to retain some of their humor when appearing in print years later).

In Box 3.1, the hard-fought campaign between Trump and Clinton takes center stage. In one joke, Stephen Colbert takes aim at Clinton's reference to some of Trump's supporters as a "basket of deplorables," while at the same time suggesting that Trump was really the one behaving badly. The comics also attack Trump for his sexism (Fallon) and deceit (Colbert).

The joke from Trevor Noah is an interesting example about how the subject of a joke is not always subject to that stinging a barb. If anything, Noah's comparison of Clinton and African Americans is more critical of policing in America than anything Clinton actually did. But jokes such as this are not the norm. Usually the humor focusing on presidential candidates is both direct and sharp, as we see in some of the other examples presented here.

## BOX 3.2 EXAMPLES OF CHARACTER JOKES DIRECTED AT DONALD TRUMP, 2016

- It turns out his modeling agency, "Trump Model Management," is being sued by a former model to say the agency charged them extremely high rent while they barely made any money. In fact, one model was so desperate for money she ended up marrying Trump. *Jimmy Fallon, September 2, 2016*
- [In reference to Trump's leaked tax returns that showed substantial business losses] It's quite a bombshell. Trump is spinning it, pretending it's a badge of honor. This is what he tweeted. "I know our complex tax laws better than anyone who's ever run for president and am the only one who can fix them." Excellent point, he knows the laws very well from trying to get around them. They should run with that and make a campaign ad out of it.

  [Parody ad] I'm Donald Trump. Only I know how to fix America, because I'm the one who broke it. Only I know how to keep illegal immigrants out because I brought thousands of them in. To build my beautiful, successful Trump Tower. Only I know how to cut ties with China. All my fantastic Trump ties are cut in China. Education? I opened a fake school. Corruption? I buy and sell politicians like baseball cards. Veteran health care? I got to dodge the draft because of a condition that could have been solved by a Dr. Scholl's. National debt? I went bankrupt six times. Nobody has a record like that. Nobody. *Jimmy Kimmel, October 3, 2016*

- We are still trying to figure out who won Monday's presidential debate. Democrats say Hillary won, while Republicans are strong in their conviction that there are still two more debates. Evidently, his staffers tried to get Trump to practice before the first debate, but say: "Mr. Trump found it hard to focus during those meetings," and "he did not seem to pay attention during the practice sessions." I don't blame Trump. I mean, White House, Oval Office? That's colors and shapes. Very difficult. What's next? What's next? What's next? Object permanence? Where does the ball go when it rolls behind the couch? There is no way of knowing! *Stephen Colbert, September 29, 2016*
- Donald Trump, he spent the weekend campaigning and complaining. He's been cam-plaining, that is what he does. Tweeting up a storm how the election is rigged by the dishonest media and he's right. You can tell the media is rigged against Donald Trump because they keep putting microphones in front of him. *Jimmy Kimmel, October 17, 2016*
- [In reference to the Access Hollywood tape] Trump has broken almost every trick in the bag of scumbaggery. Trump's scandals now are like when the first black guy joined white sports, people were, like, I had no idea that was possible. *Trevor Noah, October 10, 2016*

In Box 3.2, the emphasis turns to the humor directed at Trump, who received far more critiques from the late night comics than did Clinton. These comments, which focused on issues of character during the campaign, suggest that he was neither a kind boss or attractive to women (Fallon), not honest (Colbert), not very smart (Colbert again), his campaign's own worst enemy (Kimmel) or that he was just a horrible person (Noah). These lines of commentary reflect the character-oriented conversation that was a key part of the political discourse during 2016, and what surveys showed were a key measure of evaluation of Donald Trump.

## BOX 3.3 EXAMPLES OF POLICY AND CAMPAIGN JOKES DIRECTED AT DONALD TRUMP, 2016

### Russia

- Yesterday, in China, President Obama had a meeting with Vladimir Putin. And, before they started, Obama texted Michelle going into a meeting, "Love you." While Putin texted the same thing to Donald Trump. Isn't that weird? … [Russian accent] "Love you, kissy face." *Jimmy Fallon, September 6, 2016*

- And today, everyone is trying to figure out who won [the previous presidential debate], which is kind of a silly question to ask, okay. Both sides are going to say they won. Everybody is going to say they won. There are no points. There's no penalties. This isn't the Olympics. There are no judges. Because if there were, the Russians would have given Trump a ten. *Stephen Colbert, September 27, 2016*
- Meanwhile, Vladimir Putin is shown on the cover of this week's Time magazine wearing an American "I voted" sticker. When Vladimir Putin saw the cover, he said, "It's funny because it's true." *Jimmy Fallon, October 3, 2016*
- Did you see there's a memo from a veteran spy that says Vladimir Putin has been supporting Donald Trump for five years. After hearing this, Trump said [Trump impression]: "Oh my God, I forgot it was our anniversary. What do you get for five? Is it crystal? I hope it's not China." *Jimmy Fallon, November 1, 2016*

## Mexico and the Border Wall

- The last 24 hours of Donald Trump has been an emotional roller coaster. You must be this crazy to ride. First, he was in Mexico, looking for an ally. [Trump quote] "There are many improvements that could be made that would make both Mexico and the United States stronger and keep industry in our hemisphere." That's not softening. Trump has always called for a wall between the hemispheres – and he will make the oceans pay for it. *Stephen Colbert, September 1, 2016*
- Yes, the media is making Trump look bad. For instance, they covered this speech. It took a second. And, of course, he also played the hits, putting a new spin on this campaign classic. [Trump quote] "Remember, I said Mexico is paying for the wall, with the full understanding that the country of Mexico will be reimbursing the United States for the full cost of such a wall. Okay?" What?! "Reimburse" us for the wall? You said Mexico would pay for it! Paying for something is very different than reimbursing. You can't take a date out for dinner, make her pay, and then say, "Just send me an invoice." *Stephen Colbert, October 24, 2016*

## Trump Campaign

- In North Carolina yesterday, a fight broke out at a Trump campaign rally. Either that or a Trump campaign rally broke out in a fight. I don't know which came first. A Trump supporter grabbed a protester by the neck and tried to hit him in the face. Things got so violent some people thought they were at a taping of *Dancing with the Stars*. *Jimmy Kimmel, September 13, 2016*

- I don't have to tell you folks that Donald Trump's not doing very well with African American voters. I especially don't have to tell you folks over there. Yesterday, at a rally in North Carolina, he once again brought the black community the message of hope that all is hopeless. [Trump quote] "They are in the worst shape than ever, ever, ever." For one thing, Donald Trump might become president. *Stephen Colbert, September 21, 2016*
- Trump has come up with a new way to encourage people to donate to his campaign. [Trump quote] "I want to show you something very special. I am dedicating this wall right here in Trump Tower to a select group of donors and supporters from my campaign, and I want to add your name to this wall. Contribute today, like the great Americans here, and you'll get your name officially on the Trump donor board."That's right. Donald Trump is building a wall and making his donors pay for it. *Stephen Colbert, November 2, 2016*

In Box 3.3, the emphasis turns to selected campaign issues. While critics attacked Jimmy Fallon for not being hard enough on Donald Trump – in part a response to his hair-tousling interview that featured softball questions – Fallon was particularly effective in drawing attention to Russian President Putin's connection to the Trump campaign. Colbert took aim at the border wall issue, mocking Trump by using clips of Trump's own words, a technique used extensively during his earlier comedy career as a correspondent on *The Daily Show* and as the host of *The Colbert Report*.

One unusual development during the 2016 campaign was the unruliness of the Trump campaign rallies. Trump himself campaigned as a highly divisive figure, attacking both his fellow Republicans in the primaries and his Democratic opponent during the general election with a venom that was unusually potent. In recent decades, candidates often said their opponents were wrong about their vision for the country, but rarely did they suggest their rivals were evil people or that they belonged in jail. In 2008, for example, Republican presidential nominee John McCain shut down a questioner at one of his town halls who vilified Barack Obama, saying that his opponent was a decent man. McCain also refused to emphasize Obama's race as a means to secure a higher percentage of white votes (Ceaser et al. 2009). To be sure, McCain would never have permitted "lock him up" chants at his campaign rallies eight years before the call for incarceration of Trump's opponent became a campaign staple in 2016 and beyond.

The vigor and anger expressed by Trump campaign supporters drew considerable attention from the comics as well as the mass media. Jimmy Kimmel drew attention to the violence at and around Trump rallies by asking whether a fight broke out at a campaign rally, or a campaign rally broke out at a fight. Colbert noted that Trump tried to raise money by promising to put the names of donors on a wall he was building at Trump Tower – a wall in New York City, far, far from the US–Mexico border.

Though the buildup to the 2016 presidential election was unconventional in many respects, coverage of the major parties' nominees by late night, weekly comedy programs followed roughly the same methodology that characterized previous election cycles. Indeed, there existed an abundance of material ripe for satire, what with the rehearsed stoicism of Hillary Clinton and the bombastic, off-the-cuff approach of Donald Trump. Any candidate for elected office presents a prime target for mockery, but Trump in particular found himself the subject of ever more frequent ridicule precisely because of how unconventional a candidate he was. From his shady past business dealings to his unusual skin tone, his like had rarely been seen before, and comedians had a field day. As we turn to how some of these weekly comedy programs covered Donald Trump during 2016 we see differences and similarities with the nightly offerings discussed so far in this chapter.

## The Weekly Humor Programs

### *Saturday Night Live*

Our discussion of how the late night weekly comedy programs addressed the 2016 presidential campaign begins with *Saturday Night Live*, a show with a long tradition of political satire. Since the program's inception in 1975, its writers have sought to make light of the prevailing political issues of the time, with an ever-changing and talented cast bringing political figures to life in an unflattering and caricatured manner.

Several distinct circumstances set *SNL*'s coverage of Donald Trump apart from other programs. For instance, a notable casting change in early October marked a shift in the show's portrayal of Trump's candidacy. *SNL*'s mockery of Trump was initially more even-handed and less severe with Darrell Hammond's imitation of Trump than would be the case when Alec Baldwin took over the role. The show's format also differs somewhat from conventional late night, host-focused talk shows. While programs such as *Full Frontal with Samantha Bee* and *Last Week Tonight with John Oliver* mimic the general format of some newscasts one would find on CNN or Fox, with the added caveat of rude and crude humor, *SNL* is a 90-minute variety show. The program features various sketches, musical guests and recurring skits, only a select few of which concern political matters. Of these segments, *SNL*'s "Cold Open" and "Weekend Update" most frequently dealt with contemporary politics during the 2016 campaign. Donald Trump was brought up sporadically in the latter, as the sketch's format only allowed for quick one-liners. Far more regularly, Trump was profiled in "Cold Open," which allowed the show to offer extensive critiques several minutes in length.

Sketches featuring Trump in early 2016 were more disposed to criticize his supporters rather than him directly. Sarah Palin, a previous object of derision for the program during her 2008 vice presidential campaign, provided prime material for one of the show's "Cold Open" segments when she endorsed Donald Trump in January 2016. Tina Fey's portrayal of Sarah Palin is as over the top as it is famous, and by linking her act with Donald Trump, the show mocked the would-be president by way of association with his unhinged supporters (*Saturday Night Live* 2016a).

Similarly, the *SNL* caricature of Trump supporter Scottie Nell Hughes, then a paid commentator on CNN, was a damning indictment of those defending Trump's actions on the campaign trail. The satirizing of Nell Hughes portrayed her as a ditsy pundit who offered absurd rationalizations of Trump's mishaps in courting women voters. For instance, her defense of Donald Trump retweeting an unflattering picture of Ted Cruz's wife is that his "hands are just so big, he can't see every little tweet his fingers retweets" (*Saturday Night Live* 2016c). This is, of course, a jab at Trump's insecurity over the size of his hands, and by extension his manhood. The segment also suggests his supporters are deluded, if not members of a bizarre cult.

The show also sought to make light of the casual racism that has characterized some members of Trump's base. In a mock political ad for Trump, a handful of different "real Americans" contest the media's negative perception of Donald Trump and explain why they are voting for him. Each person appears to be engaging in menial, everyday activities, but it is revealed over the course of the ad that things are not quite what they seem. One person getting dressed later dons Nazi paraphernalia; another is ironing her Klansman robes. A third, initially framed as a painter, is writing "white power" on a house (*Saturday Night Live* 2016b). The ad closes with the phrase, "racists for Donald Trump." Likewise, a sketch featuring Michael Che provided commentary on the lack of diversity in the Republican Party, and the lack of broad appeal in the Trump platform. Che is seen playing a spoof of the popular mobile game Pokémon GO titled "Trumpémon GO," and attempts to catch "the rarest creature of them all," minorities at the Republican National Convention (*Saturday Night Live* 2016d). His struggle over the course of the sketch mocks Trump through the demographic uniformity of his supporters.

As noted above, the casting of Alec Baldwin as Donald Trump in the premier of *SNL*'s 42nd season in October 2016 marked a change in the program's portrayal of the presidential candidate. Whereas his predecessor's imitation of Trump was somewhat reserved, Baldwin held nothing back, presenting the show's audience with an even more exaggerated and cutting Trump impersonation. From his facial expressions to his mannerisms, everything about Baldwin's performances dripped with mocking contempt (*Saturday Night Live* 2016f). Even Baldwin's Trumpian accent was taken to a greater extent than that of Darrell Hammond. Likewise, the show began to rely more on direct personal insults, rather than mocking Trump through his supporters. In a mock-up of a presidential debate, Baldwin's Trump repeatedly refers to the African American moderator as "jazz man," speaking to Trump's alleged tone deafness and insensitivity regarding racial matters. Trump, as Baldwin portrays him, also frequently comes across as inarticulate and unintelligent. Instead of answering direct questions, Baldwin's Trump prefers to blame all problems on Barack Obama and Hillary Clinton in increasingly nonsensical ways, a nod to Trump's actual "birther" and "lock her up" political themes (*Saturday Night Live* 2016e).

Even when dealing with the postelection reality of a Trump presidency, *SNL* did not tone things down, much less reverse course. If anything, the show's writers took even greater pleasure in presenting the president-elect as moronic and childish. From November on through the end of the year, Trump was depicted as stumbling from one blunder to the next as he prepared for life in the Oval Office. His lack of preparation for the presidency and his perceived low intelligence were targeted in one such sketch, where after discussing strategy with the Joint Chiefs of Staff, a concerned Trump, not knowing what ISIS is, asks Siri, "how do I kill ISIS?" (*Saturday Night Live* 2016g). He was also frequently shown exhibiting blatant ignorance to what was going on in his administration, delegating all tasks to his underlings and on one occasion even asking if he could be president just three days a week (*Saturday Night Live* 2016h). *SNL* also began to insinuate that the president-elect was beholden to Vladimir Putin in some way, as allegations began to mount that the Trump campaign conspired with Russia to harm the Clinton campaign. In the program's Christmas special, Putin came down Trump's chimney as if he were Santa to express his overwhelming delight that "the best candidate, the smartest candidate, the Manchurian candidate" was elected president (*Saturday Night Live* 2016g).

## *Full Frontal with Samantha Bee*

In keeping with the other comedy programs discussed here, the TBS show *Full Frontal with Samantha Bee* found ample material in covering the tumult of the Trump campaign. Bee brought to the table her own abrasive, crass brand of humor that stands in stark contrast to the situation-based *SNL*. She is by her own admission an unabashed liberal, and rarely held back in her criticisms of Donald Trump. Far more than *SNL* and *Last Week Tonight*, Bee was prone to jest in solidarity with her like-minded audience when confronted with the threats posed by Trump's candidacy.

Following the shock of the November election, she underscored the uptick in instances of intimidation and harassment of minority groups, noting that every member of her staff experienced or witnessed disgusting behavior immediately after the election (*Full Frontal* 2016i) Indeed, much of her show's content considered the human impact of Trump's incendiary rhetoric throughout 2016. This unique agenda serves to build Bee's rapport with her liberal audience and gives her work a personal touch that endears her to like-minded consumers of late night political humor. Additionally, her joining of vulgarity and news makes for unexpectedly pointed political commentary, as when she described the rise of Trump following his nomination by the Republican Party. "Trump isn't desecrating the Republican Party," she explained, "he's just peeling back the glossy exterior to reveal the hideous symbiont [i.e. the racist wing of the GOP] that has been lurking there for decades" (*Full Frontal* 2016a).

Samantha Bee's treatment of the Trump campaign was not simply limited to the man himself; she found both Trump's campaign team and his supporters to be highly attractive targets for her humor throughout 2016. Even when she had exhausted recent subject matter concerning Trump, there often remained a rich supply of material relating to the people Trump chose to surround himself with during the campaign. In presenting unflattering profiles of some of the names touted for cabinet positions in the new administration following Trump's victory, Bee associated their various shortcomings with the man elected to the White House. She labeled this group of people, which included prominent members of the Trump transition team, a "parade of misfits, deplorables, zealots, and extremists" (*Full Frontal* 2016h).

*Full Frontal with Samantha Bee* is often interspersed with different types of segments, such as interviews, field pieces, and lengthy examinations of different news stories, providing a number of different avenues to vilify Trump supporters. One particularly humorous segment was a profile on "Latinos for Trump" founder Marco Gutierrez, known as the "taco truck guy." The piece repeatedly highlights what Bee sees as the absurdity and hypocrisy of Gutierrez's views, describing him as an "anti-Mexican immigrant Mexican immigrant," and provides some information on his background as a shady mortgage broker. Ultimately, many comparisons are drawn between the man who describes himself as a "minute Donald Trump" and Trump himself, essentially mocking the presidential candidate by associating him with his deluded supporters (*Full Frontal* 2016c). Samantha Bee was also prone to draw attention to the influx of white nationalist rhetoric into US political discourse and the threat it poses to minorities, by extension disparaging Trump for embracing this aspect of the American electorate and his refusal to disavow white supremacy (*Full Frontal* 2016g).

*Full Frontal*'s humor was heavily insult-based when covering Donald Trump's candidacy. Everything was fair game, from his physical appearance to his personality. It was not uncommon for Samantha Bee to intersperse her show with quick jabs at the so-called "orange supremacist at the top of the (Republican) ticket" (*Full Frontal* 2016a). Indeed his skin tone regularly drew her attention. In consoling her largely sympathetic audience after Trump's generally unexpected November victory, Bee explained the surprise turn of events as if the nation hacked up "a marmalade hairball with the whole world watching" (*Full Frontal* 2016e).

Bee was also prone to framing Donald Trump as childish and unintelligent. For instance, she repeatedly poked fun at how the GOP was tearing itself apart because it nominated a "sociopathic 70-year-old toddler" (*Full Frontal* 2016b), and even ran a mock investigative journalism piece where she suggested that Trump could not read (*Full Frontal* 201d).

Above all else, Samantha Bee sought to portray Trump as a dangerous person, one both inept and underqualified for the presidency. She merged political humor with political commentary perhaps more than any other late night comedian did. This framing became especially pertinent after Trump was actually elected president. In one segment that aired the day after the 2016 election, Bee offered a window into the rapidly approaching dysfunction about to consume the White House. She highlighted the dearth of substantive policy discussion from Trump during the election by profiling Pratik Chagoule, the disillusioned head of a failed policy shop the Trump campaign set up in Washington.

That former Trump staffer, a Yale-educated conservative lawyer, shared stories of mismanagement, dysfunction and an overall ambivalence on the part of the campaign (*Full Frontal* 2016f). This interview, of course, served to show Trump in a bad light, making him appear incurious and willfully ignorant when it came to formulating real policy to deliver on his lofty campaign promises. Bee also bemoaned what she saw as Trump's willingness to tell whatever lies were necessary to serve his purposes. She portrayed it as unbecoming of a president-elect, exclaiming that "one of the major questions being debated in our country today is whether it's okay for the president to lie his f**king face off 24 hours a day" (*Full Frontal* 2016j). Overall, Bee's postelection humor was centered on commiserating with her audience and underscoring how unconventional the Trump presidency is.

## *Last Week Tonight with John Oliver*

Of the weekly comedy programs considered here, HBO's *Last Week Tonight with John Oliver* most closely resembles a traditional newscast. Oliver spends large portions of the show looking into a particular story or subject in some depth, rather than moving from joke to joke as is the case with *SNL* and *Full Frontal*. *Last Week Tonight* is certainly the most professionally staged of the three, with Oliver's lengthy policy-oriented segments often supplemented by real data. Oliver takes a more even-handed approach than do some other purveyors of late night humor, and is somewhat less overt in displaying his political persuasions. His insights, no matter how comically framed, often carry the weight of traditional journalism rather than being simple throwaway lines.

Such was the case when Oliver tried to parse through Trump's immunity to the adverse effects of saying outrageous things on the campaign trail. Oliver lists a handful of statements made by Trump in the past week alone, of which two were unquestionably false, which was entirely what Oliver was driving at. To that point in the campaign, Oliver observed, Trump had made not one but thousands of ludicrous statements, each of which would have been sufficient to disqualify him, yet every subsequent statement served to "blunt the effects of the others" (*Last Week Tonight* 2016e).

*Last Week Tonight* also had a lot in common with other humor programs during 2016, particularly when it came to covering Trump's candidacy. In many of the segments mimicking investigative journalism, John Oliver sought to expose Donald Trump as a fraud and an unabashed racist, especially early in the year. One segment in late February actually saw him tout the virtues of Trump as a candidate, before brutally exposing these appealing qualities to be false. "Donald Trump," he explained, "can seem appealing until you take a closer look; much like the lunch buffet at a strip club, or the NFL, or having a pet chimpanzee" (*Last Week Tonight* 2016a). He also delved into the logistics behind one of the presidential candidate's few policy proposals: the border wall. Not only did Oliver present the proposal as being firmly motivated by racism and xenophobia, but he also sifted through the math behind the proposal, concluding that it was extremely costly and ineffective in dealing with the immigration issues it was purported to fix (*Last Week Tonight* 2016b).

John Oliver also frequently outlined the various scandals and past mishaps that were a regular feature of Trump's candidacy. There was an entire segment devoted to detailing and weighing the different scandals that plagued both the Trump and Clinton campaigns, in order to help viewers sift through things and choose the better candidate for themselves. Of course, his conclusion was not surprising. That is not to say Oliver's analysis was entirely one-sided. He asserted that the scandals surrounding Clinton were irritating rather than nefarious, and that "not being as bad as Trump [was] a low bar to clear" (*Last Week Tonight* 2016f). Furthermore, in explaining to his audience the Trump organization's history of vexatious litigation, Oliver listed every single cable television show featuring lawyers as major characters. The tally of the combined episodes of each show still didn't match the number of lawsuits the Trump organization filed in the last decade alone, prompting Oliver to exclaim, "Trump's lawsuits exceed the limits of the f*cking genre" (*Last Week Tonight* 2016h).

Overall, the way in which John Oliver poked fun at Donald Trump involved less build up and fewer drawn-out jokes. His style involved more frequent one-liners aimed at insulting the presidential candidate. As was the case with Samantha Bee, this could take the form of anything from making fun of his appearance to attacking his disposition. He too joked about Trump's skin tone, when he posed the question "where exactly are you from, because you look like you came out of the clogged drain at a Wonka factory" (*Last Week Tonight* 2016h). Oliver also took a jab at Trump's insecurity as well as his philandering past when he said that "anything Trump's tiny fingers touch turns into an ex-wife or an abandoned casino" (*Last Week Tonight* 2016h). In one opening quip following the conclusion of the Republican National Convention, Oliver led on his audience by saying one could call Trump a true visionary, because for the longest time, "he was the only one who envisioned himself as a presidential nominee" (*Last Week Tonight* 2016c).

Most frequently, John Oliver harped on Trump's personality and psychology. He repeatedly framed Trump as a bigot, an egomaniac and an all-around bad person, even going so far as to suggest he was in league with the devil. After the shock of the 2016 election, Oliver played a clip of reporters listing the Trump agenda, before cutting it off short to interject, "it sounds like you are reading the to-do list on Satan's refrigerator, which of course Satan no longer needs now that hell has frozen over" (*Last Week Tonight* 2016g). In the same vein, Oliver poked fun at Trump's use of the hit R.E.M. song "It's the End of the World" as a lead-in to a speech he gave on the Iran nuclear deal. "That is just too perfect," Oliver scoffed, "Trump may as well have been riding out on stage with the three other horsemen of the apocalypse" (*Last Week Tonight* 2016d).

Our analyses of these three weekly shows were not systematic. Overall, however, it seems likely that the weekly programs were, if anything, even more anti-Trump than the weeknight shows in their comic material. Samantha Bee certainly made no bones about her detestation of Trump, and the formats of *SNL* (sketch comedy) and *Last Week Tonight* (a lengthy study on a single topic) favored a focus on only one politician a night, and that politician was usually Donald Trump. There may also be a structural element involved. Three of the four weeknight shows we examined aired on broadcast television networks, which still require larger and more diverse audiences than cable programs in order to survive. You need higher ratings to survive on CBS than you do on TBS. And HBO's audience of subscribers frees politically oriented hosts like John Oliver (and Bill Maher) from worrying about advertisers. Of course, *SNL* airs on NBC, but its political sketches are just one piece in a diverse mix of comedy sketches. All in all, the weekly talk shows we examined add to the overall impression that late night comedy is an anti-Trump zone.

## It's a Wrap

Our study of the attention late night comics paid to politicians during late 2015 and 2016 confirms the impression that Donald Trump was in a class by himself. He ranked first in terms of the number of jokes he received during all eight months of the primary study period, which started well before he was seen as a favorite for the nomination. The blustering billionaire may be a rich source of material for comedy, and it seems the attention he received from the late night comics varied little depending on his poll standings or his record in primary contests. When the two major party nominees squared off in the general election, the comics remained consistent: all four daily late night hosts focused primarily on Trump, with relatively little to say about Clinton. Our qualitative analysis of the weekly programs we examined suggests the same pattern on the once-a-week programs.

While Hillary Clinton was the second most frequent source of humor during late 2015, the relative attention paid to her declined during the winter and spring of 2016. Although Sanders proved an unexpectedly strong threat, Clinton remained consistently ahead in pledged Democratic convention delegates during the process and was always the favorite to win the nomination. As her path to the nomination became clearer in early 2016, she was the subject of less attention from the comics, a sharp contrast to the more consistent way Trump was treated across the eight months of primary jokes examined here. Perhaps the length of time she had been in the public eye – she was First Lady for eight years, a US Senator from New York for another eight years, a failed presidential candidate in 2008, and Secretary of State for Barack Obama's first term – meant that by early 2016 the comedians were running out of new and different ways to make fun of her. This could also be true of the general election, where voters started the campaign season more familiar with Clinton, and when Trump showed an ability to dominate both public attention and news discourse (Patterson, 2016). Finally, this fits into the long-term pattern of late night comedy in presidential elections. For all of Trump's novelty, this was the seventh consecutive time that the Republican nominee exceeded his Democratic counterpart in attracting the attention of late night comedians. Overall, the margin between him and Hillary Clinton was greater than the margin between the Republican and Democratic nominees in any of the previous six general elections (Farnsworth et al. 2017, 2018; Lichter et al. 2015).

Turning to the Democrats, one of the larger surprises of the 2016 nomination season was the relative success of Bernie Sanders, who had little support in the polls before the nomination contest began. But as he won more and more contests, the comedians took an increasingly strong interest in him, moving from fifth in the humor rankings in late 2015 to second in early 2016. As with Trump, Sanders' personality may have lent itself to humorous commentary. For example, his rumpled demeanor may have stimulated more jokes than that of a conventional, disciplined, button-down candidate. But the Sanders experience does seem to show that relative political success begets more attention from comics.

The increased attention on Cruz during early 2016 also suggests that comics respond to political success, at least for politicians who were not yet household names. Cruz ranked eighth during late 2015, when he was just another name in the crowded Republican field, but moved to third during early 2016 as he emerged as the main rival to Trump. The same pattern can be seen for Ohio Governor John Kasich, who also lasted longer in the Republican contest than most other would-be nominees. Kasich did not make the top 10 until early in 2016, as his ability to survive as a candidate throughout the nomination process became increasingly apparent. Dr. Ben Carson represents a confirmation of this pattern in the opposite direction: his political fortunes sank once the nomination contests were underway, and the comedians lost interest.

Of course, just because you are losing does not always mean comedians let up on you, particularly if your last name is Bush. Jeb Bush ranked fourth in the number of jokes during late 2015, when he seemed as likely as the other Republicans running for president to receive the nomination, and he continued to rank fourth in the number of jokes in early 2016, when his extremely well-funded campaign failed to secure even modest success in early primary and caucus states. (Bush finished sixth in Iowa and fourth in New Hampshire before suspending his campaign on February 20, 2016.)

Barack Obama's consistent sixth-place finish during the two periods we examined during the nomination cycle represents something of an anomaly for a sitting president nearing the end of his second term. In 2000, Bill Clinton placed second in the number of late night jokes he received, behind George W. Bush. In 2008, George W. Bush placed second in the number of jokes he received, behind John McCain, that year's Republican nominee (Lichter et al., 2015). Since his 2008 candidacy for the presidency, Obama has always been a difficult subject for the late night comics, perhaps because his cool demeanor did not allow for the sort of broad-brush character-related humor that flows from the humor-rich public perceptions of Bill Clinton as an aging Lothario and George W. Bush as a dim bulb (Lichter et al. 2015).

It is also true that the late night comics tend to focus on the themes in the news. Personality and political machinations routinely dominate campaign news stories, even though such topics may be less important to voters than the policy initiatives that the candidates would offer. But in the same way that some reporters may hesitate to offer much policy coverage, the comics likewise may consider policy themes too complicated or simply too unfunny to deserve much attention. This is a disadvantage for those citizens who might otherwise become informed about substantive issues as they listen to the voices of late night comedy, but it reflects the news coverage that is often the source of their inspiration.

For all the drama, suspense and unexpected turns of the 2016 elections, late night comedy differed surprisingly little in many regards from that of other recent presidential campaigns, at least insofar as we were able to measure them. There were new faces among the hosts (as there were among the leading candidates), and old routines such as Letterman's Top Ten lists gave way to new ones like Jimmy Fallon's "slow jamming the news." But these were more a matter of form than substance. The heavier focus on Republican than Democratic candidates continued for the seventh straight presidential election cycle, and (as noted above) the emphasis on personality over policy remained unchanged as well. Candidates continued to frequent the shows and were treated relatively well by their hosts, but the brief moments of civility disappeared once the guests had departed.

On the other hand, the sheer volume of jokes about Trump was certainly unprecedented; even Bill Clinton was never so frequent a target during his election campaigns (Lichter et al. 2015). At least qualitatively, there seemed more of an edge to much of the humor, as the comedians' distress and disdain toward "The Donald" sometimes seemed palpable. For example, in one routine Colbert tried to "connect the dots" among Trump's ideas and behavior on a blackboard and ended up drawing a swastika. But even this was in line with highly negative news coverage of Trump that included discussions of whether it was appropriate to call him a fascist or compare him to Hitler. Thus, Trump posed a challenge to comedians, as he did to journalists. Even when making light of Trump, there was a dark edge to the outpouring of late night comedy. In the next chapter, we consider whether the distinctiveness of late night comedians' takes of candidate Trump continues to color the treatment of President Trump.

# 4

# HOW POTUS PLAYS ON LATE NIGHT

*Co-authored with Noah Gardner and Shaelyn Patzer*

Once the elections are over and a new president takes office, comedians can focus their attention on a single political figure. No long are they looking at the two major party nominees and the occasionally colorful running mate, not to mention the cast of characters who sought the presidential nomination at the start of an election year. With the electoral contests behind them, the late night comics can focus on the new president and the new president's team. The transition from campaigning to governing does not mean the laughs stop coming. It means the laughs focus on the victorious candidate and his plans for the future.

Once in office, presidents pay considerable attention to the late night humorists who are paying so much attention to them. Of course, few presidents have devoted as much energy to attacking the late night comics as has President Trump. During his time as a candidate and as president, he routinely sought to reshape the critical late night narrative by engaging in Twitter feuds with late night comics on Twitter. Alec Baldwin, who impersonates Trump on *Saturday Night Live,* became a particular *bête noir* (Itzkoff 2018). Given these dustups, Trump has drawn more attention to his comedic critics than they could ever produce on their own. Even though Trump's own mocking, insulting style is not unlike the cutting barbs of late night comedy, he just cannot let things go. After one particularly irritating week, for example, Trump said that Alec Baldwin's Trump imitation "stinks" and "just can't get any worse" (Lee and Quealy 2019).

Trump is hardly the first president to try to redirect late night humor to his advantage, but his behavior offers a powerful contrast with the way his predecessors reacted to comedic mocking. During his time in office, President Obama focused on shaping the news narrative by interacting with comedians, even willingly participating in efforts to generate laughs on his own. He famously appeared on *The Tonight Show* to "slow-jam" the news with Jimmy Fallon, and he sat down on *Between Two Ferns* to trade insults with comedian Zach Galifianakis before promoting greater youth enrollment in the Obama health care program (Farnsworth 2018; Hopper 2017; Martinelli 2016; Scacco and Coe 2016).

Of course, Obama had a big advantage on these programs. His politics more closely aligned with those of his hosts than have recent Republican presidents. The subject of his slow jam was student loans, and the audience was a highly receptive group of University of North Carolina students. In retrospect, the sketch foreshadowed the much-criticized mutual admiration that Trump now shares with certain Fox News commentators.

Nonetheless, this rapport with humorists was not unique to Obama. In 1975, during the first season of *Saturday Night Live*, President Gerald Ford tripped and stumbled down the stairs when disembarking from Air Force One. The TV networks showed the event, and rising young *SNL* comedian Chevy Chase saw an opportunity. In skits that opened the show, Chase repeatedly parodied Ford's stumble as a pratfall, and he eventually succeeded in reframing Ford's physical image from the former All-American football player that he was to the hapless klutz Chase depicted. Nonetheless, Ford admitted to watching the show and even being entertained by it. He later reflected, "On occasion, I winced. But, on the other hand, Betty and I used to watch *Saturday Night Live* and enjoyed it. Presidents are sitting ducks, and you might as well sit back and enjoy it" (quoted in Lichter et al. 2015: 46).

Three presidencies later, George H.W. Bush even invited Dana Carvey, his *SNL* impersonator, to a holiday party for the White House staff. That day, the two shared the lectern and the laughs to the delight of Bush's team, which a few weeks earlier had lost the 1992 presidential election (Rosenwald 2018). It is difficult to imaging Donald Trump palling around with Alec Baldwin in such circumstances.

In some ways, late night humor is more consequential for presidencies than for presidential elections. While elections determine who gains power, the presidency determines how they use (or abuse) it. The opportunities for comedians are greater, for the winner brings with him a completely new cast of characters, from appointees to family members, as well as a new set of issues and policies.

To understand how this running dramedy played out in late night comedy routines, we applied the same content analysis techniques to the presidency that we did to presidential elections. Using the same CMPA coding manual, we applied this analysis to how Kimmel, Fallon, Colbert and Noah treated the first year of Donald Trump's presidency. This involved 6,337 late night political jokes by the fab four that aired from January 23 (the Monday after Inauguration Day) through December 31, 2017. Once again, we also compared these findings to a qualitative study of the weekly comedy shows featuring *Saturday Night Live, Full Frontal with Samantha Bee* and *Last Week Tonight with John Oliver*.

Finally, we compare the presidential focus of late night humor during 2017 with the drubbings endured in the first years in office of several previous presidents. Once again we relied on the CMPA political humor database, which stretches back through the first years of the presidencies of Barack Obama, George W. Bush, and Bill Clinton.

## The Nightly Humor Programs

The first year of Trump's presidency generated consistently negative public approval numbers, with much of the public frustration with Trump continuing to focus on matters of character (Newport 2017b). A July 2017 Gallup survey that examined closely the sources of public disapproval of Trump found that nearly two-third of those who disapproved or objected to the president did so on character or personality dimensions: that he was arrogant, obnoxious, ill-informed, untrustworthy, racist or sexist (Newport 2017b). Only 16 percent of Trump's critics in that survey said that their objections were based mainly on issue or policy disagreements (Newport 2017b). Supporters of Trump, while fewer in number, considered policy agreements with the new president more important a source of their evaluation than character matters (Newport 2017b).

Against that backdrop of public negativity, it should come as no surprise that Donald Trump dominated the late night humor discourse during his first year as president.

Before delving into the data, it is important to note the changing role that late night hosts sometimes claim for themselves during the Trump presidency. For decades, these shows have not offered much policy content beyond some topical jokes in the opening ten minutes or so of the program. Most of the airtime on these programs was given over to chats with celebrities and with the occasional political figure, but even then the content generally remained light. While the number of jokes, and the harshness of the topics, may have increased over the years, there remained little deep discussion of policy matters, perhaps because producers believed that getting into policy specifics in a program airing after 11 p.m. would drive away viewers seeking a little rest and relaxation before bed.

Then along came Jimmy Kimmel and the Affordable Care Act. On September 19, 2017 in his opening monologue for ABC's *Jimmy Kimmel Live!* Kimmel departed from the usual string of jokes about celebrities, current events, and public affairs to issue a point-by-point criticism of health care insurance legislation pending in Congress. He concluded by exhorting his studio and television audience to lobby against the legislation: "So if this bill isn't good enough for you, call your congressperson." *Politico* later calculated that Kimmel devoted 24 minutes of airtime in three nights to defeating the Republican bill designed to repeal the Affordable Care Act (Diamond 2017).

Heard in its entirety, Kimmel's commentary sounds considerably more like parts of a stump speech than a laugh fest. In any event, Kimmel's engagement with health care legislation illustrates the extent to which the juncture of news and entertainment in politics can quickly expand to encompass the juncture of political advocacy and entertainment. In fact, a *Newsweek* story asserted that Kimmel "has proved to be the nation's most effective critic of the Graham-Cassidy bill that would repeal and replace the Affordable Care Act" (Nazaryan 2017).

Neither Johnny Carson nor Jay Leno would ever have made such a personal appeal regarding such a divisive political issue, nor would either have discussed it in the deeply personal terms Kimmel employed. Indeed, a dozen or so years earlier Kimmel himself might have seemed a very unlikely choice to weigh so forcefully in on serious public policy matters. He rose to national prominence on *The Man Show*, a cable-based celebration of the raunchier aspects of maleness, including frequent discussions of beer, women and adult entertainment that few would consider intellectually stimulating (Garber 2018). When the show debuted in 1999, Kimmel himself promised it would be "a joyous celebration of chauvinism!" (quoted in Garber 2018). Kimmel's public policy activism during the Trump years has also focused on exhortations regarding school gun violence after the mass shootings in Las Vegas and Parkland, Florida (Garber 2018).

Reports of Kimmel's policy influence in the health care debate are indicators of agenda setting and priming, as Kimmel linked his own infant son's need for expensive heart surgery to such insurance problems as coverage of preexisting conditions and lifetime caps on coverage. All this also fed into a media narrative about the politicization of late night entertainment, in particular the frequent focus of comedians on Donald Trump and his administration during its first year in office. As former *New York Times* writer and historian of late night entertainment Bill Carter put it, "There's no example of any kind of sustained attack like this on a politician ... There's a horde of writers writing jokes about Donald Trump every single night" (Quoted in Rutenberg 2017).

A generation ago, late night hosts did not want to go too far and risk offending Middle America. Now the tables have turned. These days, these hosts face criticism, both (from conservatives) for being too partisan in their remarks and (from liberals) for not being partisan enough. This happened to Jimmy Fallon during the 2016 general election, after he had Trump as a guest and did a routine that culminated with him tousling Trump's hair. After a deluge of articles and social media posts that accused him of "normalizing" Trump, a contrite Fallon insisted that he had intended not to "humanize" his guest but to "minimize" him, saying that people "have a right to be mad" at his 2016 interview with Trump (quoted in Andrews 2017).

Once again, however, these themes follow from the perceptions of journalists and pundits generalizing from particular incidents, rather than any systematic study. Moreover, it is not obvious on its face that the animus toward Trump is in fact historically unprecedented. Earlier frequent targets of late night humor include Bill Clinton, Dan Quayle and Sarah Palin. Nevertheless, Trump has blasted talk show hosts with all the fervor that he applies to denouncing the news media. He has gone so far as to demand equal time to balance the comedians' "one-sided" treatment of his administration (Associated Press 2017).

Of course, Trump is the latest in a long line of media bashers on the right side of the political spectrum. Republicans and conservatives, for whom demonizing the "liberal news media" is a long-standing staple of their rhetorical repertoire, have long complained about its counterpart among Hollywood liberals, including the hosts of late night talk shows (Dagnes 2012). But the criticisms prior to 2016 were mostly intermittent and episodic, in contrast to the steady drumbeat of Trump's attacks on the late night comics during his presidency.

In fact, our content analysis suggests that, like the news media, late night comedy threatens to feature all Trump, all the time. Table 4.1 shows Trump was the focus of almost half of all political jokes (3,128 out of 6,337, or 49 percent) on the top four late night programs during his first year in office. Trump's staggering total of jokes exceeded the rest of the top 20 joke targets combined. Finishing a very distant second was a cluster of policy issues, which attracted a combined 208 jokes. The Trump Administration collectively generated 166 jokes. The individual who garnered the most laughs after Trump was his former Press Secretary Sean Spicer, who was the subject of 162 jokes on the four programs.

(General categories like the Trump Administration refer to jokes that focus on a group collectively rather than on a specific individual. As a result, jokes about Trump or Spicer or any other administration official identified by name register as focused on that individual. Such a joke would not be part of the Trump Administration category. Similarly, jokes are coded as primarily about policy when no individual or nation is named. Many jokes do include a policy dimension, but they do so in the context of a joke aimed at a particular individual. A story on Trump and health care, for example, counts primarily as a Trump joke.)

Only eight individuals or topics were the subject of more than 100 jokes during the year, and other than policy issues, and those eight included Trump himself, members of the Trump family and other Republican office-holders and candidates. In fifth place was Roy Moore, a Trump-endorsed Republican Senate candidate in Alabama who lost after allegations emerged about his interactions with teenage girls when he was in his 30s. Presidential son Donald Trump Jr. took sixth place; First Lady Melania Trump ranked ninth. Attorney General Jeff Sessions ranked eighth, while Vice President Mike Pence ranked tenth.

Defeated presidential candidate Hillary Clinton was the top-rated Democrat, ranking 12th, behind Anthony Scaramucci, who briefly served as White House Communications Director, and just ahead of Steve Bannon, a top Trump political advisor. Former President Barack Obama was the second highest Democrat, ranking 17th with 48 jokes, just behind Russian President Vladimir Putin.

Putin and North Korean leader Kim Jon-un were the only foreign figures to crack the top 30 humor targets. Among other leading foreign targets, Pope Francis ranked 36th and Russia generally ranked 39th.

Few members of the Trump family escaped attention from the late night hosts. In addition to President Trump, Donald Trump Jr. and Melania Trump, who all made the top 10, "First Son-in-law and White House advisor Jared Kushner ranked 17th, son Eric Trump ranked 22nd and daughter Ivanka Trump, another top White House advisor in the family, ranked 29th. Daughter Tiffany Trump,

**TABLE 4.1** Leading Targets of Late Night Humor, 2017

| *Donald Trump* | *3128* |
|---|---|
| Policy Issues | 208 |
| Trump Administration* | 166 |
| Sean Spicer | 162 |
| Roy Moore | 160 |
| Donald Trump Jr. | 108 |
| Congressional Republicans* | 106 |
| Jeff Sessions | 104 |
| Melania Trump | 96 |
| Mike Pence | 80 |
| Anthony Scaramucci | 73 |
| Hillary Clinton | 71 |
| Steve Bannon | 69 |
| Kellyanne Conway | 58 |
| Ted Cruz | 50 |
| Vladimir Putin | 49 |
| Barack Obama | 48 |
| Jared Kushner | 43 |
| Congress* | 41 |
| James Comey | 40 |
| Michael Flynn | 39 |
| Eric Trump | 37 |
| Paul Ryan | 36 |
| Betsy DeVos | 35 |
| Voters | 35 |
| Paul Manafort | 35 |
| Rex Tillerson | 34 |
| Kim Jong-un | 34 |
| Ivanka Trump | 31 |
| Mitch McConnell | 30 |
| Bernie Sanders | 27 |
| Chris Christie | 25 |
| Ben Carson | 25 |
| John Kelly | 23 |
| Neil Gorsuch | 23 |
| Pope Francis | 21 |

| *Donald Trump* | *3128* |
|---|---|
| Al Franken | 21 |
| Reince Priebus | 20 |
| Russia* | 19 |
| Bill O'Reilly | 19 |
| Fox News* | 18 |
| Robert Mueller | 16 |
| Steve Mnuchin | 16 |
| George W. Bush | 16 |
| Stephen Miller | 16 |
| Republicans* | 15 |
| Sarah Huckabee Sanders | 13 |
| Dennis Rodman | 13 |
| Tim Murphy | 12 |
| Lindsey Graham | 12 |
| North Korea* | 12 |
| Bob Corker | 11 |
| Kayla Moore | 11 |
| Devin Nunes | 10 |
| Anthony Weiner | 10 |
| Arnold Schwarzenegger | 10 |
| John Conyers | 10 |
| Media* | 10 |

*General categories are used for jokes that focus on the institution rather than a specific individual. Jokes that name individuals are coded as jokes directed at that individual.

Note: Only individuals and institutions that were the subject of at least 10 jokes are included here. N = 6337. Totals include late night jokes aired during January 23–December 31, 2017 on *Jimmy Kimmel Live!, The Daily Show with Trevor Noah, The Late Show with Stephen Colbert* and *The Tonight Show Starring Jimmy Fallon.*

currently a student at Georgetown Law School, and son Barron Trump, years away from adulthood, generally were spared these barbs, perhaps because of their youth and their relative distance from both the White House and from the family real estate business.

Critics have long faulted network television for focusing on the executive branch and providing relatively little attention to the other branches of government in its news reports (Farnsworth and Lichter 2006). Our data here reveal that late night humor does little better in covering the range of governmental actors in Washington. For the current and potential members of the legislative branch, the most jokes (160) targeted defeated Senate candidate Roy Moore. Congressional Republicans in general ranked seventh with 106 jokes, while Republican Texas Senator Ted Cruz ranked 15th, with 50 jokes. Congress as a collective ranked 19th with 41 jokes, while House Speaker Paul Ryan (R-WI) and Senate Majority Leader Mitch McConnell (R-KY) were the subject of 36 and 30 jokes respectively.

The judicial branch was even less likely to be in the sights of the late night comics. Neil Gorsuch, nominated and confirmed to the Supreme Court during Trump's first year in office, was the leading member of the judicial branch in terms of late night humor, ranking 35th with 23 jokes during 2017. No other member of SCOTUS ranked among the top 60 subjects of late night humor. Since the justices as individuals generally receive news coverage only during their nominations, confirmations and resignations, late night comics probably find these largely unknown figures to be a poor source of humor for a mass audience. (Of course, our study ended prior to the media circus surrounding the nomination and confirmation of Brett Kavanaugh to the Supreme Court.)

In Table 4.2, we look at the targets of late night humor on a month-by-month basis. Once again, Donald Trump dominates, finishing first during every single month of 2017, with at least double the joke totals of the second-place finisher every single month of the year. (The January jokes considered here are those that aired starting the Monday after Trump's inauguration on Friday, January 20. So the January monthly totals included in our analysis – and reported here – cover roughly one-third of that month.)

Being a public relations specialist for Trump made one relatively visible, and therefore a key target of the comics. This was particularly true if a spokesperson put forth easily debunked claims. Press Secretary Sean Spicer, who first sprang to public attention with his wildly inaccurate description of the size of the crowd on the Washington Mall that attended Trump's inauguration, ranked second or third as a joke target during the first four months of the year. White House public relations aide Kellyanne Conway likewise generated significant ridicule in the early days of the Trump presidency for what she dubbed "alternative facts," a term she used in the wake of those same erroneous White House claims about the crowd size at the inauguration (Sinderbrand 2017). She ranked as a top-five target for humor during the first three months of 2017. Anthony Scaramucci, who lasted less than two weeks as the White House communications director, ranked third as a humor target in July, during his extremely brief star turn in Washington.

Allegations of scandalous behavior also put political figures in the sights of the humorists. Statements from victims that Senate candidate Roy Moore of Alabama pursued teenagers for dates while in his 30s made him the second-ranked source of humor in November and December, behind only the president who endorsed him in that failed Senate bid. (Moore also made the top five in September, when the scandals regarding his personal behavior first generated considerable public attention.) Education Secretary Betsy DeVos, whose unusually rocky confirmation hearings early in the year revealed that she knew little about public

**TABLE 4.2** Leading Targets of Late Night Humor by Month, 2017

| *Top Five Targets Mentioned During Each Month* | | | | | | | |
|---|---|---|---|---|---|---|---|
| **January** | | **February** | | **March** | | **April** | |
| D. Trump | 62 | D. Trump | 230 | D. Trump | 224 | D. Trump | 247 |
| Spicer | 15 | Spicer | 26 | P. Ryan | 24 | Spicer | 23 |
| Conway | 5 | Conway | 20 | Spicer | 21 | Kushner | 13 |
| B. Obama | 5 | M. Trump | 13 | Sessions | 19 | M. Trump | 11 |
| Voters | 4 | B. DeVos | 13 | Conway | 14 | Pence | 11 |
| **May** | | **June** | | **July** | | **August** | |
| D. Trump | 435 | D. Trump | 242 | D. Trump | 243 | D. Trump | 237 |
| Trump Adm* | 42 | Issues | 67 | D. Trump Jr. | 58 | Issues | 31 |
| Cong. Rep* | 33 | Sessions | 31 | Scaramucci | 57 | Trump Adm* | 17 |
| Issues | 32 | Comey | 24 | Cong. Rep* | 17 | Putin | 10 |
| Spicer | 27 | Cong. Rep* | 24 | Spicer | 12 | Jong-un | 10 |
| **September** | | **October** | | **November** | | **December** | |
| D. Trump | 320 | D. Trump | 415 | D. Trump | 321 | D. Trump | 152 |
| Issues | 25 | Trump Adm. | 35 | Moore | 76 | Moore | 67 |
| Cruz | 22 | Tillerson | 21 | D. Trump Jr. | 18 | Issues | 24 |
| H. Clinton | 21 | Manafort | 15 | Congress* | 18 | Flynn | 15 |
| Moore | 17 | Issues | 15 | Sessions | 16 | K. Moore | 11 |

Source: CMPA

*General categories are used for jokes that focus on the institution rather than a specific individual. Jokes that name individuals are coded at the individual level.

Note: Totals include late night jokes aired during January 23–December 31, 2017 on *Jimmy Kimmel Live!*, *The Daily Show with Trevor Noah*, *The Late Show with Stephen Colbert* and *The Tonight Show Starring Jimmy Fallon*.

education (Huetteman and Alcindor 2017), cracked the top five in February. Attorney General Jeff Sessions, who angered Trump by refusing to oversee the investigation into possible collusion between Russia and the Trump campaign, found himself in the top five targets for humor during March and June. Former Trump campaign chairman Paul Manafort, subsequently jailed over a variety of money laundering and fraud violations relating to his failure to report the details of his business dealings with pro-Russian government officials in Ukraine and other matters, ranked fourth as a humor target in October 2017. Former National Security Advisor Michael Flynn, who pled guilty on December 1, 2017 to charges stemming from Mueller's Russia investigation, ranked fourth that month (Leonnig et al. 2017). Thus, Trump's presence in the nightly monologues was reinforced by a host of subordinates who served him.

Donald Trump also dominated the late night jokes when each humorist is examined individually. As shown in Table 4.3, all four programs provided at least eight times as many jokes about Trump as any other topic, institution or individual during 2017.

Despite their general similarities, these are not four cookie-cutter late night humor programs. Indeed, it is important to examine these programs as separate entities. For example, Jimmy Fallon has been seen as less critical of Trump than the other late night hosts, particularly Stephen Colbert (Hartung 2017; Itzkoff 2017; Merry 2016; Poniewozik 2017), and different hosts have different orientations to political comedy, as we illustrate below.

In addition to telling more jokes overall and more jokes directed at Trump than his three leading competitors, Colbert has focused far more on the Trump family and the Trump governing team. His 75 jokes on the Trump Administration were double the number of any one of the other three programs examined here, as were his 50 jokes on Attorney General Sessions. His 77 jokes on Donald Trump Jr. far outpaced the other three hosts, with Kimmel's 13 jokes in second place. Colbert likewise found much mirth to share regarding White House political advisor Stephen Bannon, the subject of 48 jokes on his program, as compared to 14 jokes on *The Daily Show*, and far less elsewhere.

Of course, other programs had other targets of particular interest. Trevor Noah regularly turned to Senator Ted Cruz (R-TX), the source of 25 jokes on the *The Daily Show*, which represented more than double the number of jokes told about that failed 2016 candidate than any of the other three shows. Noah also offered more jokes about Obama than the other programs, perhaps because the other three hosts, who are white, might have been less comfortable joking about the first African American president. Noah's program also focused more on policy matters than did the other late night programs.

Fallon, who saw his ratings drop in response to what some viewers felt was a too favorable treatment of Trump during the 2016 campaign, spent 2017 offering more humor directed at former presidential candidate Hillary Clinton, Russian President Vladimir Putin and Vice President Mike Pence than his nightly comedy competitors did. The continued Clinton attacks offered a way to retain some of *The Tonight Show* viewers who might not respond to the sharper treatment of Trump on Fallon's show during 2017.

The joke data suggest that Fallon was responding to audience pressures, as the percentage of political jokes he told about Trump during 2017 accounted for 55 percent of his political jokes, a higher percentage than either Colbert or Noah,

**TABLE 4.3** Leading Target Frequency by Program, 2017

| *Topic* | *Kimmel* | *Noah* | *Colbert* | *Fallon* | *Total* |
|---|---|---|---|---|---|
| Donald Trump | 598 (54.5%) | 689 (46.3%) | 1151 (46.3%) | 690 (54.5%) | 3128 |
| Issues | 268 | 85 | 70 | 27 | 20 |
| Trump Admin.* | 26 | 34 | 75 | 31 | 166 |
| Sean Spicer | 42 | 26 | 60 | 34 | 162 |
| Roy Moore | 38 | 32 | 71 | 19 | 160 |
| Donald Trump Jr. | 13 | 9 | 77 | 9 | 108 |
| Congressional Rep.* | 7 | 35 | 55 | 9 | 106 |
| Jeff Sessions | 14 | 24 | 50 | 16 | 104 |
| Melania Trump | 31 | 17 | 14 | 34 | 96 |
| Mike Pence | 9 | 15 | 23 | 33 | 80 |
| Anthony Scaramucci | 4 | 9 | 39 | 21 | 73 |
| Hillary Clinton | 14 | 15 | 13 | 29 | 71 |
| Steve Bannon | 1 | 14 | 48 | 6 | 69 |
| Kellyanne Conway | 15 | 9 | 23 | 11 | 58 |
| Ted Cruz | 10 | 25 | 5 | 10 | 50 |
| Vladimir Putin | 9 | 7 | 12 | 21 | 49 |
| Barack Obama | 12 | 19 | 9 | 8 | 48 |
| Jared Kushner | 16 | 10 | 15 | 2 | 43 |
| Congress* | 5 | 11 | 16 | 9 | 41 |
| James Comey | 2 | 10 | 23 | 5 | 40 |
| Michael Flynn | 3 | 10 | 23 | 3 | 39 |
| Eric Trump | 2 | 12 | 13 | 10 | 37 |
| Paul Ryan | 0 | 18 | 11 | 7 | 36 |
| Betsy DeVos | 3 | 0 | 7 | 25 | 35 |
| Paul Manafort | 1 | 7 | 24 | 3 | 35 |
| Voters* | 6 | 15 | 10 | 4 | 35 |
| Total | 1097 | 1487 | 2487 | 1266 | 6337 |

*General categories are used for jokes that focus on the institution rather than a specific individual. Jokes that name individuals are coded at the individual level.

Note: Only the subjects of at least 35 jokes are included. Totals include late night jokes aired during January 23–December 31, 2017 on *Jimmy Kimmel Live!, The Daily Show with Trevor Noah, The Late Show with Stephen Colbert* and *The Tonight Show Starring Jimmy Fallon.*

each of whom focused on Trump in 46 percent of their political jokes. Kimmel matched Fallon, with 55 percent of his political jokes aimed at the president during 2017. Colbert's sheer number of jokes about Trump dwarfed those told by the other three hosts, but Fallon's total number of Trump jokes was almost identical to Noah's. Even so, Fallon's increasingly critical treatment of Trump jokes in 2017 may have had less of an impact on his ratings than his relatively cozy approach to Trump during the 2016 campaign, a matter that generated considerable media attention at the time. You only get one chance to make a first impression, and Fallon's more generous treatment of Trump during 2016 apparently reduced his audience share during these polarized times, and his shift in 2017 may not have been seen by those who had already stopped watching the program.

Kimmel, whose program received considerable attention during 2017 as he talked about health care in the context of his sick infant son (France 2017), actually did not emphasize policy that much in his jokes during Trump's first year in office. (Kimmel's emotional, personal and lengthy discussion about his family's health crisis contained relatively little humorous content, and therefore was the source of few jokes here. The CMPA coding system did pick up the occasional zinger during Kimmel's emotional personal appeals, however.) Kimmel's 26 jokes relating to policy matters were far below the totals on Noah's and Colbert's programs during 2017. Kimmel's favorite targets, after President Trump, were Sean Spicer, Roy Moore and Melania Trump. As a whole, though, the results in Table 4.3 demonstrated that Kimmel was the least likely late night host to make a political joke. Fallon ranked third in terms of number of jokes, behind Colbert and Noah.

Many of the jokes that focused on Trump and the Trump White House had significant policy dimensions, even though the main target of the humor was the president rather than the policy itself. Among joke topics identified in Table 4.4, all four humorists found Russia a more compelling policy matter for humor than any other issue, as that topic ranked first for each of the four comedians. Stephen Colbert, who had more policy-focused humor than the other three hosts did, joked about Russia as much as all three other hosts combined. (This topic included Russian interference in the 2016 elections.) Colbert and Noah had notably more policy-oriented humor than did Kimmel and Fallon.

Once again, there were some significant differences in choices made by the various programs. While all four hosts joked about racism, Jimmy Fallon only focused on the topic for three jokes as compared to double-digit numbers of jokes on this topic by the other three hosts. (That pattern of limited discussion of racial matters might jibe with the preferences of some late night viewers less critical of Trump, viewers who might find Fallon's less contentious history with Trump as a presidential candidate a reason to select his program.) Colbert joked far more about immigration than his rivals, and he told even more jokes than they did about the budget – a risky wonk-ish topic to put frequently before a potentially tired late night audience. Noah focused more attention on the alt-right, who triggered a fatal clash in Charlottesville, Virginia during August 2017, the event that promoted Trump to talk about "very fine people on both sides" of the race riot there (Blake 2019).

Noah emphasized jokes about climate change more than the other hosts did, and he had notably less to say regarding North Korea. Kimmel said less about health care than one might expect, given the very visible and newsworthy comments he made about the Trump Administration's efforts to repeal the Affordable Care Act, also known as Obamacare.

**TABLE 4.4** Policy Topics by Program, 2017

| *Topic* | *Kimmel* | *Noah* | *Colbert* | *Fallon* | *Total* |
|---|---|---|---|---|---|
| Russia | 64 | 154 | 324 | 84 | 626 |
| Sex | 46 | 65 | 94 | 30 | 235 |
| Health Care | 23 | 57 | 83 | 26 | 189 |
| North Korea | 36 | 9 | 40 | 14 | 99 |
| Racism | 23 | 13 | 35 | 3 | 74 |
| Immigration | 11 | 11 | 40 | 12 | 74 |
| Taxes | 3 | 22 | 19 | 15 | 59 |
| Border Wall | 10 | 16 | 12 | 14 | 52 |
| Climate Change | 4 | 19 | 10 | 6 | 39 |
| Alt-Right | 1 | 19 | 1 | 0 | 21 |
| Budget | 0 | 3 | 13 | 0 | 16 |
| Election | 3 | 4 | 5 | 0 | 12 |
| Puerto Rico | 0 | 0 | 9 | 0 | 9 |
| Terrorism | 0 | 6 | 2 | 0 | 8 |
| Net Neutrality | 0 | 2 | 6 | 0 | 8 |
| Marijuana | 1 | 1 | 0 | 6 | 8 |
| Opiods | 3 | 3 | 0 | 0 | 6 |
| Gun Control | 0 | 3 | 1 | 1 | 5 |
| Multiple Policies | 0 | 3 | 1 | 0 | 4 |
| LGBT Rights | 0 | 0 | 2 | 2 | 4 |
| Environment | 0 | 0 | 2 | 0 | 2 |
| Energy | 0 | 1 | 0 | 0 | 1 |
| Deregulation | 0 | 0 | 1 | 0 | 1 |
| Football | 0 | 1 | 0 | 0 | 1 |
| Economy* | 0 | 0 | 0 | 1 | 1 |
| Birthers | 1 | 0 | 0 | 0 | 1 |
| First Amendment | 0 | 0 | 1 | 0 | 1 |
| PBS | 1 | 0 | 0 | 0 | 1 |
| Israel | 0 | 1 | 0 | 0 | 1 |
| Grand Total | 230 | 413 | 701 | 214 | 1558 |

Source: CMPA

*The economy category excludes jokes about taxes and budgets, which are separate categories.
Note: N = 6337. Totals include late night jokes aired during January 23–December 31, 2017 on *Jimmy Kimmel Live!*, *The Daily Show with Trevor Noah*, *The Late Show with Stephen Colbert* and *The Tonight Show Starring Jimmy Fallon*.

**TABLE 4.5** Political Jokes by Program, 2017

*Jokes About Trump*

| | Not Political | Political | Total Jokes |
|---|---|---|---|
| *Jimmy Kimmel Live!* | 253 | 347 | 600 |
| *The Daily Show with Trevor Noah* | 307 | 385 | 692 |
| *The Late Show with Stephen Colbert* | 411 | 743 | 1154 |
| *The Tonight Show Starring Jimmy Fallon* | 383 | 313 | 696 |
| Total Jokes | 1354 | 1788 | 3142 |
| Total Percentage | 43% | 57% | 100% |

*Jokes Not About Trump*

| | Not Political | Political | Total Jokes |
|---|---|---|---|
| *Jimmy Kimmel Live!* | 200 | 297 | 497 |
| *The Daily Show with Trevor Noah* | 316 | 479 | 795 |
| *The Late Show with Stephen Colbert* | 582 | 751 | 1333 |
| *The Tonight Show Starring Jimmy Fallon* | 342 | 228 | 570 |
| Total Percentage | 45% | 55% | 100% |
| Total Jokes | 1440 | 1755 | 3195 |

Note: N = 6337. Totals include late night jokes aired during January 23–December 31, 2017 on *Jimmy Kimmel Live!, The Daily Show with Trevor Noah, The Late Show with Stephen Colbert* and *The Tonight Show Starring Jimmy Fallon.*

These choices correspond relatively closely to the policy issues of greatest public concern, as revealed in surveys taken at that time. In Table 2.5, for example, Americans said their main policy concerns in 2017 included health care and the budget, a difficult-to-explain topic that nevertheless generated a significant amount of political humor. While hunger, homelessness and crime were also issues of great public concern in the survey, these topics seem even less accessible to humor than budgetary matters. Other issues survey respondents emphasized did receive some attention from the comics, including race relations and immigration.

While it ranked first in terms of policy topics employed in political comedy during Trump's first year as president, Russia does not appear among the major concerns of voters in the 2017 Gallup survey presented in Table 2.5. Nor did Russia emerge as a major source of why voters approved or disapproved of Trump's job performance as of mid-2017, as revealed in Table 2.2 and Table 2.3. Even so, all four comics invested significant attention in jokes in relation to Putin and Russia, a reflection of significant news attention to the issues relating to Russian efforts to interfere in the 2016 election and potential Russian influence in the Trump Administration, both of which were subjects of the Mueller investigation. In other words, most policy-related jokes relate to issues that are major public concerns or frequent topics of the mass media, or both. Rarely does one see much comedic attention to issues that do not have some connection to current public opinion or news coverage.

In Table 4.5, we see some key similarities in the way the four comics dealt with political jokes. Overall 57 percent of the jokes about Trump were political, almost identical to the 55 percent of the jokes about someone or something else. There was, however, one important difference: a majority of the jokes Fallon told about Trump were not political in orientation, while the other three hosts all focused more on political rather than nonpolitical humor relating to Trump. Fallon also emphasized the nonpolitical in jokes about people and things other than the president, again in contrast to the other three programs. Once again, the findings suggest less political fare on NBC when compared to the other three late night offerings.

In Table 4.6, we see that all four hosts focused on the personal in jokes about President Trump: fully 94 percent of the jokes told at the president's expense focused

**TABLE 4.6** Personal Jokes by Program, 2017

*Jokes About Trump*

| | Not Personal | Personal | Total Jokes |
|---|---|---|---|
| *Jimmy Kimmel Live!* | 35 | 565 | 600 |
| *The Daily Show with Trevor Noah* | 35 | 657 | 692 |
| *The Late Show with Stephen Colbert* | 93 | 1061 | 1154 |
| *The Tonight Show Starring Jimmy Fallon* | 35 | 661 | 696 |
| Total Jokes | 198 | 2944 | 3142 |
| Total Percentage | 6% | 94% | 100% |

*Jokes Not About Trump*

| | Not Personal | Personal | Total Jokes |
|---|---|---|---|
| *Jimmy Kimmel Live!* | 87 | 410 | 497 |
| *The Daily Show with Trevor Noah* | 168 | 627 | 795 |
| *The Late Show with Stephen Colbert* | 222 | 1111 | 1333 |
| *The Tonight Show Starring Jimmy Fallon* | 71 | 499 | 570 |
| Total Jokes | 548 | 2647 | 3195 |
| Total Percentage | 17% | 83% | 100% |

Note: N = 6337. Totals include late night jokes aired during January 23–December 31, 2017 on *Jimmy Kimmel Live!, The Daily Show with Trevor Noah, The Late Show with Stephen Colbert* and *The Tonight Show Starring Jimmy Fallon.*

on personal attributes, like his weight, his hair, his preference for long ties, his allegedly small hands and his bombastic and sometimes erratic demeanor. There was little difference in emphasis: over 90 percent of the Trump-related humor on all four shows focused on personal matters. Jokes about people and institutions other than Trump still involved a highly personal focus, but the 83 percent of jokes about personal matters was a slightly lower total than those directed at Trump.

In Table 4.7, we see just how much the humor relating to Donald Trump differs from that of his predecessors in the Oval Office. While presidents usually

**TABLE 4.7** Jokes Targeting Presidents and Presidential Candidates, 1992–2017 (Presidential Election Years and First Years in Office)

| *Year* | *Candidate* | *Party* | *Jokes* | *Rank* |
|---|---|---|---|---|
| 1992 | George H.W. Bush | R | 616 | 1 |
| | Bill Clinton | D | 421 | 2 |
| 1993 | Bill Clinton | D | 440 | 1 |
| 1996 | Bob Dole | R | 839 | 1 |
| | Bill Clinton | D | 657 | 2 |
| 1997 | Bill Clinton | D | 808 | 1 |
| 2000 | George W. Bush | R | 905 | 1 |
| | Al Gore | D | 546 | 3 |
| 2001 | George W. Bush | R | 546 | 2 |
| 2004 | George W. Bush | R | 1169 | 1 |
| | John Kerry | D | 505 | 2 |
| 2005 | George W. Bush | D | 657 | 1 |
| 2008 | John McCain | R | 1358 | 1 |
| | Barack Obama | D | 768 | 3 |
| 2009 | Barack Obama | D | 936 | 1 |
| 2012 | Mitt Romney | R | 1061 | 1 |
| | Barack Obama | D | 401 | 2 |
| 2016* | Donald Trump | R | 1817 | – |
| | Hillary Clinton | D | 506 | – |
| 2017* | Donald Trump | R | 3128 | 1 |

Programs included: 2016–2017: *The Tonight Show* (NBC), *The Late Show* (CBS), *Jimmy Kimmel Live!* (ABC), *The Daily Show* (Comedy Central); 2012: *The Tonight Show* (NBC), *The Late Show* (CBS), *The Daily Show* (Comedy Central), *The Colbert Report* (Comedy Central); 2008–2009: *The Tonight Show* (NBC), *The Late Show* (CBS), *The Daily Show* (Comedy Central), *The Colbert Report* (Comedy Central), *Late Night* (NBC); 2004–2005: *The Tonight Show* (NBC), *The Late Show* (CBS), *The Daily Show* (Comedy Central), *Late Night* (NBC); 2000: *The Tonight Show* (NBC), *The Late Show* (CBS), *Politically Incorrect* (ABC), *Late Night* (NBC); 1996: *The Tonight Show* (NBC), *The Late Show* (CBS), *Politically Incorrect* (ABC), *Late Night* (NBC); 1992: *The Tonight Show* (NBC), *The Late Show* (CBS), *Arsenio* (Fox).

rank at or near the top of the rankings of late night jokes, the sheer amount of attention Trump received defies the norm. The 3,128 jokes told about Trump during his first year in office exceeds the number of jokes told during the first years of Presidents Bill Clinton in 1993, George W. Bush in 2001 and Barack Obama in 2009. Obama ranked second in the first-year humor sweepstakes in 2009 with 936 jokes, followed by Bush with 546.

Bill Clinton, a joke-generating and scandal-surviving president like few others, was fortunate to have been president during a time when political humor was less barbed, and he only had to endure 440 jokes in 1993 (Lichter et al. 2015). The number of jokes directed at Clinton during subsequent years in office increased, particularly during the Clinton–Lewinsky scandal that emerged during Bill Clinton's second term. But even during controversy over the president's sexual behavior and the subsequent impeachment debate, the humorists never found as much to mock with Clinton as they did with Trump during his first year in office (Lichter et al. 2015).

Trump, during his time as a presidential candidate, also had shattered previous records. The 1,817 jokes directed at him during 2016 (coded from January 1 through November 11, shortly after he became president-elect), was far above the 1,358 jokes directed at 2008 Republican nominee John McCain and the 506 jokes directed at Hillary Clinton in 2016, when she lost the election to Trump. (And the gap is even greater between Trump and McCain when one considers that the McCain jokes covered a 12-month period of analysis and Trump's jokes only involved about 10.5 months of late night humor.)

## BOX 4.1 JOKES ABOUT TRUMP'S CHARACTER AND PHYSICAL APPEARANCE

### Trump's Character

went to Disneyland. Yeah, which wasn't really a good choice, because everywhere I looked, I couldn't escape the thought of Donald Trump. I saw this cartoon idiot named Donald with a big red tie everywhere I went. *Trevor Noah, February 27, 2017*

To make sure Trump reads his daily briefings for this trip, sources say that for this trip, National Security Council officials have strategically included Trump's name in "as many paragraphs as we can because he keeps reading if he's mentioned." That is a true story. Apparently, the only thing that can overcome Trump's short attention span is his crippling narcissism. But, of course, if they want to explain that to him, they'll have to call it his crippling Trumpicism. *Stephen Colbert, May 19, 2017*

Good afternoon. Before the fake news media reports any more inaccuracies, the White House would like to clarify, Secretary of State Tillerson did not call the President a "moron." He also did not call him any of the following: idiot, bonehead, nincompoop, imbecile, empty jack-o-lantern, suntanned ham loaf, so stupid he got his hair stuck in a cotton candy machine and called it a hairstyle, dumb dumb, dumb [bleep], [bleep] for brains or racist sweet potato. Thank you. We'll have an update on this tomorrow. *Jimmy Kimmel, October 4, 2017*

And today, and today, we learned that [Senator] Corker might be onto something because, according to *Politico*, White House aides use delays and distraction to manage Trump. Chief of Staff John Kelly has tried to limit bad decisions by blocking information from the President's desk. And sometimes, staffers would even distract him with a visual aid "like charts on how farmers might feel about ending the North American free trade agreement." And an executive with the Trump organization explains that "you either had to just convince him something better was his idea, or ignore what he said to do and hoped he'd forgot about it the next day." Because, like a toddler, Trump lacks object permanence. *Stephen Colbert, October 10, 2017*

## Trump's Personal Attributes

Trump is a lot like the Knicks – he's from New York, he's orange and always finds a way to lose on the court. Always. The only difference, I like the Knicks. Did you say that ain't right? *Trevor Noah, February 6, 2017*

Actually, it turns out, President Trump is a big fan of the Irish. That's why yesterday he sported the colors of their flag. There you go. He's got green tie, white shirt, orange chin. It's perfect. The whole combo. That was very thoughtful. *Jimmy Fallon, March 17, 2017*

Mr. Trump, your presidency, I love your presidency. I call it "des grace the nation." You're not the POTUS, you're the blotus, you're the glutton with the button. You're a regular gorge Washington. You're the presi-dunce, but you're turning into a real prick-tator. Sir, you attract more skinheads than free Rogaine. You have more people marching against you than cancer. You talk like a sign language gorilla who got hit in the head. In fact, the only thing your mouth is good for is being Vladimir Putin's [bleep] holster. Your Presidential Library is going to be a kid's menu and a couple of Jugg's magazines. The only thing smaller than your hands is your tax returns. *Stephen Colbert, May 1, 2017*

Everybody was looking forward to the former F.B.I. Director testifying about all the juicy details of his meetings with Donald Trump. Because, remember, Comey wrote everything down. And all his memos are going to be collected in his new children's book: "James and the Guilty Orange." Heart warming. A lost masterpiece. Tim Burton's going to make a movie of it. *Stephen Colbert, June 8, 2017*

At a dinner last night, President Trump told Republican senators that if they didn't vote for the healthcare bill, they'd look like dopes. And he combed his neck hair over the top of his head and walked away with his tie dragging on the floor. *Jimmy Fallon, July 18, 2017*

Good press conference. This back and forth between us and North Korea, it's become frightening. Donald Trump and Kim Jong-un do not like each other at all, which is a shame because they actually have a lot in common. And not just the terrible haircuts. *Jimmy Kimmel, 14 August, 2017*

Box 4.1 offers a sample of late night presidential humor offered during 2017 that related to who Trump is: his character and his physical appearance. These boxes offer examples of the sort of humor directed at the president. The lists are not representative samples, but rather try to provide a flavor of the some of the lines of mockery that humorists employed. Several of the jokes relate to unusual aspects of Trump's appearance, including his unorthodox hairstyle, his highly tanned appearance and his decision to wear extra-long ties. Several of these clips are particularly harsh. For example, on October 4, 2017, Jimmy Kimmel used the debate over whether then–Secretary of State Rex Tillerson called Trump a "moron" as an opportunity to launch into a very intense list of all the other insults that could be lobbed at the president. On May 1, 2017, Stephen Colbert offered a list of insults relating to how ways to describe Trump that demonstrate he is a disgrace to the nation. There is also a reference to Trump as an angry narcissistic child trapped inside a senior citizen's body. (This was part of a joke by Colbert on October 10, 2017 about how White House staffers try to distract the president when he has a bad idea.)

## BOX 4.2 JOKES ABOUT TRUMP AND SEX

But Trump's already settling in. In fact, on Friday, the White House changed the curtains and the rug in the Oval Office. And Trump said that wasn't what he meant when he asked the secretary "does the carpet match the drapes?" *Jimmy Fallon, January 23, 2017*

Wow, guys. You see what's happened? Trump used to be the care-free rich guy, and now he and Obama have switched lives. It's like they got hit by lightning while peeing in the same fountain. Or maybe like Trump made a wish on a monkey's paw while he was being peed on. All I know is there was pee involved. That's all I'm saying. *Trevor Noah, February 7, 2017*

On Tuesday, Brooke Shields appeared on Andy Cohen's *Watch Andy Cohen Happen Live* and told this story about Donald Trump asking her out in the 1990s.

SHIELDS: He called me right after he'd gotten a divorce, and he said, "I really think we should date because you're America's sweetheart and I'm America's richest man, and the people would love it."

Really? That was his pickup line? No wonder he prefers women who speak English as a second language. *Stephen Colbert, October 6, 2017*

Here [Trump] is on Howard Stern bragging about how he handled STDs in the New York dating scene:

TRUMP: It is a dangerous world out there, it's scary, it's like Vietnam, sort of like—

STERN: It is, it's like your personal Vietnam isn't it? You've said that many times.

TRUMP: I feel like a great and very brave soldier.

I know it sounds bad, and it is, but he's right. Sex with Trump is like Vietnam. It's a bungled operation launched on false pretenses without a satisfying ending. *Stephen Colbert, October 23, 2017*

Now of course there are still people asking, how could President Trump support the man credibly accused of sexual misconduct by so many women. Well, it's simple, people. Birds of a feather molest together. *Trevor Noah, December 12, 2017*

Box 4.2 offers a sample of late night humor related to sex. The humorists mocked the president's sexism, the narcissistic, tone-deaf pickup line Trump used to express his interest in dating the much-younger movie star Brooke Shields after his first divorce, and Trump's remark that trying to avoid sexually transmitted diseases in New York City in the 1970s dating scene represented his own personal Vietnam.

On February 7, Trevor Noah made a veiled reference to the "pee tape," a reference to an alleged tape – never made public by anyone as of the publication of this book – that purportedly showed Trump watching women urinate on each other in a Moscow hotel (Parker 2018). Rumors of the existence of such a tape had been circulating in Washington since before the 2016 presidential election, and Noah's urine-related joke presumes a high level of political awareness on the part of viewers about a possible compromising tape (as well as a preference for scatological humor). For his part, Trump denied he engaged in such behavior in Moscow, noting that he fears germs.

## BOX 4.3 JOKES ABOUT TRUMP AND POLICY MATTERS

### Trump and Russia

Trump's not worried about the testimony of Sally Yates or the testimony of former intelligence director James Clapper, tweeting: "Director Clapper reiterated what everybody, including the fake media, already knows – there is 'no evidence' of collusion with Russia and Trump." Um, Mr. President, a little tip: When you put "no evidence" in quotes, it really makes you seem "Innocent." *Stephen Colbert, May 9, 2017*

This is potentially illegal, maybe even very illegal. Fortunately this morning Trump re-tweeted the story from *Fox & Friends* that said Jared didn't do it, so.

That's a relief. Senator John McCain, fellow Republican, said he doesn't like this at all, he says allegations of ties between Trump's campaign and Russia are reaching Watergate size and scale. And that, you know – I understand what Senator McCain is saying. But Watergate was different. Watergate was some guys breaking into a hotel. This is a guy with a hotel breaking into the White House. *Jimmy Kimmel, May 30, 2017*

This is pretty big, though. Yesterday, White House officials said Russia targeted election systems in 21 states last year. Trump was furious. He said, "I paid for all 50." *Jimmy Fallon, June 22, 2017*

The meeting took place at Trump Tower and included Jared Kushner and then–Trump campaign manager Paul Manafort. And that proves that at least some in the campaign were willing to accept Russian help. So it's not a smoking gun, but it is a gun meeting with a Russian bullet about their mutual desire to smoke. *Stephen Colbert, July 10, 2017*

## Trump and North Korea

So, now, as much as I hate to admit it, it's all in the hands of Donald Trump. I hope that he has a well thought-out plan.
TRUMP: We'll handle North Korea. We're going to be able to handle them. They will be – it will be handled. We handle everything. Thank you very much. And flight back to Africa, booked! *Trevor Noah, August 1, 2017*

This problem with North Korea and the nukes is not an easy one to fix for anyone. President Clinton, President Bush, President Obama all tried different strategies and they didn't work. And so far Trump's strategy of playing multiple rounds of golf and watching *Fox & Friends* is not working either. *Jimmy Kimmel, August 9, 2017*

Here's the thing about North Korea. They have a fundamental misunderstanding of what Americans care about. They're always like, your president is a dangerous simpleton pig! We're like, yeah, yeah, we know. *Jimmy Kimmel, October 5, 2017*

## Trump and Health Care

Here's what – here's what people are talking about, you guys. I saw that yesterday, President Trump said that Obama copied him by calling the Republican health care bill "mean." And then Obama said Trump copied him by spending the last six months doing nothing. *Jimmy Fallon, June 26, 2017*

While they've pulled the bill, Republicans say they're going to come back with something better. So, they're going to – what do you call it? – repeal and replace their bill. And there's a lot of blame to go around. In fact, today, *The*

*New York Times* said Donald Trump "Faltered in his role as a closer." Yeah, usually, he's a great closer. Just look at his casinos. *Stephen Colbert, June 28, 2017*

Trump told reporters he was being unfairly judged because he's only been in office six months and people are expecting him to deliver a health care bill. And he has a point. I mean, where did anyone get the idea that passing health care was going to be easy? *Jimmy Kimmel, July 20, 2017*

For the last 24 hours, Donald Trump has been the President of busy town. This morning, he signed an executive order to get rid of some key provisions of Obamacare. For instance, the care part. *Stephen Colbert, October 12, 2017*

Box 4.3 provides some policy-oriented jokes relating to three key subjects of presidential humor during 2017: Russia, North Korea and the effort to repeal the Affordable Care Act, which eventually failed when a few Republican senators rejected Trump's plan to repeal Obama's health care expansion law. These Russia jokes, and many others not included in this illustration, presumed at least some members of the Trump team were guilty long before the Mueller investigation was completed – or even before Michael Flynn, a former general who served briefly as Trump's national security advisor, admitted to lying to the FBI regarding contacts with the Russians (Leonnig et al. 2017).

The 2017 jokes relating to the impasse with North Korea drew attention to Trump's lack of ability to express a plan for dealing with the regime. Comedians noted how he vacillated from talking about the "fury" he would release on the nation to holding summits with the North Korean dictator – as well as joking about Trump's lack of interest in doing his foreign policy homework.

The jokesters also focused on Trump's failure to convince enough fellow Republicans to support his plan to reverse the Affordable Care Act. They mocked his original claim that creating a replacement health care bill would be easy, while also noting that Trump did more to close casinos than he did to close the deal on repealing the health care law.

## BOX 4.4 JOKES ABOUT THE TRUMP ADMINISTRATION AND FAMILY MEMBERS

### Trump Administration

The big news since last we were together and talking has been from the Senate, where they've been debating the nomination of Trump's attorney general and baby-grandpa hybrid, Jeff Sessions. Well, they can do amazing things with genetics now. *Stephen Colbert, February 8, 2017*

He wouldn't do it [be alone with a woman] unless there's a chaperone? Why? Is he afraid they'll start banging in the middle of dinner? How irresistible does Mike Pence think he is? He's sitting there, like, there is no way we can be in this room and not have sex. How do you think my hair got so white? I (bleep) the color out of it. *Trevor Noah, April 3, 2017*

This administration is like organized crime, except for the organized part. It's "Not Very Good at This Fellas." *Stephen Colbert, July 28, 2017*

And that's not all. Trump also released a list of other rule changes he thinks the NFL should make. They're pretty interesting. I'll show you what I mean. For example, Trump's first rule is that someone has to get sacked every five minutes, just like at the White House. *Jimmy Fallon, September 25, 2017*

## Trump Family Members

Today, Trump sent Ivanka to Berlin to participate in a women's conference, making her the first Trump to attend a women's conference that didn't include a swimsuit competition. *Stephen Colbert, April 25, 2017*

So then because these were uncomfortable conversations, [FBI Director] Comey told the Attorney General, Jeff Sessions, he did not want any future direct communication with President Trump. Melania said the same thing by the way. *Jimmy Kimmel, June 8, 2017*

Donald Jr. hired a lawyer yesterday. This lawyer, in the past, represented members of the mafia, which actually makes sense – the Trumps are like the Corleone family if all of them were Fredo. Every one of them. *Jimmy Kimmel, July 11, 2017*

Meanwhile, I saw that Donald Trump Jr. just got his Secret Service protection back. While his brother Eric is still on one of those child leashes you see at the mall. "Put that down, Eric. Don't eat that. Don't put that in your mouth. Spit it out, Eric. It's a candle." *Jimmy Fallon, July 29, 2017*

Box 4.4 demonstrates that the late night comics provided equally harsh treatment for Trump Administration officials and family members. Stephen Colbert mocked Attorney General Sessions as a "baby-grandpa" hybrid, Trevor Noah ridiculed Vice President Pence's policy of not meeting women alone for dinner or meetings, and Jimmy Fallon made light of the extremely frequent turnover of the White House staff. Colbert also compared the Trump White House to a mob operation that he described as "Not Very Good at This Fellas," a reference to the Martin Scorsese mob film *Goodfellas* (1990).

Kimmel turned to the mob reference when talking about Trump's son Donald Jr., noting that the Trump family seems to consist of one Fredo after another, a reference to the least competent of the Corleone brothers in the *Godfather* film series. Younger brother Eric Trump received even harsher treatment from Fallon, who on July 29 compared Eric to a wild, dangerous toddler who needs a leash when being taken to a shopping mall.

## The Weekly Humor Programs

Like their daily humor program brethren, hosts of the weekly comedy programs found Trump to be a highly attractive target for their humor during 2017. While any president is likely to be subject of considerable mockery by late night comics, the rocky start to the presidency of Donald Trump provided copious amounts of material to discuss and mock. A close reading of these three prominent once-a-week shows demonstrates that they generally offered quite similar material to the comedy shows examined above, which are broadcast four or five times a week.

One potential problem that weekly shows faced, particularly when compared to the nightly comics, was that the barrage of daily news often added to an immense amount of material deserving attention during the seven days between episodes. As a result of the news deluge, they had to boil down an immense amount of joke-worthy material with enough time to provide context and offer humorous content. The weekly late night shows examined here, *Saturday Night Live, Full Frontal with Samantha Bee*, and *Last Week Tonight with John Oliver*, have distinct formats that gave rise to somewhat different approaches to covering the first year of the Trump presidency.

### *Saturday Night Live*

We start our discussion of the once-a-week programs with *Saturday Night Live*, the dean of weekly late night political humor. By using Twitter to criticize Alec Baldwin's imitation of him as unfunny, Trump has elevated the show's salience to contemporary political conversations (Waisanen 2018). Of course, the show has long featured political content and mocked political figures. From the Chevy Chase pratfalls during his imitations of President Ford to the presidential candidate cameos of Al Gore and George W. Bush in 2000, this weekly comedy program has offered a heavy dose of political content that had secured the attention and sometimes the respect of presidential candidates and presidents (Lichter et al. 2015; Parkin 2018).

*Saturday Night Live*'s format differs significantly from *Full Frontal* and *Last Week Tonight*. While Samantha Bee's and John Oliver's respective shows are both host-focused talk shows, *SNL* is a 90-minute variety show featuring various sketches, musical guests and recurring segments. The cast engages in extensive sketches, while the other two programs are more inclined to offer commentaries on news footage.

One recurring *SNL* segment that would seem more familiar to regular viewers of the other weekly programs is "Weekend Update," a regular segment that more closely resembles the news satire of *Full Frontal* and *Last Week Tonight*. In "Weekend Update," comedians Colin Jost and Michael Che review the biggest news stories of the previous week while providing biting commentary on the week's key political events.

"Weekend Update" touched on many of the biggest news stories of Trump's first year in office. However, given that this was just one segment in a larger show, its coverage was often more abbreviated than the news roundups on *Full Frontal* and *Last Week Tonight*. Many stories received just a few sentences, often following a formula of giving a roughly one-sentence explanation of the news story followed by a single joke. These segments frequently featured one story emphasized beyond the others, receiving several minutes of discussion. As with the other weekly late night shows, the rapid pace of the news cycle became a subject for some humor, such as when Jost remarked, "I know I said this last week, but this week was crazy" (*Saturday Night Live* 2017j). Some of the news stories covered by "Weekend Update" were President Trump's executive orders on immigration (*Saturday Night Live* 2017c), Republican attempts to repeal and replace the Affordable Care Act (*Saturday Night Live* 2017g), US military strikes in Syria (*Saturday Night Live* 2017h), developments in the various investigations of the Trump campaign (*Saturday Night Live* 2017j) and relations with North Korea (*Saturday Night Live* 2017i).

*SNL*'s sketches, in contrast to the rapid-fire commentary of "Weekend Update," would sometimes nod at recent events but generally focused more on mocking the individuals involved in these news stories. News coverage was certainly not the purpose of these sketches. Rather, news stories framed the sketches. For example, when the US Court of Appeals for the Ninth Circuit challenged the legality of President Trump's immigration executive order, *SNL* produced a sketch in which Trump, as portrayed by Alec Baldwin, challenged the appeals court ruling on the reality court show *The People's Court* (*Saturday Night Live* 2017d). Another example is a sketch showing Trump making a surprise visit to the home of Trump's former campaign manager Paul Manafort, produced after the real-life Manafort was charged with a number of crimes by Special Counsel Robert Mueller (*Saturday Night Live* 2017l). While these sketches drew from real news stories, they presented fictionalized events and focused mainly on making jokes at the expense of the people portrayed in the sketch.

Like *Full Frontal* and *Last Week Tonight, SNL* mostly relied upon personal insults for its jokes about Trump and his administration. *SNL* found plenty of humor in Trump's physical appearance. "Weekend Update," for example, joked about Trump's weight. When Trump ended his remarks on his executive orders on crime by saying, "A new era of justice begins, and it begins right now," the hosts of "Weekend Update" joked that he spent the next twenty minutes struggling to squeeze into a Batman costume (*Saturday Night Live* 2017e). *SNL*'s sketches expanded upon the mocking of Trump's physical appearance through

Alec Baldwin's portrayal. Baldwin emphasized and exaggerated aspects of Trump's appearance as a form of mockery, squinting his eyes and pushing out his lips in extreme versions of Trump's facial expressions. Baldwin also mimicked Trump's hunched-over posture, as well as his hand gestures. Furthermore, the use of makeup to match Trump's skin tone and wardrobe choices such as long ties both served to help Baldwin look the part as he mocked Trump's appearance.

As was the case on the other late night shows, *SNL* sometimes framed Trump as a bigot, a misogynist, an egomaniac and a fool. One sketch, entitled "Through Donald's Eyes," suggests that Trump's self-obsession and insecurity are so intense that they alter his perception of the world (*Saturday Night Live* 2017f). The sketch shows a day in Trump's life through his eyes, beginning with Trump awakening and watching a Fox News anchor on TV saying "Huge, huge success. Fantastic. Victory. Landslide. Fox News" (*Saturday Night Live* 2017f). When Trump later sees a celebrity criticizing him on TV, his previously friendly aides start to insult him and Trump sees his own hands shrink (*Saturday Night Live* 2017f). This sort of mocking of Trump's personality and psychology was present throughout *SNL*'s coverage of Trump's first year in office, in both sketches and "Weekend Update."

*SNL*'s sketches also targeted numerous people surrounding Trump. Kate McKinnon portrayed Kellyanne Conway, counselor to President Trump, as a somewhat sinister character obsessed with appearing on television. In one memorable example, Conway's character is crossed with the evil clown Pennywise from the film *It* as she attempts to lure CNN anchor Anderson Cooper into a sewer (*Saturday Night Live* 2017k). Melissa McCarthy portrayed Press Secretary Sean Spicer as an antagonistic liar wearing an ill-fitting suit in parodies of White House press briefings (*Saturday Night Live* 2017b).

By showing the Trump White House as a den of wacky and perhaps sinister self-serving characters, *SNL* mocks Trump by way of association. Another recurring character in *SNL* sketches about the first year of the Trump presidency was Russian President Vladimir Putin, played by Beck Bennett. Sketches featuring Putin generally suggest that the Russian president was largely responsible for Trump's election and that the president is under Putin's control (*Saturday Night Live* 2017a). These sorts of jokes aim to undermine the legitimacy of Trump's presidency while also striking at Trump's ego by suggesting he is not in control. Since Putin often appears in these sketches without a shirt, he also represents a macho contrast to the flabby and less fit image of Trump favored by late night comedians.

## *Full Frontal*

*Full Frontal with Samantha Bee* runs on TBS for 30 minutes each week, including commercial breaks. The show typically contains an opening monologue that briefly runs through the previous week's top stories and then any of a variety of different types of segments. These segments can be interviews, field pieces, lengthy examinations of recent news stories, or something a bit more unconventional. When the show found that a would-be job candidate for *Full Frontal* was actually trying to run a sting for Project Veritas, Bee created an advocacy segment on the spot that ridiculed the conservative group's effort to infiltrate the show. The segment also offered an element of feminist empowerment and advocacy not regularly encountered on the mostly male world of late night comedy (Waisanen 2018).

As was the case with the other comedy programs examined here, *Full Frontal* sought to cover many of the major news stories in the first year of the Trump presidency. The show tackled the executive orders on immigration (*Full Frontal* 2017c), the investigations into Russian interference in the 2016 election (*Full Frontal* 2017f), various attempts by congressional Republicans to pass a health care reform bill (*Full Frontal* 2017i) and the firing of FBI Director James Comey (*Full Frontal* 2017i). The show also touched on any number of smaller stories that had occurred in the week prior to the filming of an episode.

At times, the show's struggle to get through all of the week's key items was apparent. The opening news roundups of some episodes sped through several news stories within just a few minutes. While the nightly talk shows were able to give certain news stories more coverage, the limitations of *Full Frontal*'s weekly format became obvious as Bee was forced to rush through the news. In fact, the rapid pace of the news cycle became the subject of jokes itself, such as when Bee joked only a few weeks after Trump's inauguration that he had managed to complete his first 100 days in office in just 19 (*Full Frontal* 2017d).

*Full Frontal* also featured profiles of various members of the Trump Administration such as Sebastian Gorka, who worked briefly as a presidential aide (*Full Frontal* 2017g), White House Chief of Staff John Kelly (*Full Frontal* 2017l), and Trump's daughter and advisor Ivanka (*Full Frontal* 2017e). These sorts of profiles gave the show an expanded cast of characters to ridicule, while also mocking Trump by association. By characterizing members of the Trump Administration as absurd and devoting time to the tensions between them, the show treated the Trump White House as if it were an over-the-top soap opera. Bee made this framing explicit when she called the Trump Administration a "batsh*t telenovela" (*Full Frontal* 2017k).

As a host, Samantha Bee is forthright with her political views. She is essentially the Rachel Maddow of late night humor – very openly liberal, as evidenced by her attendance at and positive coverage of the Women's March (*Full Frontal* 2017b). Bee also makes her personal politics clear in the way she discusses President Trump and his agenda. In her coverage of the first year of the Trump presidency, Bee had no kind words for the president or his policies. She was consistently critical of Trump's words, actions and proposals.

*Full Frontal*'s humor was heavily insult-based when covering Trump in his first year in office. Everything about Trump from his physical appearance to his personality and behavior was fair game. Bee joked about numerous aspects of Trump's personal appearance, mocking his weight through the extensive use of unflattering pictures (*Full Frontal* 2017l). Trump's odd hairstyle and bizarre orange-ish skin tone were also the subject of considerable mockery. Even Trump's physical movements generated jokes, such as when she described his walking style as "lurching" (*Full Frontal* 2017h).

President Trump's personality and psychology were the targets of numerous jokes on all these programs, and they received considerable attention from Samantha Bee. *Full Frontal* frequently portrayed Trump as a bigot and misogynist, as well as intensely insecure, fearful and childish. For example, Bee described the Trump presidency as an "experiment in toddlerocracy" (*Full Frontal* 2017j). In a jab at Trump's perceived insecurity, Bee repeatedly suggested that he might not be in charge at the White House. Following Trump's inauguration speech, Bee joked that then Chief Strategist Steve Bannon was filling Trump's mouth with "more Nazi code than Enigma" (*Full Frontal* 2017a). Bee's numerous mentions of the supposed "pee tape" also suggested that Trump was beholden to Russian President Vladimir Putin.

Trump's behaviors, past and present, also provided *Full Frontal* with a great deal of comedic material. His predatory behavior towards women was a frequent topic of commentary. When British Prime Minister Theresa May visited the White House during Trump's first months as president, she was pictured holding her host's hand while descending a set of stairs. This prompted Bee to comment, "Honestly, Theresa May is lucky all he grabbed was her hand" (*Full Frontal* 2017c).

Trump's past business practices also provided comedic material. When he threatened to withhold federal funds from cities that declared themselves "sanctuary" locations for illegal immigrants, Bee made a joking reference to Trump allegedly not paying contractors who had completed work for him: "Well, he did say he'd run the country the same way he runs his business" (*Full Frontal* 2017d). Bee also repeatedly mocked Trump for his frequent and often inaccurate Twitter commentary.

*Full Frontal* even tapped into very specific, odd features of Trump for humor. His preference for well-done steaks served with ketchup was brought up repeatedly for mockery (*Full Frontal* 2017f). Bee even joked about the illegibility of Trump's signature, likening it to a "polygraph malfunction." (*Full Frontal* 2017c). All of the above listed subjects for jokes about Trump demonstrate just how insult-based *Full Frontal*'s humor was during the first year of the Trump presidency.

## *Last Week Tonight*

*Last Week Tonight*'s format is somewhat different from *Full Frontal*. While both shows last half an hour, *Last Week Tonight* is on HBO, meaning that it has no commercial breaks. John Oliver has shaped the content of his show in accordance with this unique format. He begins episodes with a brief review of the past week's news and then spends a large portion of the show looking at a particular story or subject in some depth. Because of this, Oliver seems to be attempting to appeal to viewers who use late night comedy shows as a news source. Indeed, the program's relatively long policy-oriented segments may resemble investigative journalism as much as political humor, suggesting to some scholars that the program has broken new ground in bringing together satire and journalism (Fox 2018).

Overall, *Last Week Tonight* is much less joke dense than *Full Frontal.* Oliver often speaks at length on subjects while making few quips. This lower joke density, in tandem with the show's long segments focusing on specific topics, might make the show seem potentially more reliable as a news source to members of its audience. Because HBO is a special subscription cable channel, the program's visibility comes not just through cable television but also through YouTube, a video service that provides more public access to Oliver's program.

The weekly format offers *Last Week Tonight* the opportunity to move beyond the indexing norm of the nightly political humor shows, which have little time or inclination to develop the sort of investigative content commonly offered on Oliver's HBO program (McKain 2005). Even so, Oliver is clearly not trying to offer the sort of objective news one finds on conventional news programs: the show's segment examines complicated economic, social and political issues with an emphasis on holding elites to account (Fox 2018).

John Oliver also pushes against the boundaries in late night humor through his personal behavior, such as when he purchased at a large discount a total of $15 million in uncollected medical debts of 9,000 people. He then paid off those obligations to demonstrate how easy it is to start up a debt-collection company focusing on low-income Americans (Waisanen 2018). This public donation had a serious edge, and a significant component of philanthropy, as Oliver investigated the ongoing debt crisis (Waisanen 2018). The segment also demonstrated how a relatively small amount of money directed at a public policy concern could go a long way.

This program also has a good deal in common with other humor programs, particularly when it comes to its treatment of Trump. Much like *Full Frontal, Last Week Tonight* covered many of the major news stories that occurred during the first year of the Trump presidency. Oliver at least touched on many major news items in the opening news roundup of each episode, though these segments frequently rushed through several stories within the span of a few minutes. Like *Full Frontal*, the pace of news stories itself became a subject for jokes on *Last Week Tonight*, such as when Oliver joked that Trump "seems to be bending the space-time continuum in order to fill a week with more news than it can scientifically contain" (*Last Week Tonight* 2017g).

In the longer segments, Oliver offered extensive coverage of a number of stories relating to the Trump presidency. He dedicated substantial time to stories like the proposed American Health Care Act of 2017 (*Last Week Tonight* 2017b), Trump's decision to remove the US from the Paris Climate Accord (*Last Week Tonight* 2017e) and developments in the US's relationship with North Korea (*Last Week Tonight* 2017h). He also reported on the investigation of possible collusion between the Trump campaign and the Russian government, a scandal that Oliver dubbed "Stupid Watergate" (*Last Week Tonight* 2017d). *Last Week Tonight* also covered stories that had less direct connections to Trump, including an examination of the state of the US coal industry that Oliver tied to Trump's promises to help the industry (*Last Week Tonight* 2017f).

Oliver's particular style of humor is also somewhat different from Bee's. He occasionally finds humor in simply pointing out the inherent absurdity of something. This particular style of humor was frequently used when discussing President Trump's stream-of-consciousness speeches. For example, Oliver played a roughly 30-second monotone reading of a transcript of a Trump speech on the Iran nuclear deal, evoking much laughter from the studio audience due to its unfocused, rambling style (*Last Week Tonight* 2017i). Another example of this style of humor occurred in a segment on Trump's numerous lies. In one episode, Oliver marveled at a clip of a reporter speaking on the difficulties of covering Trump in which the reporter asked, "What does he [Trump] mean when he says words?" (*Last Week Tonight* 2107a).

Of course, insult-based jokes are the bread and butter of late night political humor, regardless of format. Oliver was true to form, mocking various aspects of Trump's physical appearance, including his hair and skin tone. He also made numerous jokes about Trump's weight and poor diet. For example, when President Trump announced via Twitter his intention to ban transgender people from the US military, Oliver joked that the long-time gaps between the three tweets making this announcement were due to the fact that Trump was finishing his breakfast of "deep-fried Big Macs and mashed Doritos" (*Last Week Tonight* 2017g).

*Last Week Tonight* also featured a number of jokes at the expense of the president's personality and psychology. As was done on the other programs examined here, Oliver generally portrayed Trump as a bigot, a misogynist and an egomaniac. Oliver, like Bee, joked about Trump being like a child, such as when he remarked after playing a clip of a Trump speech, "I don't speak 'Toddler Pyschopath'" (*Last Week Tonight* 2017c). Oliver also joked about Trump seeming unhinged, such as claiming that Trump has the temperament of a wet cat (*Last Week Tonight* 2017h). He also mocked Trump for seeming out of touch, as seen in jokes about Trump's awkward attempt to pantomime coal mining at a rally (*Last Week Tonight* 2017f).

*Last Week Tonight* also made numerous jokes about Trump's apparent lack of knowledge and experience upon entering office. This is best exhibited in a series of television advertisements Oliver produced and actually broadcast on various cable channels aimed specifically at President Trump. In the first episode of *Last Week Tonight* in 2017, Oliver noted that Trump seemed to be a regular viewer of morning cable news shows. Following this observation, Oliver announced that he had purchased ad time during those same shows to broadcast ads parodying a real medical catheter ad, except that Oliver's ads provided useful information such as an explanation of the nuclear triad and the difference between weather and climate (*Last Week Tonight* 2017a). The show reprised this joke in the last episode of the year, announcing a new series of ads explaining to Trump the error of his own public statements. The ads noted that Frederick Douglass is dead (referring to a remark Trump made about the 19th century abolitionist using the present tense), that it is dangerous to look directly at a solar eclipse (Trump did precisely that), and that the Virgin Islands has a governor, not a president (another Trump gaffe) (*Last Week Tonight* 2017i). These jokes all served to portray Trump as an inexperienced fool.

## The Evolution of Trump Humor

As a candidate and as a president, Donald Trump has dismissed presidential norms. His prolific use of Twitter and his great interest in employing personal attacks have made him popular with his base (Schier and Eberly 2017). But the aggressive fact-checking about the president and his very public presidency have also made him an immensely popular target for the humorists of late night talk shows. Everything about Donald Trump that seems larger than life – his gilded lifestyle, his private resorts and golf courses, his abandonment of policy consistency in favor of being able to declare momentary victories – allow humorists to have a field day. If the calm, cool, self-controlled introvert Barack Obama was a profound challenge for late night comedy writers a decade ago, then Trump is their dream come true. Indeed, joke writers who might like to exaggerate for humorous effect might find the need to do little more than read the headlines to poke fun at this inconsistent man of immense appetites who loves to see the spotlight turned towards the White House.

As our findings demonstrate, late night comedians found a huge payoff during the opening acts of the Trump presidency. Regardless of format, frequency and host style, mocking Trump has become a growth industry for late night humor. With obvious glee, the current generation of last night comedy hosts have torn into Trump from a multitude of directions: they make fun of his physical appearance, his clothing style, his chaotic administration, his policy ignorance, inconsistency in his statements, his neediness, his narcissism and his volatile temperament.

While some wonder whether the tidal wave of anti-Trump comedy will be sustainable over a four-year presidency, the constantly changing scandals and cast of characters surround the president and his administration create fresh opportunities for mockery almost daily. But there may be limits to the size of the market for political humor, even in the age of Donald Trump. Comedy Central canceled Larry Wilmore's *The Nightly Show*, a successor program in the time slot after *The Daily Show* once occupied by Stephen Colbert, when the network said it failed to attract a sufficiently large audience (Butler 2016).

Media observers who have examined these comedy shows have noted important differences in their treatment of the new president. As discussed above, no one seems to have changed more than Fallon between the 2016 campaign and the soft treatment of a fellow NBC star from *The Apprentice* – and 2017 (Farnsworth et al. 2018; Itzkoff 2017; Merry 2016; Poniewozik 2017). While much of the late night audience skews young and more liberal, Fallon offers a slightly different product: one a bit more hospitable to a mainstream audience less critical of Trump than viewers drawn to the sometimes blistering barrage and extreme harshness of the anti-Trump jokes most notably offered by Trevor Noah and Stephen Colbert.

The mixture of experimentation with new formats that marked the first year of the Trump presidency, as well as the president's inability to take a joke without striking back, are likely to keep the humorists on the air and make their programs key parts of the political conversation in the years to come.

This chapter and the one before it offered information on what the nation's most prominent comics said about the 2016 election and the first year of the Trump presidency. The next question to consider is the impact of this humor. In Chapter 5, we consider who watches late night comedy and whether these programs have an influence regarding political interest, political knowledge and political action.

# 5

# POLITICAL CONSEQUENCES OF LATE NIGHT HUMOR

Over the past several years, late night comedians have been getting more attention from candidates and presidents as well as from journalists who cover politics and political campaigns. Even as traditional news formats like print newspapers and network television newscasts have lost significant shares of their audiences, the late night talk shows continue to command substantial attention, as viewers turn to those shows at the traditional late evening hours or increasingly at their own convenience via online media sharing available 24/7. Even before the start of the 2016 election, all the prominent late night comics had their own YouTube channel to allow for the replaying of late night content. Some, including Jimmy Fallon's *Tonight Show*, ranked in the top 100 most popular channels on YouTube (Baumgartner and Becker 2018).

While Donald Trump is not the first president to wish to avoid the mockery of late night humor, the ferocity with which he criticizes these humorists, and his talk of using federal regulatory powers to curb their attacks on him, draw attention to these comics in a way previous presidents considered unproductive. To Trump, the stakes for late night programming are high. If not, why would a president, with so many global and domestic crises and concerns to address, invest as much time and energy as Trump has on picking fights with Stephen Colbert, Alec Baldwin and others of their ilk? Trump, who excels at treating his political rivals with the very same personal attacks and undermining of individual reputations that are the bread and butter of late night humor, seems to believe that these critical voices are undermining public respect for his personal character and his presidency. But is that true?

This chapter examines previous scholarly research as well as a public opinion survey on late night political humor, which was conducted by the Pew Research Center at the outset of the 2016 election campaign, to consider possible political impacts of late night comedy. We ask whether personal criticism on late night programming damages the reputations of its targets. We then ask whether any such impact may affect more than just the individuals who are skewered. For example, does late night comedy undermine trust in the news more generally? Does political humor affect political learning more positively, as the desire to understand the jokes may increase the audience's political sophistication? We also consider the partisan impact of late night humor. Does the particularly harsh treatment conservatives and Republicans face from late night humor trigger a greater hostility to this genre from the political Right?

## Late Night Humor and Political Support

Long before there were late night television comics, indeed long before there was television, there were citizen frustrations with government. The US political system itself was created by revolutionaries with deep skepticism about human nature and the capacity of self-government. Even though American history includes many political, social, economic, cultural and military successes, political figures have learned repeatedly that it is not easy to keep citizens happy. Political humor can be a way to focus, codify and perhaps even respond to the gap between what people would like to see from government and what the government actually delivers. Late night comedy programming is a popular enough format to have survived decades of changes in politics and culture, and is now thriving in a variety of communication channels.

The commitment to free speech in democratic societies encourages higher levels of critical discourse aimed at the government. For this reason, public expressions of frustrations with government are particularly intense in modern Western democracies. Of course, our ancestors would be amazed at what today's citizens expect from government. The capacity of the modern democratic state to provide general satisfaction regarding the traditional and comparatively modest public expectations of a national government (that is, to secure a healthy economy and keep the nation's enemies at bay) is no longer enough.

Today, citizens in modern Western democracies possess a variety of higher-level and harder-to-satisfy public demands dealing with quality of life issues like environmental regulation, health care provision, and navigating the conflicting tax and service demands of the modern welfare state (Habermas 1973; Inglehart 1990). These contemporary, harder-to-resolve policy challenges represent a sort of "demand overload" for government as it concentrates on areas where there is less public consensus about how to proceed – and where government itself has less experience in addressing the policy matters at issue (Inglehart 1977, 1981, 1988, 1990). Some of the harshest political battles over recent decades have been over how to deal with "post-materialist" demands regarding the government's relatively new social welfare responsibilities, including health care, housing, welfare and the environment (Cohen 2006; Hopper 2017; Schwartz 2014; Skocpol

1997). When governments fall short on these measures – and how can they not? – we can expect the late night comics to take note.

As modern Western governments descend deeper into gridlock, there is also a level of "procedural frustration," where the focus of discontent is at least as much on the procedures as the outcomes (Bond and Fleisher 2000; Campbell 2016; Mann and Ornstein 2012; Mayer and Canon 1999). At the core of this public objection is the sense that government is not responsive to public demands and should do more to provide fair access to the policy process for everyone (Tyler 1988; Tyler and Rasinski 1991). This frustration was a key component of public support for the self-proclaimed outsider Donald Trump, whose election in 2016 represented a populist reaction to the sense that elites were mainly looking out for themselves rather than ordinary Americans (Abramowitz 2017; Ceasar et al. 2017; Schier and Eberly 2017). Still others frustrated by government may turn inward; they are tuning out, or "bowling alone," in response to what some citizens feel is a society unraveling before their eyes (Putnam 2000).

These theories of citizen discontent dovetail with significant components of the late night jokes directed at American presidents generally, and at Donald Trump's time in public life in particular. As we saw in previous chapters, the late night comedians delight in skewering the national government's dissatisfying policy outcomes, its inability to resolve policy disputes, this president's erratic behavior, and the dubious qualifications of some of Trump's friends and family members placed in positions of great authority and influence.

The late night comics regularly make use of the fact that cynicism regarding people in power seems to be part of our political DNA; they have made the cultivation of that cynicism an art form. Aggressive questioning or even mocking people in power is not necessarily a bad thing, to be sure, as "those who are overready to approve of government are overready to yield to it" (Sniderman 1981: 148).

Given the combativeness of today's late night comics, there seems little chance that the above description of faith-based support for government would apply to large numbers of their viewers. Indeed, previous research has shown that the overwhelmingly negative nature of political humor can lead to more negative evaluations of the political figures being skewered (Baumgartner and Morris 2006; Morris 2009; Young 2004). A study of the impact of *The Daily Show* during the 2004 presidential campaign found that viewership led to lower evaluations of candidate John Kerry (Baumgartner and Morris 2006). A focused study of *The Daily Show*'s coverage of the 2004 national party conventions found that the show was more critical of the Republican convention (Morris 2009). The study also found that evaluations of Bush and Vice President Dick Cheney fell more among viewers of that program than did evaluations of Democrats John Kerry and John Edwards, whose nominating convention was treated more gently (Morris 2009). Tina Fey's treatment of 2008 vice presidential nominee Sarah Palin likewise lowered evaluations of Palin among viewers of *Saturday Night Live* (Baumgartner et al. 2012). Late night humor directed at the news media also undermined public assessments of the journalism profession (Morris and Baumgartner 2008).

The process of increasingly negative evaluations of political figures seems most powerful with respect to the least informed viewers of the late night shows. A study of the impacts of late night humor on public perceptions of Al Gore and George W. Bush during the 2000 election found that low-knowledge viewers developed more negative assessments of both candidates after seeing them skewered by the late night comics (Young 2004). Some researchers have found that critical political humor lowers public assessments of the political system generally, as well as evaluations of the candidates targeted by late night comedy (Baumgartner 2013). There is a sense in some research that political humor can generate "blowback" that undermines the general social fabric at the same time it may also increase political interest (McClennen 2018).

Because political humor contains policy content, some researchers believe such political messaging is particularly effective in shaping viewer preferences because of the process described by the Elaboration Likelihood Model (ELM) of persuasion. Humorous messages are particularly effective because they are processed through the peripheral (noncognitive) route without being subject to highly critical and analytical brain pathways involved in scrutinizing the accuracy of the claims made within the jokes (Petty and Cacioppo 1986). In other words, a viewer's focus is on getting the joke rather than evaluating the truthfulness of the comments that comprise it. This alternative persuasion path increases the chances of viewer agreement and therefore can increase the impact of the joke on a viewer's perceptions of the target of the humor (Becker 2018; Petty and Cacioppo 1986).

## *Politicians Can Tell Jokes Too*

Of course, candidates and elected officials do what they can to reduce the damage of late night ridicule. Politicians often try to minimize the negative impact, or even to "work the refs" of political comedy, by appearing on these late night shows as guests or by criticizing their content on social media (Farnsworth 2018; Lichter et al. 2015). The operative theory here is that of "inoculation," where a self-deprecating joke by a prominent political figure can deflect the more hostile humor that others would aim at him or her (Compton 2018). In other words, if an elected official is willing to appear on a given program, its host may treat a current or recent guest more kindly. Even if the host would not offer gentler treatment, at least the public would respect a politician who has the fortitude to face their late night critics across a desk. If you do not appear, particularly after promising to do so, you run the risk of weeks of mocking comparable to what David Letterman directed at John McCain, the GOP's 2008 presidential nominee (Farnsworth and Lichter 2011a).

For evidence of just how effective self-deprecating humor can be, consider Ronald Reagan's use of a humorous remark during the second presidential debate of the 1984 presidential election. Few presidents were as good at inoculation as Ronald Reagan, who during his decades in political life joked about his aversion to hard work, his age, his film career and even the content of his speeches (Cannon 1991). His comfort in front of the camera stemmed from his years as a movie actor and as a pitchman for the General Electric Co. before entering elective politics (Cannon 1991). Despite his extensive public-oriented experience, which also included his first term as president, Reagan struggled at some points during the first presidential debate in 1984, raising questions about whether the elderly president had the fortitude to take on the challenges of a second term. Reagan planned his counterattack with a one-liner prepared for deployment at the second debate. When the opportunity arose, Reagan pounced, saying, "I will not make age an issue of this campaign. I am not going to exploit, for political purposes, my opponent's youth and inexperience" (quoted in Stewart et al. 2018: 123). After making that absurd quip about how he would not focus on the age of Democratic rival Walter Mondale, a highly experienced former vice president and senator, would it not seem unduly harsh for Mondale or other Democrats to offer further questions about Reagan's fitness for office and alleged mental decline? In the moments after Reagan's joke, even Mondale chuckled, and the exchange threw the challenger off his stride during the rest of the debate (Compton 2018; Gergen 2000).

In an instant, arguably the most threatening challenge to Reagan's re-election, questions over the aging president's mental health, simply evaporated. Reagan's joke did not just undermine concerns that had arisen in the weeks before the second debate. The quip also protected the president – like an injection in a doctor's office – from subsequent threats along these same lines: that by 1984 Reagan may have lacked the intellectual capacity and vigor for a second term (Compton 2018).

Self-deprecatory humor serves a politician's purposes in trying to preempt and redirect potential critical lines of attack. It also serves the process of making the political figure more likeable. The explicit public discussion of one's own flaws signals that the speaker does not take himself or herself too seriously or place himself on a higher level than the public he or she seeks to serve (Stewart et al. 2018).

Self-deprecating humor is a common approach employed by presidents. When a desperately ill Franklin Roosevelt ran for an unprecedented fourth term in 1944, he chose to respond to a Republican attack on the use of a destroyer to pick up the president's dog, Fala, which had been left behind by accident on a presidential trip. The Republican attacks on this incident, which implicitly raised questions about an ailing and potentially forgetful president as well as the potentially improper use of taxpayer resources during wartime, could easily have been ignored (Burns and Dunn 2001; Goodwin 1994). But FDR saw the opportunity to offer a humorous statement that would belittle his opponents by redirecting the conversation back to Fala, who FDR joked, had a sharper temper and was more upset about the expense and the controversy than the president himself.

> Then came his rebuttal of the Fala story, his dagger lovingly fashioned and honed, delivered with a mock-serious face and in the quiet, sad tone of a man much abused. "These Republican leaders have not been content with attacks on me, on my wife, or on my sons. No, not content with that, they now include my little dog, Fala. Well of course I don't resent attacks, and my family doesn't resent attacks, but Fala – being Scottish – *does* resent them!" Some reporters saw this as the turning point of the campaign.
>
> *(Burns and Dunn 2001: 482; emphasis in original)*

Another example of self-deprecating humor, discussed earlier in this book, was how Barack Obama responded with humor to the birth certificate dispute, raised by his opponents during the 2008 election and kept alive during his time in office. After Obama had released the official "long form" birth certificate demanded by his critics to show the proof of his birth in Hawaii, he aired a segment from the film *The Lion King* at the 2011 White House Correspondents Dinner. He then claimed, with tongue in cheek, that the animated film clip of a newly born royal lion cub was in fact the video of his own birth. By doing so, Obama made light of both the high public expectations his 2008 campaign generated and the critics (including Donald Trump, who was in the audience) who had sought to make the birth certificate issue such a long-running and absurd controversy. The humorous segment was a double play: a self-deprecating remark to endear himself to the public, combined with a simultaneous skewering of his critics.

A president who makes jokes on the public stage is one thing, but joking while appearing on someone else's show is quite another matter. It is open to question whether efforts at inoculation on late night comedy programs are worth the trouble, particularly for Republicans. The consistently harsher treatment that conservatives receive from the late night comics could be a powerful argument for Republican candidates to stay away from their programs. For example, in 2012 Mitt Romney held out against appearing on these shows throughout much of the general election, feeling that he would not get a fair treatment. His aides finally convinced him to go on *The Tonight Show*.

However, numerous other Republicans candidates appeared on those programs, going back to Ronald Reagan, who appeared on Johnny Carson's *Tonight Show* during his failed 1976 effort to wrest the GOP nomination from incumbent president Gerald Ford. Other presidential nominees who were guests include George W. Bush in 2000 and John McCain in 2008. As we noted earlier, however, canceling an appearance can have dire consequences, as John McCain discovered in 2008. A late cancelation of his appearance on *The Late Show* brought a profusion of anti-McCain jokes from an angry David Letterman, which ended only when a contrite McCain appeared on the show and delivered an abject apology for his earlier absence.

Even Donald Trump, who has been by far the president most hostile to late night comics, engaged in the same efforts to try to tame or at least temper the hosts while a candidate. Before the 2016 election, Trump appeared on *The Tonight Show* and *Saturday Night Live*, and it probably did not hurt that both shows aired on NBC, the same network that aired Trump's own reality show offerings. (During his time as president, Trump so far has avoided personal appearances on the late night humor shows. As previous chapters demonstrate, though, the shows' hosts have plenty to say about him whether he appears onstage or not).

In practice, though, Trump's appearance on *The Tonight Show* in 2016 triggered a backlash, the opposite of any inoculation. In fact, our data shows that the hit to Fallon's ratings after Trump's appearance in 2016 came before Jimmy Fallon's more critical treatment of Trump in 2017.

Trump's own use of political humor, again employed away from the late night programs, tends toward "sarcastic and exaggerated comments," far from the self-deprecating humor that Reagan used to charm the country three decades earlier (Stewart et al. 2018). During the 2016 candidate debates, both Trump and Clinton used the opposite of the Reagan humor strategy – employing aggressive humor to "diminish the stature of the opposition" rather than using self-deprecation to make themselves look more appealing (Stewart et al. 2018: 128).

Inoculation may involve more than a politician's use of humor, whether on a comedy program or not. Fame may be a particularly effective prophylactic against mockery that generates changes in public opinion. There is some evidence in support of the idea that better-known political figures have more stable public evaluations. In 2004, for example, critical comments of President George W. Bush on *The Daily Show* did not have as much of an impact on his public evaluations as did similar comments directed at Democratic nominee John Kerry, who was less well known than the incumbent president (Baumgartner and Morris 2006). Voters who were less informed regarding Al Gore and George W. Bush in 2000 were more easily persuaded via new information than more informed voters, who tended to have more fixed opinions about that year's major party nominees (Baum 2005).

A study examining political humor regarding more known and less well-known candidates during the 2016 primaries revealed that public evaluations regarding well-known front-runners Donald Trump and Hillary Clinton were highly resistant to change, while clips that focused on Bernie Sanders and Ben Carson had greater impacts on public assessments (Baumgartner 2018). The study provides further evidence that comedy's impact is the smallest where public knowledge is the greatest.

> Those who think or hope that Trump's approval ratings (or Trump himself) may be affected by the constant barrage of jokes made at his expense may be

> disappointed. While there may be a correlation between public opinion, negative news and the number of jokes told at the president's expense, this research suggests the correlation may be weaker when the public holds definite opinions about the president ... It is probably the case that one either loves or hates him, irrespective of what the satirists are saying.
>
> *(Baumgartner 2018: 72)*

## Late Night Humor, Information and Participation

Late night political humor has gained in attention and influence as people reduce their consumption of traditional media, such as the daily newspaper and the broadcast television networks' evening news shows. This trend has been particularly pronounced among younger adults, many of whom have been turning to soft news as an alternative source of political information for two decades now (Baumgartner and Morris 2011; Feldman and Young 2005; Hoffman and Thomson 2009; Mitchell et al. 2014).

Following the audience declines plaguing traditional news outlets, particularly among young adults, some scholars believe that the late night television talk shows, particularly *The Daily Show*, deserve to be considered as an alternative news source (Baym 2005). As we noted earlier, during his heyday as host of the Comedy Central program, survey respondents identified Jon Stewart as one of the most trusted journalists in America, comparable to Tom Brokaw or Anderson Cooper (Baumgartner and Morris 2011). As a result, presidential candidates have increasingly treated these talk shows as a means of reaching potential voters who have relatively modest interest in traditional political news but do not mind receiving campaign information on infotainment programming. For a candidate's appearance on late night talk shows to be valuable, the viewer must possess some political knowledge.

Growing cynicism regarding traditional news outlets has enhanced the status of these late night comedy programs, a response to the so-called "trust deficit" that legacy media have endured in recent years (Feldman and Young 2005; Pew Research Center 2016b, 2017). As a result, presidential candidates and presidents seek to reach voters who have moved away from traditional news outlets and make use of the late night comedy programs as supplemental vehicles to promote their policies and themselves (Brewer and Cao 2006; Farnsworth 2018). During the wide-open 2008 campaign, for example, presidential candidates and their family members responded to the growing importance of these programs by making 80 appearances on these shows (Lichter et al. 2015).

In addition to an individual's previous political knowledge, selective news exposure by consumers also may limit the impact of the late night comic takedowns on the public's estimation of established political figures. Because the first and/or most significant exposure some news consumers receive about political figures is provided by partisan media sources, the impact of late night skewering may be quite modest (Iyengar and Hahn 2009; Pew Research Center 2014; Stroud 2008; Taber and Lodge 2006). A 2014 Pew Research Center survey, for example, found that liberals were more likely to trust and conservatives more likely to distrust *The Colbert Report* and *The Daily Show*, two of the late night comedy programs included in its survey (Mitchell et al. 2014). In addition, some critics of talk shows believe the hosts have gone too soft on political figures (Kinsley 1992).

Despite the disagreements over the potential impact of political humor, there is a consensus regarding the learning opportunity these programs offer their audiences. Researchers have found these humor programs to be informative, providing current events information to viewers (Young 2013). They also make use of the information to shape their understanding of politics. Viewing political comedy can encourage citizens to "connect the dots between the comedy they view and what they already know from traditional news sources" (Becker 2018: 80). Indeed, research into the content of such programs has found that they do a better job of talking about substantive issues during presidential campaigns than do journalists on television, who place greater emphasis on the campaign horse race and the candidates' strategies and tactics as well as candidate sound bites and gaffes (Farnsworth and Lichter 2011a; Lichter et al. 2015).

On balance, research has found that viewing late night political humor is associated with higher levels of political knowledge (cf, Brewer and Cao 2006). A study that compared learning from interviews with political figures on a late night comedy program compared with a traditional news program found higher recall of basic information among the comedy program viewers (Becker 2013). According to another study, the political comedy shows led to information acquisition at the same level as network television news, but network news was a more effective source for learning the relative importance of policy matters (Becker and Bode 2018).

These late night political conversations appear to increase political knowledge by providing information in a digestible and interesting manner (Xenos and Becker 2009; Young 2006, 2013). One key component of that learning stems from prior expectations: viewers who watched *The Daily Show* and *The Colbert Report* as news programs or news/entertainment hybrid programs were more likely to engage with the program content than those who did not see a news dimension to the shows (Feldman 2013). Those who are motivated to consume the comedy for the political content or those who possess a general affinity for political humor are more inclined to say they draw links between the news and the jokes (Becker 2018). In addition, individuals who have an interest in the political topics being explored by the late night hosts have an increased appreciation for the jokes involving themes that match their personal interests (Grill 2018).

The comedy programs also shape political participation activities of their viewers in a variety of dimensions (Moy et al. 2005). These increased political activities may be a result of increased internal political efficacy, which is associated with viewing late night political humor (Baumgartner and Morris 2006). There may even be a sense of self-satisfaction derived from the consumption of political humor, which can reinforce boundaries between those who "get" the jokes and those who do not (McClennen 2018). By attacking ideas and behaviors tagged as "stupid, illogical, arrogant or manipulative," the late night humorists underscore these divisive group identities between those laughing with the comics and those being laughed at by the comics – and their viewers (McClennen 2018: 141). As one would expect, citizens who resent the choice of comedic targets do not appreciate the political humor itself, further increasing the divisions (Grill 2018).

> Not all satire has the same bite. Colbert's satirical comedy, for example, has far more of a playful edge than the searing mockery of Bill Maher or the righteous rage of Samantha Bee. But in the end, regardless of its edge, satire is about criticizing attitudes, beliefs, worldviews and behaviors that the satirist wants to target.
>
> *(McClennen 2018: 141)*

Along these same lines, one somewhat under-considered aspect of political humor's impacts concerns people who are allied with the joke target (McClennen 2018). Might these people be more inclined to defend their ally, that joke's target, as the mockery increases? After all, jokes aimed at Donald Trump are at least indirectly aimed at the people who support Donald Trump and those who agree with him on many policy issues. The anger many Trump supporters direct at elites and the status quo seems unlikely to be quelled by late night mockery. In fact, the elite media voices in New York and Los Angeles who mock the man standing before a sea of "Make America Great Again" red caps probably intensify the anger and harden the support of those who start out supporting Trump. Research into hostile audience counter-reactions might well explain why Trump and other controversial political figures seem to face little consequences to their reputations when they are attacked on late night comedy (Baumgartner 2018).

## Late Night Humor and Learning about Politics in 2016

To examine what political humor teaches viewers about real-world politics, we turn now to a 2016 national survey from the nonpartisan Pew Research Center (2016a). The Pew Center routinely conducts public opinion polling regarding US politics and policy. This nationally representative survey, which was in the field during January and February of 2016, included 4,339 online respondents and 315 mail respondents, for a total sample size of 4,654. This unusually large sample makes it possible to compare differences between smaller groups than is usually the case. In addition, prominent national research firms rarely ask about political learning and political humor. Pew was one of the few that did so during the 2016 campaign.

The survey asked a variety of questions about acquiring information, asking respondents whether they learned something about the presidential campaign during the previous week from 11 possible news sources, including cable television news, social media, local television and network television news as well as several other media formats, including late night comedy. The survey was conducted during some of the most intense parts of the 2016 presidential nominating campaign. It was a time when Donald Trump was winning some key primaries on the way to an easier-than-expected nomination victory. Meanwhile, Hillary Clinton was still struggling to fend off a tougher-than-expected challenge from Bernie Sanders. The wording of the questions can be found in the appendix at the end of this chapter.

## *Hypotheses*

Based on the research discussed above, we would expect to find support for the following hypotheses relating to political humor in the Pew Research Center (2016a) survey:

**H1:** people who identify as Democrats were more likely to report learning something from late night comedy than Republicans were.

**H2:** the more liberal the respondent the more likely one would report learning something from late night comedy during the previous week.

These two hypotheses are consistent with the growing use of partisan media sources, which are likely to discourage Republicans from using late night humor given the discrepancy between their preferences and the comedic targets of late night (Gill 2018; Pew Research Center 2014; Stroud 2008; Taber and Lodge 2006).

**H3:** the more closely one followed the news the more likely one would report learning something from late night comedy during the previous week.

**H4:** The more frequently one discussed the news the more likely one would report learning something from late night comedy during the previous week.

**H5:** the more trust one had in national news content the more likely one would report learning something from late night comedy during the previous week.

These three hypotheses are consistent with research that finds people consuming news in a variety of outlets can "connect the dots" between the humor and the news, thereby enabling them to appreciate the humor (Becker 2018; Young 2013). This process of making use of a variety of media outlets that one respects can create a sense of self-satisfaction regarding one's own political learning (Baumgartner and Morris 2006; McClennen 2018).

## *Results*

The survey captures the degree to which the American public was fascinated by an unusual campaign that was already full of surprises. Ninety-one percent of those surveyed said they had learned something about the campaign from at least one

**TABLE 5.1** Sources of Learning about the 2016 Presidential Election

| *Percentage of US adults learning something about the election in the previous week from …* | |
|---|---|
| **Television (net)** | **78** |
| Local TV news | 57 |
| Cable TV news | 54 |
| National night network TV news | 49 |
| Late night comedy shows | 25 |
| **Digital (net)** | **65** |
| News websites or apps | 48 |
| Social networking site | 44 |
| Issue-based group websites/apps/emails | 23 |
| Candidate/campaign websites/apps/emails | 20 |
| **Radio (net)** | **44** |
| **Print newspaper (net)** | **36** |
| Local daily newspapers in print | 29 |
| National newspapers in print | 23 |

Note: The Pew Research Center (2016a) national survey conducted January 12–February 8, 2016. N = 4654.

information source during the previous week. Among this group, nearly half said they learned something from five or more sources, and another one-third said they learned something from three or four sources (Pew Research Center 2016a).

As for the media included in the survey, fully 78 percent said they learned something about the campaign from television, with 57 percent saying they learned something from local television news, 54 percent saying they learned from cable news and 49 percent saying they learned from the broadcast network newscasts. (Because each potential news outlet was a separate question, the total percentages far exceed 100.)

By comparison, one out of every four respondents (25 percent) said they learned something about the presidential election from the late night comedy shows. That may seem a relatively small number compared to cable and broadcast sources, until we remember that all the other outlets included in the survey are news outlets. It is striking that late night comedy, which exists to entertain audiences, is a source of information about politics for about half the number of viewers who turn to television news. Moreover, the effects are strongest among millennials. One out of three adults under 30 said they learned about the presidential campaign via infotainment, double the number (17 percent) who learned from their local print newspaper, and nearly double the 19 percent who learned from a national paper.

As a group, digital news sources lagged somewhat behind television as a source for political learning, with 65 percent saying that they learned something from at least one digital outlet. News websites and apps were the most frequently cited news outlet online, with 48 percent saying they learned something there, while 44 percent said they learned something about the campaign from a social networking site, such as Facebook or Twitter. More partisan online outlets, including websites focused on campaigns and specific issues, were less important for political learning. Finally, radio was a source of campaign information for 44 percent of those surveyed, while 36 percent said they learned something from a print newspaper.

The results demonstrate that television remains the most prominent source of information about presidential campaigns, even as online media outlets finished a strong second and continue to grow in influence over voters every four years. (In addition, much of the online learning reported in this survey is likely to come from the online offerings of the traditional news outlets that existed in the pre-Internet age, including CNN, CBS News and the *Washington Post*.)

In Table 5.2, respondents identify the source that mattered most for learning about politics. As expected, the dominant sources are a combination of several traditional news outlets, like cable news and local television news, with newer online sources, including social media and news websites and apps. As expected, late night comedy, created primarily to entertain, not inform, finished far back in the pack. Even so, the humorists finished ahead of local and national newspapers.

Table 5.2 also breaks down media use by age group. As expected, television matters most for the oldest respondents and social media outlets matter most for

**TABLE 5.2** Key Sources of Learning about the 2016 Presidential Election by Age (among the 91 percent of those surveyed who learned something in the previous week)

| *Percentage naming each source type as most helpful* | | | | | |
|---|---|---|---|---|---|
| All | | 18–29 | 30–49 | 50–64 | 65+ |
| 24 | Cable TV news | 12 | 21 | 25 | 43 |
| 14 | Social Media | 35 | 15 | 05 | 01 |
| 14 | Local TV News | 10 | 14 | 19 | 10 |
| 13 | News website/app | 18 | 19 | 10 | 05 |
| 11 | Radio | 11 | 13 | 13 | 05 |
| 10 | Network TV News | 04 | 07 | 14 | 17 |
| 03 | Late Night Comedy | 06 | 04 | 02 | 01 |
| 03 | Local paper in print | 01 | 02 | 05 | 06 |
| 02 | National paper in print | 01 | 02 | 02 | 05 |
| 02 | Issue-based group website | 02 | 01 | 02 | 02 |
| 01 | Candidate/campaign website | 01 | 01 | 01 | 01 |

Note: The Pew Research Center (2016a) national survey conducted January 12–February 8, 2016. N = 4654.

the youngest adults. For those 65 years of age or older, 43 percent named cable television news as their top source for information, with network television newscasts finishing second among that age group with 17 percent identifying those once-dominant news outlets as their most important news source. For those between the ages of 18 and 30, 35 percent identified social media as the most important choice for campaign information, as compared to 18 percent for news websites, 12 percent for cable news and 11 percent for radio.

Overall, 3 percent ranked late night comedy as their most helpful source for news, with 6 percent of those under 30 years of age and 4 percent of those between 30 and 49 identifying it as their top source.

Table 5.3 examines whether there are partisan differences among those who learned something about the election from the late night comedy programs and those who did not. This table, and the ones that follow, employ the question about learning from late night comedy used in Table 5.1. These cross-tabulation reports use that question to mark the columns. The rows will relate to the other variables in the two-variable comparisons; for example the top half of Table 5.3 relates to partisanship and the bottom half of Table 5.3 relates to ideology. The percentages reported in Table 5.3 and in the cross-tabulation results that follow are row percentages. People who refused to answer specific questions are dropped from the relevant part of the analysis, so the total number of respondents in the individual cross-tabulation analyses in this chapter will vary slightly. Even so, all cross-tabs discussed here are based on at least 4,400 respondents, far more than the roughly 1,000 person surveys that are the standard size for US survey data analysis projects.

With respect to partisanship, the survey broke respondents out into three groups – Republicans, Democrats and independents. Those classified as Republicans said they identified with that party or leaned in its direction, while those counted as Democrats identified with or leaned toward that party. Independents were those who did not identify with or lean towards either major party. Table 5.3 shows that just under 14 percent of Republicans said they learned something from the comedy programs, almost identical to the 14 percent of independents. By contrast, 29 percent of Democrats learned about politics. Thus, Democrats were almost exactly twice as likely as Republicans and independents to learn about politics from late night humorists.

The overall response patterns for the two variables are examined systematically via a chi-square test, which identified the statistical results as highly significant. The Tau-c test likewise confirms that there is a statistically significant relationship between party identification and whether one learned something from late night comedy. These findings provide empirical support for H1.

The bottom half of Table 5.3 looks at the role of politics in the context of ideology rather than party preference. It considers the intersection of ideology and political learning from late comedy using a five-point ideology scale. As hypothesized, the more liberal one considers oneself to be, the more likely one is

**TABLE 5.3** Partisanship, Ideology and Learning from Comedy Programs

| *Partisanship* | | *Learned* | *Did not* | *Total* |
|---|---|---|---|---|
| Republican (includes leaners) | | 262 | 1675 | 1937 |
| % within Party | | 13.5% | 86.5% | 100.0% |
| Independent | | 40 | 237 | 277 |
| % within Independents | | 14.4% | 85.6% | 100.0% |
| Democratic (includes leaners) | | 648 | 1590 | 2238 |
| % within Party | | 29.0% | 71.0% | 100.0% |
| Total | | 950 | 3502 | 4452 |
| | | 100.0% | 100.0% | 100.0% |
| Chi-square significance | .000 | | | |
| Tau-c | –.154*** | | | |

| *Ideology* | | *Learned* | *Did not* | *Total* |
|---|---|---|---|---|
| Very conservative | | 44 | 411 | 455 |
| % within Ideology | | 9.7% | 90.3% | 100.0% |
| Conservative | | 150 | 988 | 1138 |
| % within Ideology | | 13.2% | 86.8% | 100.0% |
| Moderate | | 448 | 1395 | 1843 |
| % within Ideology | | 24.3% | 75.7% | 100.0% |
| Liberal | | 229 | 543 | 772 |
| % within Ideology | | 29.7% | 70.3% | 100.0% |
| Very liberal | | 121 | 219 | 340 |
| % within Ideology | | 35.6% | 64.4% | 100.0% |
| Total | | 992 | 3556 | 4548 |
| | | 100.0% | 100.0% | 100.0% |
| Chi-square significance | .000 | | | |
| Tau-c | –.170*** | | | |

Statistical significance: * $p < .05$ ** $p < .01$ *** $p < .001$

Note: The Pew Research Center (2016a) national survey conducted January 12–February 8, 2016. N = 4654.

to have learned something about the election via the discussions on late night comedy programs. The question asked respondents to place themselves on a five-point scale ranging from very conservative (1) to very liberal (5). Each point along the scale involved a higher percentage of people learning something about the presidential election from Fallon, Colbert et al. For those who said they were very conservative, 10 percent said they learned something from late night comedy. For self-described moderates, the comparable figure was 24 percent. For the very liberal, it rose to 36 percent. Thus, the most liberal viewers were nearly four times as likely as the most conservative viewers to learn about the election from late night jokes. These findings provide empirical support for H2.

With Table 5.4, we turn from the political predispositions of viewers to their interest in the news. Previous researchers have said that late night viewers must be relatively knowledgeable about people and events in the news in order to understand and enjoy the jokes the comedians tell about them. The first half of Table 5.4 examines how political learning from comedy corresponds to how closely one follows the news. As expected, the more closely one follows the news, the more likely one was to have learned something from the late night programs. It did not take a lot of interest in the news to have an effect.

The difference between following the news very closely and learning from the comedy shows (24 percent) is not a great deal more than those who followed the news somewhat closely (23 percent) or not very closely (21 percent). But all three groups are far more likely to take new information from late night jokes to bed with them than are viewers who follow the news "not at all" closely (5.9 percent). These findings provide empirical support for H3.

The second half of Table 5.4 examines not how closely late night viewers follow the news but how frequently they discuss it. A similar pattern appeared, as one out of four respondents (25 percent) who discussed the news nearly every day said they learned something from the comedy shows during the previous week. That one-quarter figure compared to 18 percent of those who talked about the news a few times a month and only 10 percent of those who talked about the news less frequently. Thus, it seems clear that people who are interested in the news – who follow and discuss it – are most likely to bring the same interest and learning to bear on late night comedy. But it doesn't take a lot of interest to have this effect. Even an occasional interest or discussion of the news seems to promote learning from late night relative to those who almost never follow or discuss the news. These findings provide empirical support for H4.

Finally, Table 5.5 examines the relationship between faith in the national media and political learning from the entertainment shows on late night TV. When we study this relationship, a familiar pattern appears. Among those with a high level of trust in the content produced by national news outlets, 27 percent said they learned something in the previous week from the comedy programs. The comparable figure for those with "some" trust was 22 percent, above the 20 percent of those who said they had "not too much" trust in national news

**TABLE 5.4** Media Use and Learning from Comedy Programs

| *Following news* | | *Learned* | *Did not* | *Total* |
|---|---|---|---|---|
| Very closely | | 362 | 1146 | 1508 |
| % within following news | | 24.0% | 76.0% | 100.0% |
| Somewhat closely | | 464 | 1583 | 2047 |
| % within following news | | 22.7% | 77.3% | 100.0% |
| Not very closely | | 158 | 596 | 754 |
| % within following news | | 21.0% | 79.0% | 100.0% |
| Not at all closely | | 16 | 253 | 269 |
| % within following news | | 5.9% | 94.1% | 100.0% |
| Total | | 1000 | 3578 | 4578 |
| | | 100.0% | 100.0% | 100.0% |
| Chi-square significance | .000 | | | |
| Tau-c | .057*** | | | |

| *Discussing news* | | *Learned* | *Did not* | *Total* |
|---|---|---|---|---|
| Nearly every day | | 338 | 1011 | 1349 |
| % within discussing news | | 25.1% | 74.9% | 100.0% |
| A few times a week | | 478 | 1531 | 2009 |
| % within discussing news | | 23.8% | 76.2% | 100.0% |
| A few times a month | | 139 | 631 | 770 |
| % within discussing news | | 18.1% | 81.9% | 100.0% |
| Less often | | 45 | 396 | 441 |
| % within discussing news | | 10.2% | 89.8% | 100.0% |
| Total | | 1000 | 3569 | 4569 |
| | | 100.0% | 100.0% | 100.% |
| Chi-square significance | .000 | | | |
| Tau-c | .083*** | | | |

Statistical significance: * $p < .05$ ** $p <.01$ *** $p <. 001$

Note: The Pew Research Center (2016a) national survey conducted January 12–February 8, 2016. N = 4654.

**TABLE 5.5** Media Evaluations and Learning from Comedy Programs

| *National news trust* | *Learned* | *Did not* | *Total* |
|---|---|---|---|
| A lot | 217 | 590 | 807 |
| % within news trust | 26.9% | 73.1% | 100.0% |
| Some | 593 | 2097 | 2690 |
| % within news trust | 22.0% | 78.0% | 100.0% |
| Not too much | 163 | 657 | 820 |
| % within news trust | 19.9% | 80.1% | 100.0% |
| Not at all | 27 | 234 | 261 |
| % within news trust | 10.3% | 89.7% | 100.0% |
| Total | 1000 | 3578 | 4578 |
| | 100.0% | 100.0% | 100.0% |
| | | | |
| Chi-square significance | .000 | | |
| Tau-c | .064*** | | |

Statistical significance: * p < .05 ** p <.01 *** p <. 001
Note: The Pew Research Center (2016a) national survey conducted January 12–February 8, 2016. N = 4654.

content. The most obvious difference appeared at the lowest level of trust. Only 10 percent of those who said they had "no trust" in national news content reported learning anything from the late night shows. These findings provide empirical support for H5.

## Surveying the Survey

Our analysis of the 2016 Pew survey on people learning shows that several key components of one's background and media consumption are linked to learning about politics from comedy. The analysis shows that late night comedy is indeed a key component of presidential election discourse, especially for younger viewers. Of course, one would not expect the late night comics to have as *great* an impact on political learning as news organizations explicitly designed to inform the public, like cable news, local TV news, and the television network newscasts and news websites. Even so, the comics had an impact on learning that was comparable to local and national newspapers in print. Not long ago print newspapers were one of the top two sources of campaign news (Farnsworth and Lichter 2011a). That more people are learning about politics from watching Jimmy Kimmel and Stephen Colbert than from reading the print editions of their local paper or the *New York Times* and *Washington Post* is a sign of how rapidly both politics and the media are changing. Another piece of evidence regarding the importance of the late night comics concerns their influence compared to the issue-based and campaign-based modes of communication asked about in this Pew survey. As Table 5.1 demonstrates, both of these information formats finished behind the late night comics in providing campaign information during 2016.

News consumers of a certain age might wish to see a greater influence commanded by print newspapers, which (as content analyses have consistently shown) do a more substantive job of providing information about political developments than television's briefer and less substantive focus (Farnsworth and Lichter 2004, 2005, 2006, 2011a, 2012a, 2012b, 2016). But the stories produced by journalists working for legacy publications do obtain a second life, in outlets ranging from their employers' social media accounts to the joke writers on late night talk shows.

The results here also suggest the utility of Trump's attacks on political comedy. Among the factors that predicted political learning from late night comedy, partisanship was the strongest. In these highly partisan times, the president's criticism of his critics helps solidify partisan loyalties and even intensify them. Partisanship is a particularly powerful lens through which voters and viewers see the political world. The president's combative approach towards the late night comics, in other words, is another example of the political strategy that is at the core of his approach: appealing to his political base at nearly every opportunity (Ceaser et al. 2017; Cohen et al. 2016; MacWilliams 2016; Parker 2016).

The second most important factor in turning political jokes into political information was discussing the news. This is consistent with research that finds people consuming news in a variety of outlets can "connect the dots" between the humor and the news, thereby enabling them to appreciate the humor (Becker 2018; Young 2013). This process of making use of a variety of media outlets that one respects can create a sense of self-satisfaction regarding one's own political learning (Baumgartner and Morris 2006; McClennen 2018).

The study also revealed that late night viewers were not replacing traditional political news with political humor. They were more rather than less likely to find interest and value in political news. Their interest in late night humor was an expression of general interest in political information, just as those who discussed the news more frequently were drawn to other nontraditional sources of political information.

As with any public opinion survey, there are some limitations regarding a specific area of scholarly interest, in this case public opinion regarding political humor. The survey does not ask how much political humor a survey participant consumed before it asked about the importance of late night humor to the respondent's political learning. Given that the survey asked for information about nearly a dozen information sources, as well as seeking information about an individual's community involvement and orientation towards international, national, state and local matters, understandably there was no opportunity to delve more deeply into the precise questions of information channel use for each outlet considered in the survey.

Even so, the findings here, which are based on one of the rare publicly available national surveys to pay any attention to political comedy, demonstrate that political humor played an important part in political learning during the early phases of the 2016 presidential election. Further, it did so in the ways identified by previous researchers who looked at public opinion and political humor consumption in previous election cycles.

In this work's final chapter, we turn our attention to the future of late night comedy. What is the future shape of political humor, both during the remainder of Donald Trump's presidency and in the years that follow?

## Appendix: Pew Survey Questions

Survey details: the 2016 Pew Research Center's American Trends Panel (Wave 14) was a national survey that was in the field from January 12 to February 8, 2016. Total N = 4,654 (Web N = 4,339, Mail N = 315).

### *Table 5.1 – Sources of Learning about the 2016 Presidential Election*

Now in the past week did you learn something about the presidential campaign from each of the following sources? Now in the past week did you learn something about the presidential campaign from each of the following sources?

Cable television news (such as CNN, the Fox News Cable Channel, or MSNBC)
Social Media
Local TV News
News websites or apps
News on the radio
Network nightly TV news
Late Night Comedy
Your local newspaper in print
National newspaper in print
Issue-based group websites, apps or emails
Candidate/campaign websites, apps or emails

### *Table 5.2 – Key Sources of Learning about the 2016 Presidential Election by Age*

Of all the places you learned something about the presidential campaign or candidates in the past week, which one would you say has been most helpful to you?

### *Table 5.3 – Partisanship, Ideology and Learning from Comedy Programs*

Now in the past week did you learn something about the presidential campaign from each of the following sources? [late night comedy]

Party Identification options: Republican (including Strong Republicans, Weak Republicans, Leaning Republicans); Independents, Democrats (including Strong Democrats, Weak Democrats, Leaning Democrats),

Ideology options: Very conservative, conservative, moderate, liberal, very liberal.

### *Table 5.4 – Media Use and Learning from Comedy Programs*

How closely do you follow the national news?
(Very closely, Somewhat closely, Not very closely, Not at all closely)
How often do you discuss the news with others?
(Nearly every day, A few times a week, A few times a month, Less often)

### *Table 5.5 – Media Evaluations and Learning from Comedy Programs*

How much, if at all, do you trust the information you get from national news organizations?
(A lot, Some, Not too much, Not at all)

# 6

# THE (NEAR) FUTURE OF POLITICAL HUMOR

For years, survey results and academic analyses have found that the late night comedy programs promote political learning. The effect is greatest on young adults, but it is not confined to them. Recent research into adolescents' consumption of political humor likewise has found a great affinity for this form of comedy, as they follow the lead of their parents, peers and somewhat older family members (Edgerly 2018).

These trends also increase the likelihood that the late night television comedy programs will remain commercially successful for at least another generation (Edgerly 2018). As with adults, political humor is not generally the dominant form of news exposure for adolescents, but it is an important component of political learning even for those too young to vote (Edgerly 2018).

Thus, as late night comedy seems to be picking up another generation of future viewers, we will consider the trajectory of humor during the remainder of the Trump presidency and its aftermath. To what extent have the norms of late night comedy changed permanently in response to a president who represents an unusually target-rich environment?

## The Coarsening of Political Humor

Throughout this book, we have talked about how political comedy in the Trump era is qualitatively and quantitatively different from what came before it. While it once seemed impossible that any president would generate more white-hot "burns" on late night than the aging Lothario Bill Clinton, Trump has set a new standard for the volume of comedic attacks. The president is mocked as a sexual libertine like Clinton, to be sure, but Trump is also routinely referred to as a liar, a fraud and sometimes even a criminal. Given the extent to which these attacks have increased the attention paid to late night – and they have – one can hardly imagine a return to the jovial banter of the Carson years and Chevy Chase's good-natured ribbing of Gerald Ford's alleged clumsiness.

In the short term, we can expect little change in the behavior of this president or the late night comics who mock him to the near exclusion of anyone else. In many ways, Trump and the current crop of comedians are perfect foils for each other. Business is good for them, particularly when they attack Trump, so they will likely offer more of the same mockery during his remaining time in office. Trump's attacks on the late night comics also pay off in terms of retaining the loyalty of his political base, and distracting them from trickier topics such as Russia, the costs to consumers of tariffs and trade wars, and the various scandals and indictments emerging from his campaign team and his administration.

In one of his many attacks on late night humor, Trump complained on Twitter in March 2019 that the comics offered "one-sided hatred." In response, Jimmy Kimmel replied that the Trump presidency was so extraordinary that he and his fellow hosts had no alternative but to make the jokes they do.

> I don't want to talk about Donald Trump every night. None of us do. But he gives us no choice. If he sat in the White House all day quietly working on things, I would almost never mention him, because it's not interesting … But today — not even today, before 10 a.m. today, before 10 o'clock this morning, his former campaign chairman was sentenced to prison for the second time in a week, he called himself the most successful president in history and he tweeted to let people know his wife hasn't been replaced with a body double. I'm not supposed to mention that?
>
> *(Kimmel, quoted in Russonello 2019a)*

Stephen Colbert also believes that Trump brings all the negative comedy content upon himself with all the lies he tells the country. Colbert has presented his role as that of a watchdog and fact checker.

> Trump consumes the news cycle, and our mandate, as we've established for ourselves, is that I want to inform the audience of my opinion about what they've been thinking about all day. … I'm going to do my best to stand in the teeth of that particular [expletive] hurricane and make jokes about how we're all being lied to. For my own heart's ease, I'm not going to pretend that Trump is not lying to me. The alternative is to stick your head in the sand.
>
> *(Colbert, quoted in Marchese 2019)*

Thus, Colbert's and Kimmel's justifications for their political material sound similar to the way journalists define their roles, as watchdogs who serve the public by holding the powerful to account. This may seem presumptuous, but it recalls a joke by Will Rogers: "Everything is changing. People are taking their comedians seriously and their politicians as a joke" (quoted in Schwartz 2011).

So, expect the volume of political humor directed at Trump to remain high for the near future. The coarsening of political humor, which has intensified during Trump's presidency, also seems unlikely to revert to more modest past norms during the remainder of his time in office or the tenure of future presidents. Even if the personal life of the next president does not encourage comedic crassness, other political figures and their personal missteps will offer alternatives for late night mockery. When George W. Bush replaced Bill Clinton and Bush's quiet personal life offered comparatively little material, the comics simply continued to talk about Clinton's foibles. During Bush's first year in office, there were more jokes about Bill Clinton, the outgoing president, than there were about his successor (Lichter et al. 2015: 49). Since the late night humorists like to play a winning hand for as long as it works, Trump as an ex-president will likely face at least as much mockery after his time in office as Clinton did when he left office in 1993. As was the case with Clinton, the comics may miss Trump when he is gone.

That being said, the late night comics have suggested that the president might benefit from a tougher skin, or at least try to do a better job of being president. As Jimmy Kimmel said of Trump, "Obama wore mom jeans one time and we made jokes about it for six straight years. How about this: You stop being terrible, we'll stop pointing it out, O.K.?" (quoted in Russonello 2019a).

For all of Trump's bluster about Alec Baldwin's imitation, critics have suggested that the impersonation is not as harsh as it could be. In fact, many of Baldwin's treatments of Trump portray him more overwhelmed and befuddled than sinister. Trump also comes across in Baldwin's portrayal as relatively introspective and wistful (Canellos 2019).

> By giving Trump qualities he's shown little evidence of in public—conscience, introspection, even regret—*SNL* does him an enormous favor. It offers a glimmer of sympathy about his motives, inviting the generous assumption that there's a better and more self-aware man lurking behind the Twitter feed. In portraying the president as a beleaguered figure, it even allows the conclusion that the real threat to democracy isn't Trump's venomous rhetoric or disregard for constitutional norms, but the ruthlessness of the Washington system that confronts this blustering, fumbling uncle.
>
> *(Canellos 2019)*

In other words, despite Trump's many complaints about Baldwin's impersonation, it could have been far worse. Even so, this portrayal of Trump as befuddled may be problematic to Trump, who bristles at the news reports suggesting the president is not in full command of his administration – or his temper (Miller and Riechmann 2019; Parker and Rucker 2019). His visible anger leads to frequent insults of the late night comics, treating them almost as if they were rival presidential candidates. This then draws even more attention and higher ratings to his most persistent and most visible critics (Marchese 2019).

Trump's public speaking style, with his apparently off-the-cuff insults and some false statements that he apparently wishes were true, helped him win the White House (Ceaser et al. 2017). Given the success of this approach in the 2016 campaign, he is not likely to change. In fact, he recently said as much. At a 2019 appearance at the Conservative Political Action Committee (CPAC) meeting in Washington, Trump said he was sticking with what worked for him, regardless of the consequences.

> "This is how I got elected, by being off script," the president said, briefly walking a half circle away from the podium, as if to physically illustrate just how far he had veered from his teleprompter remarks. "And if we don't go off script, our country is in big trouble, folks." Little of what Trump said was factual — he made 102 false or misleading claims in the speech, according to an analysis by *The Washington Post*'s Fact Checker — yet to this crowd and millions of supporters around the country, his broader points rang true and carried the imprimatur of authority because he delivered them.
>
> *(Parker and Rucker 2019)*

Trump's own coarse and misleading rhetoric, and his expressed lack of interest in doing things differently in the future, is part of the reason why the coarsening of the political debate on late night and elsewhere is not going away anytime soon, neither on late night nor in more general political discourse. Without the lies, there is much less opportunity to offer Trump humor, according to Stephen Colbert. The nature of those presidential deceits, he argues, shapes the nature of the jokes.

> When you make jokes about politicians, there's what they say and what they do. It's hard to make jokes about someone who says something and then kind of does it. But with a guy who points east with his words and west with his action, that's where all the jokes live. Now, what are the things he's lying about? If the things he's lying about have a moral component, then your jokes will have a moral component. In other words, you don't choose the flavor. The flavor is chosen by politics itself.
>
> *(Colbert, quoted in Marchese 2019).*

Trump's use of humor during the 2016 presidential debates focused attention where Trump wanted it focused, on the shortcomings of his rivals rather than his own. While his jokes might have been sharper than jokes by some of the late night critics, Trump's humor was effective in rallying supporters and disarming critics. Trump, in other words, used harsh comments to build a rapport with the audience watching his rallies and debates in ways that were somewhat similar to the ways the hosts of late night comedy build a rapport with the audience watching their programs. As one scholar noted in an analysis of Trump's humor during a debate with Hillary Clinton:

> Trump's sarcastic and hostile humor, when combined with his multiple interruptions used to discombobulate, may be seen as a successful strategy to focus scrutiny on Clinton with audience collaboration through their laughter, while avoiding examination of his substantive shortcomings. While Clinton's humor responded in kind, she was not able to respond in volume; this may have had greater and more strategically debilitating results on the election by focusing on style, not policy substance. Whereas entering into the debate, the stage appeared to be Clinton's domain, stylistically Trump made it his own through the studio audiences' support.
>
> *(Stewart et al. 2018: 129)*

Whatever the future brings for Trump, he has already shown how to diminish rivals and opponents via brief and pointed verbal dismissals. This builds him up and keeps his supporters enthusiastic about him and fearful or dismissive about his adversaries. Even years into his presidency, Trump was still building up energy at his rallies by talking about "Crooked Hillary" and encouraging "Lock her up" chants that were staples of his 2016 campaign rallies. Even though the 2016 nomination campaign is even further in the past, Republican rivals like "low energy" Jeb Bush and "Lyin'" Ted Cruz are still marked by the insults Trump hurled at them several years ago (Allsop 2019).

Though sometimes brutal, Trump's humor is effective because it responds to core dynamics of human nature. Above all, these personal insults feed deep human desires for a world that is simple, where there is good on the one side and evil on the other – with few shades of gray found in between. Like tabloid journalists, the screeching voices of cable television and talk radio, as well as the late night comics, Trump appreciates that entertainers need to avoid complexity to maximize their audience, and their influence (Postman 1985). As a result, Trump offers his audience what one critic calls the modern equivalent of traditional children's stories, tales that contain sharply drawn elements that are comforting and fear-inducing at the same time (Allsop 2017).

> Donald Trump has always spoken in fairy tale language. With a rhetorical swish, he turns complicated figures into witches, bogeymen, and, often, pumpkins, and reduces opponents—including politicians, the media, and other national leaders—to their most simplistic. At its darkest, it is a language that cleaves the world into opposing spheres of good and evil, pulling up the drawbridge to keep the hordes at bay. His dragon-like threat to rain "fire and

> fury" on North Korea is just one recent example. But it is also chauvinistic, trading in strength, moral failure, and cartoonishly rendered virtue.
>
> (*Allsop 2017*)

The personal insults connect effectively with emotional rather than intellectual dimensions of the brain. "Name-calling has always been a raw, primal assertion of power," writes Allsop (2017) in the *Columbia Journalism Review*. Given Trump's successes with employing personal insults to degrade and demonize rivals, one should not expect him to change course. The name-calling on late night comedy seems certain to keep pace with this coarsening of political commentary, as ratings for these programs have increased along with the amount of critical and often personal attacks. Trump's insults and harsh jokes are hardly the primary cause of this coarsening, but his behavior exacerbates a trend underway long before he became a presidential candidate. His own sometimes boorish behavior seems very unlikely to encourage the late night comics to reverse course. Nor will Trump do so on his own initiative.

As the 2020 campaign offered Trump a new round of political rivals to mock, including "Pocahontas" Elizabeth Warren and "Crazy Bernie" Sanders, critics increasingly are encouraging those talking about politics to move beyond the repetition of Trump's personal attacks. "Journalists may not be able to ignore these nicknames altogether, but they should stop doing Trump's dirty work for him: amplifying their power through prominent placement and frequent, unquestioning repetition," according to Margaret Sullivan (2019), the media columnist for the *Washington Post*.

For reporters, that proposal would be like asking them to walk away from a front-page byline. For comedians, it would be like asking them to give up paid public appearances. Given those professional dynamics, it seems unlikely that reporters or the late night comics will follow Sullivan's advice to go easy on the reporting of insults and ridicule. Trump's aggressive use of Twitter allows him to demonstrate daily that sarcasm counts for a lot in politics (and in the news). His tweets function as the equivalent of the assignment desk for Washington reporters and the topical agenda for the late night comics. Day after day, White House reporters chase the president's early morning tweets, and as they do, reporters and editors learn anew the marketing behemoth that is Trump. The president's tweets and the resulting stories bring news consumers to their portals, be they intense fans of the president or intense foes of him (Farnsworth 2018). In the evening, the comics take their turn, as they too have learned a vital lesson: when Trump talks, media companies hear a ringing cash register.

Trump revealed his game plan for 2020 from the moment Democrats began announcing their candidacies. For little known candidates, his barbs may represent the first thing many voters have heard about them. From there on, it's an uphill battle to change initial public impressions. For example, after Trump compared Democratic candidate Pete Buttigieg, (the mayor of South Bend,

Indiana) with "Alfred E. Neuman," the fictional cover boy of *Mad* magazine, in the spring of 2019, the characterization dominated the news cycle for days (Allsop 2019). One can understand why: what a president says is news. That the remark is somewhat odd only makes it more newsworthy. In this case, Trump made the connection between comedy and news even closer, using one of America's best-known cartoon characters (at least to people of a certain age) to insult and mock a political rival who had barely stepped onstage.

Insult narrative reports that draw on the norms of comedy – and sometimes even employ clips or quotations from the late night shows to illustrate the stories – are easy for journalists to write and produce. The ease of story construction is an important aspect of contemporary journalism, as the news business has been shrinking in size for decades. A quip from a late night comic in a news report only increases the appeal of the story in today's crowded short-attention-span media marketplace. Trump knows better than any recent president how to make himself the story of the day all day long – in the morning paper, during the afternoon cable shows, on the evening news and then on late night television. If attention on the president starts to flag, or if the news cycle veers in a direction less than appealing to the White House, Trump can always redirect the national narrative via Twitter.

Thus, Trump is both the subject of such personally oriented attacks and one of the star performers at using that approach. The similarities between the reality TV star dispatching contestants on *The Apprentice* and the president dissing rivals as he dominates the minute-by-minute news cycles all day long are legion.

Further, Trump's insults are largely consequence-free. His supporters love the attacks and those who object were not likely to support him anyway. What's more, these adjectival slurs are not likely to receive the sustained factual scrutiny that accompanies policy pronouncements (Allsop 2017). How can they? Buttigieg is obviously not the gap-toothed grinning dolt that is the personification of a youth-oriented humor magazine, so Trump's comment here hardly deserves the attention of the already overworked media fact-checkers. Nevertheless, making the link between the fictional character who personifies *Mad* magazine and the mayor clearly helps both Trump and the media business that reports on the comparison that Trump made (Allsop 2019). Of course, Buttigieg may not have been the best target for Trump to attack. At the time, he was well back in the Democratic primary field. But he was getting positive press as the first openly gay major party presidential candidate, and he was doing better than some of the other presidential candidates in the early polls. And his background as a red state Democrat who served in the military might make him a threat if his poll numbers improve (Grynbaum 2019).

A larger question is whether Democratic candidates will respond to or perhaps mirror Trump's version of humor in their own campaigns. As of this writing early in the campaign, no Democratic presidential candidate has provided an in-kind answer to the attack-joke tactics of Donald Trump. Despite Trump's obvious advantages when he uses these tactics, rival candidates have found it tough to compete in the race to the bottom of personal insults. Joe Biden, a former vice president and an early Democratic front-runner in the 2020 contest, has said that he does not want to get into a mudslinging contest with Trump, but he couldn't resist calling the president a "clown" from time to time (Allsop 2019).

But Biden's insult is hardly competitive with Trump's own description of the former vice president as "sleepy creepy" (Allsop 2019). If Biden does become the nominee, he will probably have to step up his insult game to be competitive. Trump's first efforts at labeling Biden also may have been inadequate, but Trump's record of trying out different insults for his rivals until he finds one that resonates suggests that Biden will soon face worse from Trump than the original "sleepy creepy" moniker.

Of course, one might wonder if the mockery Trump faces on late night has fully insulated him against the insults of other candidates during the 2020 election cycle. In addition, his own sarcastic commentary gets more attention than any comeback from potential rivals, potentially giving him a head start in the character destruction efforts of any challenger. What could an opponent possibly say about Trump that has not already been the subject of an insult on late night comedy?

It would be depressing if a significant part of winning over the public in a presidential campaign involved a comedic insult face-off. While such an approach may not correspond to the founders' dreams of serious political debate, Trump's electoral victory stemmed in large measure from his ability to attack opponents in ways a significant number of voters found relatable (Ceaser et al. 2017). In 2016 First Lady Michelle Obama encouraged Democrats to "go high" when people like Trump "go low." The results of the 2016 election cast doubts on whether that is a successful strategy for candidates facing Trump and his barrage of sarcasm and combative humor.

While the future seems quite likely to resemble the past where political humor is concerned, one should not entirely rule out the possibility of change. Scholars have debated one potential factor that might change the nature of political humor is the possibility that comedians lose their sense of optimism, the idea that tomorrow could be better than today. At the very core of mocking the present is the sense that the future can be different than the present (even though that may not turn out to be the case). The jokes about Trump are funny in part because he may be followed by another president soon. (For many fans of late night humor, one might add many of them wish for that change *very* soon.) Given the extremely critical treatment of Trump by the late night comics, one might wonder if they or their generally liberal audiences would fall victim to despair if their target-in-chief were re-elected. The "sense of play" that animated comedy for comics and audiences could possibly disappear or at least go into remission for some if Trump wins again. One might suppose that humor would not be as funny to those for whom the present seemed bleak and the future seemed even more so.

If history tells us anything, though, bleak times, even very bleak times, do not kill political humor. Humor is a perennial, which thrives in the sunlight of optimism and in the shadows of extremely hard times. Political humor thrives in wartime, in peace, in famines and in times of plenty. Human beings laughed during the Irish famine, during the US Civil War, as Stalin starved and tortured his people and shortly after 9/11. Concerns that the comedians of late night might never laugh again – or that half the country would be too bitter to laugh along with them – if Trump were re-elected seem misplaced. Things are never too bleak for a joke. The experience of history tells us to expect that the political humor of a second Trump term (if he is re-elected) would likely look a lot like the political humor of his first term.

## *Comedic Insulation?*

Given the size of their audiences and the apparent stability of their platforms, Trump's insults cannot do much to the late night comics. Does that insulation from Trump's rage make them the ideal choices to challenge Trump and otherwise cut him down to size? Some might argue that Trump has met his match with the late night comics, some of whom have shown themselves to be every bit as willing as Trump to engage in the politics of personal insults and character assassination. They certainly do seem to get under Trump's skin. What's more, these late night humorists are no more tied to journalism's strict standards of accuracy than is Trump himself. So far they face little in the way of a backlash because many of their viewers view Trump negatively and enjoy their attacks on him. In some ways, the loyalty of late night viewers is a mirror image of the way that Trump's supporters insulate him from a political backlash for his nasty commentaries and inaccurate statements. Both those who watch Trump's rallies and those who tune in for the sarcasm of Colbert, Noah and others enjoy the attacks. In this "battle of the insult titans," it should not surprise anyone that the nation's senators and governors, who have built careers in public policy rather than as nightclub headliners, cable jokesters and reality TV stars, find it difficult to compete in a humor discourse that mixes laughter with personal character attacks.

On the other hand, the nonstop late night attacks on the president may encourage his supporters to double-down in their defenses of Trump. These jesters personify those coastal elites who serve as effective foils of Middle America. There is a sense in parts of the Midwest and elsewhere that the educated urbanites in the Northeast and the West view residents between the coasts with contempt (Walsh 2012). Certainly some of the jokes discussed in this book contain some disdain for the unsophisticated. It's an old saying that good comedy punches up and bad comedy punches down (McClennen 2018). But who decides the point from which to determine what is up and what is down? Might the humor directed at Trump feel to his supporters like the elite voices on the coasts are punching down at working-class whites like themselves?

Since the days of court jesters, one of the advantages comedians have possessed is their sense of relative powerlessness (Gilbert 2004). That sense of separation allowed them to exercise their craft more freely, and it protected them from the wrath they could face if they were no longer seen as outsiders. Jon Stewart sometimes fended off criticism of his political views or *The Daily Show*'s public impact by insisting on his own insignificance. In an argument with a host of CNN *Crossfire*, he protested, "You're on CNN! The show that leads into me is *puppets* making crank phone calls" (quoted in Stanley 2004).

If comedians start to appear part of a partisan power structure, that sense of powerlessness may disappear, complicating their ability to withstand attacks from their critics.

## Comedians as Politicians?

In the first part of this chapter, we talked about the many links between Trump and the late night comics. The president can't stop talking about late night comedy and the late night hosts can't stop talking about him. Both parties apply insulting monikers and acidic humor to their targets, which these days are often each other. Trump's rise to national prominence involved a large number of media appearances, including more than a few on late night programs, and even through his reality television shows. He was born to compete in the media arena, and it may take someone else familiar with the media arena to beat him.

Trump's political success, more than any other political figure in recent US history, represents the convergence of media and politics. Even Ronald Reagan, who worked as a film actor and television pitchman for General Electric before entering politics, built up experience in elective office before entering the White House. Reagan's eight years as governor of California provided him with considerable governmental experience, and he knew more about governing than his critics sometimes recognized (Cannon 1991). Trump's successes, in contrast, were entirely in the private sector domains of business and media; his first day in elective office was the day of his presidential inauguration.

Is Donald Trump model for future presidential candidates? Probably not. While candidates have long had to cultivate the mass media to be successful in politics, Trump's ability to draw so much public and media attention to himself makes him a reality show president superstar, really a one-of-a-kind melding of marketing, media and politics. Finding another figure with such abilities would be a challenge. Preliminary discussions about finding a Democratic media star to compete with Donald Trump in 2020 – Oprah Winfrey, perhaps? – fizzled (Kruse and Zelizer 2019). In other words, while one might be able to beat LeBron James with the next LeBron James, finding someone that good at basketball is a tall order.

It seems unlikely the next president will have a great deal in common with Donald Trump. There is a pattern in US politics to seek a president who has qualities the current occupant lacks (Farnsworth 2018). When George H.W. Bush did not seem to appreciate the problems ordinary citizens faced in the 1991–1992 recession, Bill Clinton promised he would feel their pain. After Clinton's sexual dalliances nearly derailed his presidency, George W. Bush noted that he had long ago sown his wild oats and was a happily married family man. After Bush's multiple second-term stumbles (the bloody resistance to the occupation of Iraq, the bungled Katrina recovery and the burst housing bubble), Barack Obama offered an image of a more competent and cerebral chief executive. When Obama seemed too aloof and unemotional to many Americans, Donald Trump was the angry, populist cure. Given this pattern, it seems unlikely that US voters would replace a reality television star turned president with another celebrity turned president.

How about a comedian turned politician? The closest match so far would be Al Franken (D-MN), a *Saturday Night Live* alumnus turned US Senator from Minnesota, until he resigned under a cloud of questionable personal behavior. But he was never viewed as an aspirant or likely candidate for national office. As to the current crop of humorists, regular viewers of the late night comedy shows will note that these programs have been sharpening their policy discussions. It's happening across the program genres: John Oliver regularly produces deep dives into policy details on a variety of topics for *Last Week Tonight* on HBO, not unlike a sort of *60 Minutes* of political humor. Samantha Bee likewise drops a great deal of policy content into her critiques of the Trump presidency.

As we discussed in Chapter 4, even late night host Jimmy Kimmel has engaged aggressively in policy debates, bringing his infant son's health care troubles into the discussion of why Trump and Republican members of Congress should not kill the Affordable Care Act, also known as Obamacare (France 2017). During the legislative debate over the health care, Senator Bill Cassidy (R-LA) even proposed considering health care bills in light of what the senator called "the Kimmel test," which would provide insurance coverage to all infants, regardless of the family's ability to pay (Russonello 2017). Kimmel charged that the bill that Cassidy was promoting failed to meet that test, and he spent several minutes on air talking about how the senator had broken his word (Russonello 2017).

> We want quality, affordable health care. Dozens of other countries figured it out. So instead of jamming this horrible bill down our throats, go pitch in and be a part of that. I'm sure they could use a guy with your medical background. And if not, stop using my name, O.K.? Because I don't want my name on it. There's a new Jimmy Kimmel test for you. It's called the lie detector test. You're welcome to stop by the studio and take it anytime.
>
> *(Kimmel, quoted in Russonello 2017)*

The sharpest of Kimmel's attacks demonstrated just how political – and how aggressive – the late night shows can be in today's era of white-hot politics. Even though the repeal measure eventually failed, Kimmel has not consistently weighed in on subsequent policy debates with the aggressiveness he employed when talking about health care. Of course, he does sometimes engage in comparable fashion on a few topics. More recently, Kimmel has also expanded his serious policy discussions into challenging the Trump Administration's anti-immigration policies (Russonello 2019b).

## *Candidate Colbert?*

Then, of course, there is Stephen Colbert, who has been involved at the intersection of politics and comedy for quite some time. Throughout this work, we have focused on how this top-ranked late night host has challenged Trump as both candidate and president, just as he attacked conservative punditry with his parody portrayal on *The Colbert Report*. Among the comics actively working on television today, he has one of the longest careers focusing on the intersection of politics, media and comedy. As such, Colbert seems a particularly interesting example of how a comedian might turn to elective politics – should he wish to do so. After all, if America can elect a reality TV star as president, who is to say that electing a late night comic is a bridge too far?

In this regard, Colbert has a particularly interesting history. Nearly a decade ago, when both men hosted late night programs on Comedy Central, Colbert teamed up with *Daily Show* host Jon Stewart to host a large demonstration on the National Mall in Washington, DC, which they dubbed "The Rally to Restore Sanity and/or Fear." The 2010 event drew large cable audiences and far more attendees in person than a rally earlier that year by Glenn Beck, a prominent conservative radio and television commentator (Stelter 2010). The Stewart–Colbert rally offered satirical content, including mock media awards for promoting fear via their media content (Carr 2010). Crowd size estimates exceeded 200,000 attendees, and the Washington Metropolitan Area Transit Authority, which oversees the Washington subway system, said Metrorail set a Saturday record that day for ridership, with 825,437 trips, compared to the average Saturday Metrorail ridership of about 350,000 (Stelter 2010).

That same year, Colbert also testified in Congress, largely in his Comedy Central character of a blow-hard conservative talk show host, about the plight of migrant farm workers (Parker 2010). The media packed the congressional hearing on the issue, thanks largely to Colbert's star power. "When the comedian was challenged by one disgruntled lawmaker about his expertise, which was based on a single day spent hamming it up in a bean field for his show on Comedy Central, Mr. Colbert, keeping completely in character, said that was enough time to make him an expert on anything," the *New York Times* reported (Parker 2010).

Colbert did drop his character briefly during the hearing to address why he wished to focus on the plight of migrant workers. "I like talking about people who don't have any power, and it seems like one of the least powerful people in the United States are migrant workers who come and do our work but don't have any rights themselves," he said. "Migrant workers suffer and have no rights" (quoted in Parker 2010).

Colbert has in fact toyed with the idea, with uncertain seriousness, of running for president. In 2007, he filed papers to enter both the 2008 Democratic and Republican presidential primaries in his home state of South Carolina. But he was put off by the Republican Party's $35,000 filing fee, and the Democratic Party rejected his application (Parker 2010). With tongue apparently in cheek, Colbert created a Super PAC, "Americans for a Better Tomorrow, Tomorrow," to further his political – or comedic – ambitions (Stelter 2012). When Colbert learned that he could not run for president and run a Super PAC at the same time, he handed over control of the Super PAC to *Daily Show* host Jon Stewart, whose program preceded *The Colbert Report* on the Comedy Central late night lineup (Stelter 2012).

When he announced the decision to transfer the Super PAC to Stewart, Colbert made the discussion a teachable moment about how difficult it is to enforce laws that require separation from Super PACs and the candidates they support.

> "You cannot be a candidate and run a super PAC. That would be coordinating with yourself," Trevor Potter, Mr. Colbert's lawyer and a former chairman of the Federal Election Commission, told him on Thursday's show. But "you could have it run by somebody else," even a friend or business partner, Mr. Potter said — illuminating what critics say is an inappropriate loophole in the law. So Mr. Colbert brought out Mr. Stewart of "The Daily Show," who played along with the joke, saying, "I'd be honored to" help.
>
> Sarcastically emphasizing that they would not coordinate Mr. Colbert's real or imagined presidential race with Mr. Stewart's ad spending, Mr. Colbert said "From now on, I will have to talk about my plans on my TV show." Mr. Stewart, whose show immediately precedes Mr. Colbert's at 11 p.m., shot back, "I don't even know when it's on."
>
> *(quoted in Stelter 2012)*

While Colbert did not choose to run for president in 2012, the educational effort had an impact. A study found that citizens said they learned more about campaign finance from Colbert's discussion of Super PACs and his creation of one for his own campaign than from traditional news segments (Hardy et al. 2014).

While he might be a compelling candidate to some Americans, Colbert insists he really does not want to be one. Nor does he want to have that influential a role in selecting candidates. Colbert, who says that he has read *The Lord of the Rings* dozens of times, uses an example from that story to place his role on the outside, not seeking power.

> Question: What's been the most interesting or weirdest idea you've noticed people projecting onto you?

> Answer. That I want to be a political force. That's the weirdest thing. I said to Jon [Stewart], back in the day: "You and I are like Frodo and Samwise. We're trying to throw the damn ring in the volcano. It doesn't occur to them that we don't want to use it." Our way of throwing the ring in the volcano is to make fun of political behavior. But people got mad at me. "Oh, now he's fashioning himself as a player." And I'm like, you could not be more wrong. If you think I want that, you know nothing about me. I just want to make jokes. I care about what happens in the news. I have an audience that seems to care, too. We mesh on the jokes. It's not complicated.
>
> *(Colbert, quoted in Marchese 2019)*

The idea of electing comedians to government does not seem so odd, when one considers that America has selected a reality television star with no governing experience for the presidency, and other nations have explicitly turned to comedians in their elections. The political and economic pressures on the nations of Europe, clearly greater than those facing the United States, have been fueling the rise of both extreme and unconventional politicians for years. Italy's Five Star Movement, led by a former comedian, first demonstrated several years ago that it was a force to contend with in that nation's politics (Unger 2013), though the renegade party has been facing hard times since it became part of a governing coalition (Povoledo 2019).

In April 2019, Ukraine elected a comedian as president in a landslide. This meant turning aside an incumbent president in the midst of a highly unstable military situation with Russia, which is occupying much of Ukraine's Donbass region and the Crimea (Higgins and Mendel 2019). The election of Volodymyr Zelensky was an example of life imitating art.

> This ability to convince and connect with people made Mr. Zelensky a natural for the stage, television and now politics, said Alina Fialka-Smal, a friend from university days. "He was always a whole pile of different characters," she said.
>
> But the character that stuck — and the one that many Ukrainians now look to to clean up their graft-addled country — is that of Vasyl Holoborodko, Mr. Zelensky's role in a hit television series, "Servant of the People," about an unwaveringly honest high school history teacher who is elected president after a viral video shows him ranting against corruption.
>
> *(Higgins 2019)*

As goes Ukraine, so goes the United States? Probably not, particularly if Colbert retains his belief that he should not seek elected office. Perhaps a more politically ambitious comedian will someday have his or her chance to steer the ship of state. Given American desires for what we lack in a leader at present, though, we are probably talking about the president who takes office at least one president after Trump.

## Where is the Conservative Political Comedy?

On *The Colbert Report*, Stephen Colbert demonstrated that conservative television can be funny, at least when he parodied it. What about the real thing? Where is the political humor for conservatives and why is it not a prominent part of Fox News?

One problem that Fox News has when it comes to offering humor is that outrage does not translate well into jokes. Anger is more scary than funny, except when someone is making fun of it. Indeed, as Colbert notes, laughter is about relieving tension and fear.

> I don't know what the next day is like for anybody. If the show goes well, maybe the audience sleeps a bit better. And maybe that's all the show should be. I have said this before, but I know that when you're laughing, you're not afraid.
>
> [Question: Is that true, though? Isn't nervous laughter a laughter that comes from fear?] Nervous laughter is not the same thing as laughing, in my opinion. I would say nervous laughter is evidence that I'm right, because that is your body autonomically trying to relieve tension. If someone can do that for you from the outside, it relieves that tension and fear, and you are momentarily not afraid. If you're not afraid, you can think, and we have to think our way out of this one.
>
> *(quoted in Marchese 2019)*

One highly visible conservative attempt to recreate a *Daily Show* for the right – *The 1/2 Hour News Hour* – briefly aired on Fox News in 2007. The show generated poor ratings and was pulled off the air that same year, as critics claimed it was more political than humorous (Morrison 2015).

To the extent that Fox News hosts follow Trump's lead and increase public anxieties, they are pushing their audiences away from the release of comedy, even though conservatives – like anyone – could use a good laugh now and then.

Psychological factors are particularly important for explaining the problems of creating a conservative political humor show. One study found that conservatives possess greater fear and less appreciation of the irony or ambiguity that can be at the heart of political humor (Young et al. 2019). These differences may also reduce the number of conservatives who choose to make a career of comedy, reducing the number of potential hosts with right-of-center views (Morrison 2015). Research shows that conservatives enjoy humor as much as liberals do. But certain forms of humor, like satire – the attacking of political institutions – can be problematic for conservatives, who often are supportive of traditions and existing institutions (Hesse 2013).

> Every attempt at delivering such a program ends up being viewed even by conservatives as mostly unwatchable. (Despite featuring appearances by Anne

> Coulter and Rush Limbaugh, *The Half-Hour News Hour* was cancelled after only 13 episodes.) It's possible that the reason for this can be found in the way every single one of these short-lived programs is described, even by the creators themselves, as a "conservative version of The *Daily Show* or 'Weekend Update.'" Similar to alcohol-free beer or soy burgers, the attempt to brand yourself as a polar alternative to the product you're ideologically opposed to is rarely accepted in America.
>
> *(Hesse 2013)*

Another potential problem for conservative political humor is the issue raised earlier: that good comedy punches up and bad comedy punches down (McClennen 2018). Where is the conservative comedy that punches up? Many favorite targets of conservatives, such as poor immigrants and welfare recipients do not lend themselves to effective comedic treatment. There is also the risk of crossing lines of acceptable racial or ethnic discourse (known on the right as political correctness), if one were to attack such groups via humor (Morrison 2015).

Some political targets of the right are well-heeled or influential, like Hollywood celebrities and liberal philanthropists. But these targets may be too narrowly defined (or too unfamiliar) to offer sufficient material for a regular late night comedy program tilted in a conservative direction. One also might wonder whether some of the political humor efforts against Hollywood, in particular, might stick. Film stars play a range of characters across their careers, and therefore may have a broader appeal that extends beyond liberals. Conservatives go to blockbuster films, just as liberals do.

> There are, of course, high-profile conservative comedians in America, such as the members of the Blue Collar Comedy Tour. But these performers, who include Jeff Foxworthy and Larry the Cable Guy, tend carefully to avoid politicized topics, mocking so-called "rednecks" in the same spirit as Borscht Belt acts mocked Jewish culture.
>
> When it comes to actual political satire, one of the most well-known figures nationally is Dennis Miller, a former *Saturday Night Live* cast member who now has a weekly segment on Fox News' *O'Reilly Factor*. On a recent show, O'Reilly brought up the Democrats' election losses, and Miller took the bait. "I think liberalism is like a nude beach," Miller said. "It's better off in your mind than actually going there." His jokes are sometimes amusing, but they tend to be grounded in vague ideologies, not the attentive criticism to the news of the day that has given liberal satires plenty of fodder five days a week. The real problem, Frank Rich wrote about Miller, "is that his tone has become preachy. He too often seems a pundit first and a comic second."
>
> *(Morrison 2015)*

## A 2020 Comedy Preview

From the outset of the 2020 presidential campaign, the late night comics played a significant mediating role in shaping public assessments of the unusually large number of potential candidates. Indeed, the immense Democratic field increased the pressure for roughly two dozen presidential wannabes appearing on the late night programs (Parkin 2018). In a month-long period a full year before the 2020 Iowa Caucus, Stephen Colbert hosted a wide range of potential presidential candidates. The list included Senator Bernie Sanders of Vermont, who finished second to Hillary Clinton in the 2016 Democratic nomination process, Senator Kamala Harris of California, former Housing and Urban Development Secretary Julian Castro, and Senator Kirsten Gillibrand of New York (Stelter 2019). The range of political guests grew as the 2020 field continued to expand.

> Of course, the comedy route works better for some politicians than for others. A politician's comfort and charm in a late night setting is considered when the show's bookers work with communications directors to schedule a guest. But the list of Colbert guests since last summer tells the story. [Former Attorney General] Eric Holder visited last July. [New Jersey Senator] Cory Booker in August. [Former Secretary of State] John Kerry, [Former Congressman and then-Senate candidate] Beto O'Rourke and [2016 Democratic presidential nominee] Hillary Clinton in September. [Then-House Minority Leader] Nancy Pelosi in October. [Minnesota Senator] Amy Klobuchar in November (Stelter 2019).

Kamala Harris, who made Colbert's program one of the first stops on her book tour, was rewarded with prime comedic real estate: she was the first guest on the program, appearing right after the monologue segment. She even received the high honor of a second segment with the host, a rare privilege usually bestowed only on the most important and compelling guests (Stelter 2019).

> *Vanity Fair*'s Chris Smith, who was backstage at the theater that day, wrote that Harris "smiled and exhaled" afterward. "The senator seemed most proud of having gotten a laugh out of Colbert, a moment that happened after the TV cameras shut down," he wrote.
>
> *(Stelter 2019)*

Indeed, the prominence of late night comedy appearances, CNN and Fox News town halls, and other television and online forums may be eclipsing the traditional clout of Iowa and New Hampshire, the first caucus and primary state, respectively, in the presidential nomination process (Martin 2019). When Democratic candidates have to establish a minimum number of donors and a minimum level of public support to qualify for the televised debates, it is hard to argue that a day spent greeting voters in Iowa is better than a day spent preparing for an appearance on *The Late Show*. As Ted Devine, a veteran Democratic campaign strategist, noted, "You don't have to be in Des Moines or Manchester to have a viral moment, and if that happens, you're in front of millions of people and can raise potentially millions of dollars" (quoted in Martin 2019).

In keeping with that expending importance of late night, Colbert has evolved over his years in comedy. By the 2020 contest he was trying to balance making his viewers laugh with giving them the opportunity to learn about the candidates.

> Colbert is said to be keenly aware of his power broker status with the Democratic electorate. He pays close attention to the Democratic field of candidates, sizing them up like so many others in the media business. But Colbert also knows he is hosting a late-night talk show, not an MSNBC broadcast. He straddles both worlds – joking with Rep. Adam Schiff one minute, asking about Russian espionage the next.
>
> *(Stelter 2019)*

Of course, Colbert's is not the only show where presidential candidates can find a mass audience. The success of late night comedy in recent years has created many opportunities for candidates. Even those who may not get a lengthy opportunity – or any opportunity – to chat with Colbert on CBS can promote their campaign elsewhere (Parkin 2018).

The number of Democratic presidential candidates itself became a punch line. As Jimmy Kimmel noted in the spring of 2019: "At this point, announcing you're running for president is like announcing you're running a 5K: Good for you. No one cares. Don't post pictures" (quoted in Russonello 2019b). Kimmel even made up a song to the tune of a number from the 1964 film *Mary Poppins*, "Supercalifragilisticexpialidocious," to help recall the 23 names in the Democratic contest as of late May 2019 (Epstein 2019).

As more and more of these Democrats made their way to the sets of the late night programs, critics started to wonder whether these shows run the risk of becoming too partisan in tone. This could limit their audiences as well as making them less appealing venues for would-be presidents who are not Democrats (Parkin 2018).

> As candidates gear up for the 2020 race, they face an increasingly partisan political communications environment in which comedy programs are deciding between maintaining their impartiality or offering a satirical critique that emulates wider partisan divisions. Democratic and Republican candidates may come to believe that certain shows are "friendlier" than the others, and if interviews become increasingly partisan, viewers may see them as less legitimate in terms of their ability to offer a fresh perspective rather than just another venue for partisan acrimony.
>
> *(Parkin 2018: 287)*

Our data suggest that we may already be at that point. Late night comedy's intense attacks on Donald Trump have made these shows unappealing places for the president and administration officials to appear. Democratic candidates and other critics of the president can find a welcome home on many of these late night programs, but as a whole, the ideological offerings on late night are far less diverse than they were a generation ago. The political jokes are also more partisan and sharp edged than they were in the past.

So far, though, there is little evidence that viewers are tiring of the largely monochromatic ideology of late night comedy. Indeed, the evidence during the first two years of Trump's presidency suggests that anti-Trump commentary sells quite well on both broadcast and cable networks, as it has ever since Trump first became a national political figure (Morris 2018).

In a recent interview, Colbert said that he welcomed the start of the 2020 presidential election campaign, which provides him more material to offer jokes about a wide range of Democratic candidates.

> [Now] there are Democrats to talk about. When Joe Biden got heat for sniffing women's heads, we did an act that he was doing A.S.M.R. We make jokes about Beto O'Rourke. We make jokes about Elizabeth Warren. We make jokes about Andrew Yang. We make jokes about Pete Buttigieg. What I'm happy about is that my audience is laughing at all of them, which is good. But not everybody is as mockable as everybody else, and some mockability doesn't have consequences. Now, maybe Andrew Yang will be president — I don't know [expletive] about politics; I only know about human behavior — but his running on no circumcision, free money and legalized pot — is of no consequence compared with Donald Trump. So in terms of balance, I don't really care. I care about being honest about what people talked about today.
>
> *(Colbert, quoted in Marchese 2019)*

Perhaps the biggest challenge for late night humor is a bit further in the future: whatever will these programs do without Trump to mock?

## Conclusion

Until the 1990s, politicians had to compete with increasingly critical if not adversarial journalists to get their messages out to the public, but they were largely ignored by the entertainment media. Then an expansion of the news agenda, together with a kind of political awakening among the hosts of television talk shows, permanently altered the landscape, bringing a new source of negativity into political discourse. Today the journalists knock the politicians off their stride, and then the humorists kick them while they are down.

In this narrow sense, Donald Trump is quite right to call journalists and late night comics "the opposition party." Any other administration might have made the same claim, but Trump's evidence is particularly strong. In addition, previous presidential administrations likely would have been more reticent than the current White House team about expressing publicly this objection to late night humor. In their effort to get their messages to the public in the form and content they prefer, all presidents and presidential candidates necessarily come into conflict with the mainstream media, whose professional norms dictate that they strip the propaganda out of politicians' messages (Farnsworth and Lichter 2006). But in this endless battle between the media and politicians, late night talk shows have emerged as a second front. As a result, the culture of personal ridicule in public discourse is stronger than ever.

In fact, the format of late night comedy creates a huge advantage for the hosts when compared to traditional news reporters, who have less of an opportunity to present themselves as individuals and also face much higher standards of content accuracy. The exaggerations and objectively untrue comments that permit effective punch lines on late night make general character criticisms of political figures more accessible and more appealing to casual news consumers. ABC News, for example, could never exaggerate the way Jimmy Kimmel et al. do regarding the personal foibles of political leaders – nor could news reporters present themselves as people as intimately as does a late night host engaging in friendly banter with celebrities night after night. The best the news division can do to narrow the entertainment gap with late night is to quote the comics as part of its own news programs (as is now done with increasing regularity to maximize "clicks" from online news consumers). Even the august *New York Times* features a "Best of Late Night" column that provides a rundown of the best political jokes from the previous night's talk shows.

The personal connections these late night comics cultivate with their audiences allow them to become policy experts and more. The most notable example we discussed occurred when Jimmy Kimmel set his jokes aside and used his infant son's health care troubles to advocate for universal health care (Yahr 2017a, 2017b). For the moment, Kimmel's aggressive, personal policy engagement on health care remains the exception, even on his own program. Given the public's low esteem for reporters and politicians and their positive evaluations of the stars of late night, perhaps Kimmel's foray into policy advocacy will embolden other comics to do the same in the years ahead.

To be sure, laughing at political leaders is a healthy expression of public skepticism about the powers that be in a democratic society, as well as a safety valve for public disaffection with its leaders (and would-be leaders). The current talk show hosts are following in a tradition that stretches back well over a century ago and includes the likes of Will Rogers and Mark Twain. And there is no doubt that the failings and antics of the political class frequently deserve a good horselaugh. But in an era of heightened negativity in political discourse, the hollowing out of public support in recent years for both political and media institutions raises questions of proportionality.

Thus, in and of themselves, the nightly monologues of comedians may be all in good fun. As part of the larger universe of political communication, though, they may accentuate trends in political discourse that bode ill for a healthy polity. In the words of Neil Postman (1985), someday we may look back on these days and conclude that we were "amusing ourselves to death."

# ABOUT THE CONTRIBUTORS

**Deanne Canieso** is a doctoral student in Communication at George Mason University, and has more than 15 years' experience in project management, advocacy and strategic communications. Her research interests lie in the study of emotional contagion in mass media and in the computer-mediated context.

**Jeremy Engel** is a senior political science major at the University of Mary Washington in Fredericksburg, Virginia. He is a member of the UMW honors program, a research assistant at UMW's Center for Leadership and Media Studies, and a member of Phi Beta Kappa.

**Noah Gardner** is a 2018 graduate of the University of Mary Washington in Fredericksburg, Virginia, where he majored in political science and graduated with distinction and departmental honors. He was a research assistant at UMW's Center for Leadership and Media Studies.

**Shaelyn Patzer** is a doctoral student in Communication at George Mason University. She earned her MA from Johns Hopkins University and her bachelor's degree from the University of Pennsylvania.

# BIBLIOGRAPHY


Abramowitz, Alan I. 2017. "It Wasn't the Economy Stupid: Racial Polarization, White Racial Resentment and the Rise of Trump." In *Trumped: The 2016 Election That Broke All the Rules*, eds. Larry J. Sabato, Kyle Kondik, and Geoffrey Skelly. Lanham, MD: Rowman & Littlefield.

Adorno, Theodor, Else Frankel-Brunswick, Daniel J. Levinson, and Nevitt R. Sanford. 1950. *The Authoritarian Personality*. New York: Harper and Row.

Allsop, Jon. 2017. "Inside the Fairy Tale Mind of Trump." *Columbia Journalism Review*, September 27. https://www.cjr.org/special_report/trump-fairy-tale.php.

Allsop, Jon. 2019. "The Dangerous Power of Trump's 'Fairy Tale' Nicknames." *Columbia Journalism Review*, May 13. https://www.cjr.org/the_media_today/trump_buttigieg_neuman_nickname.php.

Anderson, Dave. 1987. "Boxing by the Boardwalk." *New York Times*, October 16. https://www.nytimes.com/1987/10/16/sports/sports-of-the-times-boxing-by-the-boardwalk.html?searchResultPosition=10.

Andrews, Travis M. 2017. "Jimmy Fallon Says People 'Have a Right to Be Mad' at His Friendly Hair-tousling of Trump." *Washington Post*, May 18. https://www.washingtonpost.com/news/morning-mix/wp/2017/05/18/jimmy-fallon-says-people-have-a-right-to-be-mad-at-his-friendly-hair-tousling-of-trump/?utm_term=.8cf5bb9fe9bb.

Associated Press. 2017. "Trump Hits Back at Late Night Shows Critical of Republicans." *Boston Globe*, October 7. https://www.boston.com/news/politics/2017/10/07/trump-hits-back-at-late-night-shows-critical-of-republicans.

Baum, Matthew A. 2005. "Talking the Vote: Why Presidential Candidates Hit the Talk Show Circuit." *American Journal of Political Science* 49(2): 213–234.

Baumgartner, Jody C. 2013. "No Laughing Matter? Young Adults and the 'Spillover Effect' of Candidate-Centered Politcal Humor." *Humor* 26(1): 23–43.

Baumgartner, Jody C. 2018. "The Limits of Attitude Change: Political Humor during the 2016 Campaign." In *Political Humor in a Changing Media Landscape*, eds. Jody C. Baumgartner and Amy B. Becker. Lanham, MD: Lexington.

Baumgartner, Jody C., and Amy B. Becker. 2018. "'Still Good for a Laugh?' Political Humor in a Changing Media Landscape." In *Political Humor in a Changing Media Landscape*, eds. Jody C. Baumgartner and Amy B. Becker. Lanham, MD: Lexington.

Baumgartner, Jody C., and Jonathan S. Morris. 2006. "The Daily Show Effect: Candidate Evaluations, Efficacy and American Youth." *American Politics Research* 36: 341–367.

Baumgartner, Jody C., and Jonathan S. Morris. 2011. "Stoned Slackers or Super Citizens? 'Daily Show' Viewing and Political Engagement of Young Adults." In *The Stewart/Colbert Effect: Essays on the Real Impacts of Fake News*, ed. Amarnath Amarasingam. Jefferson, NC: McFarland & Co., pp. 63–78.

Baumgartner, Jody C., Jonathan S. Morris, and Natasha L. Walth. 2012. "The Fey Effect: Young Adults, Political Humor and Perceptions of Sarah Palin in the 2008 Presidential Election Campaign." *Public Opinion Quarterly* 76(1): 95–104.

Baym, Geoffrey. 2005. "The Daily Show: Discursive Integration and the Reinvention of Political Journalism." *Political Communication* 22: 259–276.

Becker, Amy B. 2013. "What about Those Interviews? The Impact of Exposure to Political Comedy and Cable News on Factual Recall and Anticipated Political Expression." *International Journal of Public Opinion Research* 25(3): 344–356.

Becker, Amy B. 2018. "Interviews and Voting Motivations: Exploring Connections Between Political Satire, Perceived Learning and Elaborative Processing." In *Political Humor in a Changing Media Landscape*, eds. Jody C. Baumgartner and Amy B. Becker. Lanham, MD: Lexington.

Becker, Amy B., and Jody C. Baumgartner. 2018. "Looking Ahead to the Future: Why Laughing and Political Humor Will Matter Even More in the Decade to Come." In *Political Humor in a Changing Media Landscape*, eds. Jody C. Baumgartner and Amy B. Becker. Lanham, MD: Lexington.

Becker, Amy B., and Leticia Bode. 2018. "Satire as a Source for Learning? The Differential Impact of News versus Satire Exposure on Net Neutrality Knowledge Gain." *Information, Communication & Society* 21(4): 612–625.

Bender, Marylin. 1983. "The Empire and Ego of Donald Trump." *New York Times*, August 7. https://www.nytimes.com/1983/08/07/business/the-empire-and-ego-of-donald-trump.html?searchResultPosition=49.

Benkler, Yochai, Robert Faris, Hal Roberts, and Ethan Zuckerman. 2017. "Study: Breitbart-led Right-Wing Media Ecosystem Altered Broader Media Agenda." *Columbia Journalism Review*, March 3. https://www.cjr.org/analysis/breitbart-media-trump-harvard-study.php.

Berger, Arthur Asa. 1997. *The Art of Comedy Writing*. Piscataway, NJ: Transaction Publishers.

Berger, Arthur Asa. 2011. "Humor, Pedagogy and Cultural Studies." In *A Decade of Dark Humor: How Comedy, Irony, and Satire Shaped Post-9/11 America*, eds. Viveca Greene and Ted Gournelos. Jackson, MS: University of Mississippi Press.

Blake, Aaron. 2019. "Trump tries to re-write his own history on Charlottesville and 'both sides'." *Washington Post*, April 26. https://www.washingtonpost.com/politics/2019/04/25/meet-trump-charlottesville-truthers/?utm_term=.788e1687ff39.

Bodroghkozy, Aniko. 1997. "'The Smothers Brothers Comedy Hour' and the Youth Rebellion." In *The Revolution Wasn't Televised: Sixties Television and Social Conflict*, eds. Lynn Spigel and Michael Curtin. New York: Routledge.

Bohlen, Celestine. 2001. "In New War on Terrorism, Words Are Weapons, Too." *New York Times*, September 29. http://www.nytimes.com/2001/09/29/arts/think-tank-in-new-war-on-terrorism-words-are-weapons-too.html.

Bond, Jon R., and Richard Fleisher. 2000. *Polarized Politics: Congress and the President in a Partisan Era*. Washington, DC: CQ Press.

Boot, Max. 2018. "Trump is a Grifter, Same as Ever." *Washington Post*, May 2. https://www.washingtonpost.com/opinions/global-opinions/trump-is-a-grifter-same-as-ever/2018/05/02/5afa43d2-4e2f-11e8-84a0-458a1aa9ac0a_story.html?utm_term=.67502b804744.

Borchers, Callum. 2016. "The Amazing Story of Donald Trump's Old Spokesman, John Barron — Who Was Actually Donald Trump Himself." *Washington Post*, May 13. https://www.washingtonpost.com/news/the-fix/wp/2016/03/21/the-amazing-story-of-donald-trumps-old-spokesman-john-barron-who-was-actually-donald-trump-himself/?utm_term=.0d0fbf6099df.

Borchers, Callum. 2017a. "A *Saturday Night Live* Spinoff Would Complete NBC's Turnaround on Trump." *Washington Post*, February 7. https://www.washingtonpost.com/news/the-fix/wp/2017/02/07/a-saturday-night-live-spinoff-would-complete-nbcs-turnaround-on-trump/?utm_term=.58b6710bbafb.

Borchers, Callum. 2017b. "*Saturday Night Live* Is the Newest, Hottest Place to Punk — and Persuade — President Trump." *Washington Post*, February 11. https://www.washingtonpost.com/news/the-fix/wp/2017/02/11/saturday-night-live-is-the-place-to-punk-and-persuade-president-trump/?utm_term=.7b8df65c66b5.

Borchers, Callum. 2018. "The Forbes 400 and How Trump's Shameless Self-promotion Helped Make Him President." *Washington Post*, April 20. https://www.washingtonpost.com/news/the-fix/wp/2018/04/20/the-forbes-400-and-how-trumps-shameless-self-promotion-helped-make-him-president/?utm_term=.6bee614b8596.

Brewer, Paul, and Xiaoxia Cao. 2006. "Candidate Appearances on Soft News Shows and Public Knowledge About Primary Candidates." *Journal of Broadcasting and Electronic Media* 50: 18–30.

Brice-Sadler, Michael. 2018. "*SNL* Imagined a World Without Trump as President. Trump Was Not Amused." *Washington Post*, December 16. https://www.washingtonpost.com/politics/2018/12/16/snl-imagined-world-without-trump-president-trump-was-not-amused/?utm_term=.5161f443e647.

Brooks, David. 2011. "Why Trump Soars." *New York Times*, April 18. https://www.nytimes.com/2011/04/19/opinion/19brooks.html?searchResultPosition=54.

Brozan, Nadine. 1992. "Chronicle." *New York Times*, August 3. https://www.nytimes.com/1992/08/03/style/chronicle-456992.html?searchResultPosition=35.

Bump, Philip. 2019. "His *Fox News* Gig Was the Perfect Transition from 'Apprentice' Trump to Politician Trump." *Washington Post*, April 17. https://www.washingtonpost.com/politics/2019/04/17/his-fox-news-gig-was-perfect-transition-apprentice-trump-politician-trump/?utm_term=.81f57052a9b3.

Burns, James MacGregor, and Susan Dunn. 2001. *The Three Roosevelts: Patrician Leaders Who Transformed America*. New York: Atlantic Monthly Press.

Butler, Bethonie. 2016. "*The Nightly Show* Ends with Heartfelt Messages from Larry Wilmore and Jon Stewart." *Washington Post*, August 19. https://www.washingtonpost.com/news/arts-and-entertainment/wp/2016/08/19/the-nightly-show-ends-with-heartfelt-messages-from-larry-wilmore-and-jon-stewart/?utm_term=.5b0fdd636c36.

Campbell, Colin. 2000. "Demotion? Has Clinton Turned the Bully Pulpit into a Lectern?" In *The Clinton Legacy*, eds. Colin Campbell and Bert Rockman. New York: Seven Bridges Press, pp. 48–70.

Campbell, James E. 2016. *Polarized: Making Sense of a Divided America*. Princeton, NJ: Princeton University Press.

Canellos, Peter. 2019. "Why Trump Should Be Thanking Alec Baldwin: Once, *Saturday Night Live* Could Take Down a President. Now It's Doing Trump a Favor." *Politico*, May 17. https://www.politico.com/magazine/story/2019/05/17/trump-snl-impression-baldwin-saturday-night-live-226920?nname=playbook&nid=0000014f-1646-d88f-a1cf-5f46b7bd0000&nrid=0000014e-f10b-dd93-ad7f-f90fad5b0001&nlid=630318.

Cannon, Lou. 1991. *President Reagan: The Role of a Lifetime*. New York: Simon & Schuster.

Cappella, Joseph N., Kathleen Hall Jamieson. 1997. *Spiral of Cynicism: The Press and the Public Good*. New York: Oxford University Press.

Carr, David. 2007. "Carson-era Humor, Post-Colbert." *New York Times*, April 23. https://www.nytimes.com/2007/04/23/business/media/23carr.html.

Carr, David. 2010. "Rally to Shift the Blame." *New York Times*, October 31. https://www.nytimes.com/2010/11/01/business/media/01carr.html?searchResultPosition=9.

Carter, Bill. 1989. "Another Trump Project: A TV Game Show." *New York Times*, September 7. https://www.nytimes.com/1989/09/07/arts/another-trump-project-a-tv-game-show.html?searchResultPosition=24.

Carter, Bill. 2003. "MSNBC Cancels the Phil Donahue Talk Show." *New York Times*, February 26. https://www.nytimes.com/2003/02/26/business/msnbc-cancels-the-phil-donahue-talk-show.html.

Carter, Bill. 2009. "Leno Takes a Turn towards the Political." *New York Times*, September 20. http://www.nytimes.com/2009/09/21/business/media/21letterman.html.

Ceaser, James, Andrew Busch, and John J.Pitney, Jr. 2009. *Epic Journey: The 2008 Elections and American Politics*. Lanham, MD: Rowman & Littlefield.

Ceaser, James, Andrew Busch, and John J.Pitney, Jr. 2017. *Defying the Odds: The 2016 Elections and American Politics*. Lanham, MD: Rowman & Littlefield.

Chadwick, Andrew. 2013. *The Hybrid Media System*. Oxford: University of Oxford Press.

Clement, Scott, and David Nakamura. 2018. "Post-ABC Poll: Trump Disapproval Swells as President, Republicans Face Lopsided Blame for Shutdown." *Washington Post*, January 25. https://www.washingtonpost.com/politics/poll-majority-of-americans-hold-trump-and-republicans-responsible-for-shutdown/2019/01/25/e7a2e7b8-20b0-11e9-9145-3f74070bbdb9_story.html?utm_term=.28d8297d6193.

Cohen, Marty, David Karol, Hans Noel, and John Zaller. 2016. "Party versus Faction in the Reformed Presidential Nominating System." *PS: Political Science & Politics* 49(4): 701–708.

Cohen, Steven. 2006. *Understanding Environmental Policy*. New York: Columbia University Press.

Combs, James E., and Dan Nimmo. 1996. *The Comedy of Democracy*. Westport, CT: Praeger.

Compton, Josh. 2018. "Inoculation against/with Political Humor." In *Political Humor in a Changing Media Landscape*, eds. Jody C. Baumgartner and Amy B. Becker. Lanham, MD: Lexington.

Compton, Josh. 2019. "Late Night Television Comedy, Mid-Afternoon Congressional Testimony: Attacks on Stephen Colbert's House Judiciary Committee Appearance." *Comedy Studies*, doi:10.1080/2040610X.2019.1623439.

Cooper, Helene. 2011. "Obama Zings Trump at White House Correspondents' Dinner." *New York Times*, April 30. https://thecaucus.blogs.nytimes.com/2011/04/30/obama-zings-trump-at-gala/?searchResultPosition=9.

Craig, Stephen C. 1993. *The Malevolent Leaders*. Boulder, CO: Westview.

Craig, Stephen C. 1996. "The Angry Voter: Politics and Popular Discontent in the 1990s." In *Broken Contract? Changing Relationships Between Americans and their Government*, ed. Stephen C. Craig. Boulder, CO: Westview.

Dagnes, Alison. 2012. *A Conservative Walks into a Bar: The Politics of Political Humor*. New York: Palgrave MacMillan.

Davis, Murray. 1993. *What's So Funny? The Comic Conception of Culture and Society*. Chicago, IL: University of Chicago Press.

Davis, Richard, and Diana Owen. 1998. *New Media and American Politics*. New York: Oxford University Press.

Diamond, Dan. 2017. "Kimmel Tells Viewers: 'We Have Until Sept. 30' to Stop GOP Health Bill." *Politico*, September 21. https://www.politico.com/story/2017/09/21/jimmy-kimmel-obamacare-repeal-bill-cassidy-243002.

Doyle, Patrick. 2019. "Conan O'Brien Remembers When Trump Stormed Off His Show." *Rolling Stone*, January 22. https://www.rollingstone.com/tv/tv-news/conan-obrien-donald-trump-video-782294/.

Dullea, Georgia. 1993. "It's a Wedding Blitz for Trump and Maples." *New York Times*, December 21. https://www.nytimes.com/1993/12/21/nyregion/vows-it-s-a-wedding-blitz-for-trump-and-maples.html?searchResultPosition=17.

Edgerly, Stephanie A. 2018. "A New Generation of Satire Consumers? A Socialization Approach to Youth Exposure to News Satire." In *Political Humor in a Changing Media Landscape*, eds. Jody C. Baumgartner and Amy B. Becker. Lanham, MD: Lexington.

Eggerton, John. 2005. "No CBS News for Stewart." *BroadcastingCable.com*, April 21. https://www.broadcastingcable.com/news/no-cbs-news-stewart-71445.

Elliott, Floyd. 2014. "Satire Is What Closes on Saturday Night: The Outrage of #CancelColbert." *Huffington Post*, May 28. http://www.huffingtonpost.com/floyd-elliot/satire-is-what-closes-on-_b_5052046.html.

Epstein, Kayla. 2019. "Jimmy Kimmel Made Up a Song to Help You Remember All the 2020 Candidates." *Washington Post*, May 29. https://www.washingtonpost.com/arts-entertainment/2019/05/29/jimmy-kimmel-made-up-song-help-you-remember-all-candidates/?utm_term=.134ee918d602.

Eskenazi, Gerald. 1984. "USFL Votes to Switch to Playing Fall Schedule." *New York Times*, August 23. https://www.nytimes.com/1984/08/23/sports/usfl-votes-to-switch-to-playing-fall-schedule.html?searchResultPosition=3.

Farnsworth, Stephen J. 2001. "Patterns of Political Support: Examining Congress and the Presidency." *Congress & the Presidency* 28(1): 45–60.

Farnsworth, Stephen J. 2003a. *Political Support in a Frustrated America*. Westport, CT: Praeger.

Farnsworth, Stephen J. 2003b. "Congress and Citizen Discontent: Public Evaluations of the Membership and One's Own Representative." *American Politics Research* 31(1): 66–80.

Farnsworth, Stephen J. 2009. *Spinner in Chief: How Presidents Sell Their Policies and Themselves*. Boulder, CO: Paradigm.

Farnsworth, Stephen J. 2018. *Presidential Communication and Character: White House News Management from Clinton and Cable to Twitter and Trump*. New York: Routledge.

Farnsworth, Stephen J., and S. Robert Lichter. 2004. "Increasing Candidate-Centered Televised Discourse: Evaluating Local News Coverage of Campaign 2000." *Harvard International Journal of Press/Politics* 9(2): 76–93.

Farnsworth, Stephen J., and S. Robert Lichter. 2005. "Local Television News and Campaign 2000: Assessing Efforts to Increase Substantive Content." *Politics & Policy* 33(3): 496–520.

Farnsworth, Stephen J., and S. Robert Lichter. 2006. *The Mediated Presidency: Television News and Presidential Governance*. Lanham, MD: Rowman & Littlefield.

Farnsworth, Stephen J., and S. Robert Lichter. 2011a. *The Nightly News Nightmare: Media Coverage of US Presidential Elections, 1988–2008*. Lanham, MD: Rowman & Littlefield. Third Edition.

Farnsworth, Stephen J., and S. Robert Lichter. 2011b. "The Return of the Honeymoon: Television News Coverage of New Presidents, 1981–2009." *Presidential Studies Quarterly* 41: 590–603.

Farnsworth, Stephen J., and S. Robert Lichter. 2012a. "News Coverage of New Presidents in the New York Times, 1981–2009." *Politics & Policy* 40(1): 69–91.

Farnsworth, Stephen J., and S. Robert Lichter. 2012b. "Authors' Response: Improving News Coverage in the 2012 Presidential Campaign and Beyond." *Politics & Policy* 40(4): 547–556 (August).

Farnsworth, Stephen J., and S. Robert Lichter. 2016. "News Coverage of US Presidential Campaigns: Reporting on Primaries and General Elections, 1988–2012." *The Praeger Handbook of Political Campaigning in the United States*, ed. William Benoit. Santa Barbara, CA: Praeger, pp. 233–253 (Volume 1).

Farnsworth, Stephen J., and S. Robert Lichter. 2018. "Dominating Late Night: Political Humor and the Donald Trump Presidency." Paper presented at the American Political Science Association Pre-Conference in Political Communication. Boston, MA. August.

Farnsworth, Stephen J., S. Robert Lichter, and Deanne Canieso. 2017. "Donald Trump Will Probably Be the Most Ridiculed President Ever." *Washington Post*, January 21. https://www.washingtonpost.com/news/monkey-cage/wp/2017/01/21/donald-trump-will-probably-be-the-most-ridiculed-president-ever/?utm_term=.98d31b3485e9.

Farnsworth, Stephen J., S. Robert Lichter, and Deanne Canieso. 2018. "Donald Trump and the Late-Night Political Humor of Campaign 2016: All the Donald All the Time." In *The Presidency and Social Media: Discourse, Disruption and Digital Democracy in the 2016 Presidential Election*, eds. Dan Schill and John Allen Hendricks. New York: Routledge, pp. 330–345.

Feldman, Lauren. 2013. "Learning about Politics from *The Daily Show*: The Role of Viewer Orientations and Processing Mechanisms." *Mass Communication and Society* 16(4): 586–607.

Feldman, Lauren, and Dannagal G. Young. 2005. "Late-Night Comedy as a Gateway to Traditional News." *Political Communication* 25: 401–422.

Fisher, Marc. 2018. "Master of Celebrity: How Trump Uses—and Bashes—the Famous to Boost Himself." *Washington Post*, June 21. https://www.washingtonpost.com/lifestyle/style/master-of-celebrity-how-trump-uses–and-bashes–the-famous-to-boost-himself/2018/06/20/fef51c98-6b33-11e8-bf8c-f9ed2e672adf_story.html?utm_term=.6139373ec115.

Fisher, Marc, John Woodrow Cox and Peter Hermann. 2016. "Pizzagate: From Rumor, to Hashtag, to Gunfire in D.C." *Washington Post*, December 6. https://www.washingtonpost.com/local/pizzagate-from-rumor-to-hashtag-to-gunfire-in-dc/2016/12/06/4c7def50-bbd4-11e6-94ac-3d324840106c_story.html?utm_term=.f26c611c40e1.

Fox, Julia R. 2018. "Journalist or Jokester: An Analysis of Last Week Tonight with John Oliver." In *Still Good for a Laugh? Political Humor in a Changing Media Landscape*, eds. Jody Baumgartner and Amy Becker. Lanham, MD: Lexington Books, pp. 29–44.

France, Lisa Respers. 2017. "Jimmy Kimmel Tearfully Reveals Son's Health Crisis." *CNN*, May 3. https://www.cnn.com/2017/05/02/entertainment/jimmy-kimmel-baby-surgery/index.html.

Franzen, Carl. 2009. "Which Way Does Leno Lean?" *The Atlantic*, September 27. https://www.theatlantic.com/entertainment/archive/2009/09/which-way-does-leno-lean/348011/.

Freedman, Samuel G. 1987. "Trump Feud: Barbs Show Deeper Split." *New York Times*, July 6. https://www.nytimes.com/1987/07/06/nyregion/trump-feud-barbs-show-deeper-split.html?searchResultPosition=114.

Freud, Sigmund. 2003. *The Joke and Its Relation to the Unconscious*. Translated by J. Carey. New York: Penguin Books (originally published in 1905).

Fromm, Erich. 1941. *Escape from Freedom*. New York: Henry Holt & Co.

*Full Frontal*. 2016a. "Nativist Son." YouTube Video, 6:11. June 20. https://www.youtube.com/watch?v=A98QTdzyZA8.

*Full Frontal*. 2016b. "GÖP-erdämmerung." YouTube Video, 7:40. July 25. https://www.youtube.com/watch?v=zQuFPxCb-_o.

*Full Frontal*. 2016c. "This Week in WTF: Latinos for Trump." YouTube Video, 6:02. September 12. https://www.youtube.com/watch?v=cYgo4gsD-38.

*Full Frontal*. 2016d. "A Totally Real, 100% Valid Theory." Full Frontal with Samantha Bee." YouTube Video, 8:35. October 31. https://www.youtube.com/watch?v=7LFkN7QGp2c.

*Full Frontal*. 2016e. "The Morning After." YouTube Video, 7:41, November 9. https://www.youtube.com/watch?v=s1SaD-gSZO4.

*Full Frontal*. 2016f. "Something that Actually 'Existed': Trump Policy Shop." YouTube Video, 6:01. November 9. https://www.youtube.com/watch?v=sxf4dFINMTY.

*Full Frontal*. 2016g. "Steve Bannon: Trump's Alt-Right Hand Man." YouTube Video, 4:17, November 14. https://www.youtube.com/watch?v=dbKT22idntg.

*Full Frontal*. 2016h. "Trump's New Cabinet Installation." YouTube Video, 4:48, November 14. https://www.youtube.com/watch?v=yve_oz-D5nI.

*Full Frontal*. 2016i. "Sore Winners." YouTube Video, 4:43, November 14. https://www.youtube.com/watch?v=XpDjqbPyqRM.

*Full Frontal*. 2016j. "The Big Lie." YouTube Video, 6:47, December 5. https://www.youtube.com/watch?v=Z4jz4mLvsWY.

*Full Frontal*. 2017a. "Coronation Street." YouTube Video, 7:30. January 25. https://www.youtube.com/watch?v=k1AvNnJRMts.

*Full Frontal*. 2017b. "Who March the World? Girls." YouTube Video, 8:10. January 25. https://www.youtube.com/watch?v=kY6aUo2PkaM.

*Full Frontal*. 2017c. "The Not-A-Muslim-Ban Muslim Ban." YouTube Video, 7:12. February 1. https://www.youtube.com/watch?v=4RM2HtvLSLs.

*Full Frontal*. 2017d. "Donald and the Terrible, Horrible, No Good, Very Bad Sanctuary Cities." YouTube Video, 8:12. February 8. https://www.youtube.com/watch?v=vypzrtAHyXk.

*Full Frontal*. 2017e. "Heir to the White House Throne." YouTube Video, 7:05. April 5. https://www.youtube.com/watch?v=AzeL_8bdrQA.

*Full Frontal*. 2017f. "We Told You So: Russian Hacking." YouTube Video, 6:47. April 5. https://www.youtube.com/watch?v=L6tVjqflXFY.

*Full Frontal*. 2017g. "Dr. Sebastian L. v. Gorka, Trump Whisperer." YouTube Video, 7:26. April 12. https://www.youtube.com/watch?v=398HJb0_PFg.

*Full Frontal*. 2017h. "AHCA: Winners & Die-ers." YouTube Video, 6:14. May 10. https://www.youtube.com/watch?v=DeAziTKb7vQ.

*Full Frontal*. 2017i. "Our Weekly Constitutional Crisis: Comey Edition." YouTube Video, 6:48. May 10. https://www.youtube.com/watch?v=3NxenCGfxEk.

*Full Frontal*. 2017j. "The War on Drugs Reboot." YouTube Video, 7:19. June 7. https://www.youtube.com/watch?v=Ex-hyHZulNY.

*Full Frontal*. 2017k. "The Mooch Will Set Trump Free." YouTube Video, 7:12, July 26. https://www.youtube.com/watch?v=kY6aUo2PkaM.

*Full Frontal*. 2017l. "John Kelly Is NOT the Adult." YouTube Video, 5:44. November 1. https://www.youtube.com/watch?v=F8-pY3n3MAs.

Garber, Megan. 2009. "Shocker of the Day: Stewart (Still) Most Trusted Newscaster in America." *Columbia Journalism Review*, July 23. http://archives.cjr.org/the_kicker/shocker_of_the_day_stewart_sti.php.

Garber, Megan. 2018. "Forgiving Jimmy Kimmel: It's a Thoroughly Modern Irony: The Host Who Will Set the Tone for the #MeToo Oscars Got His Start on a Show that Gleefully Ogled Women." *The Atlantic*, March 2. https://www.theatlantic.com/entertainment/archive/2018/03/forgiving-jimmy-kimmel/554675/.

Geist, William E. 1984. "The Expanding Empire of Donald Trump." *New York Times*, April 8. https://www.nytimes.com/1984/04/08/magazine/the-expanding-empire-of-donald-trump.html?searchResultPosition=57.

Geist, William E. 1986. "Pssst, Here's a Secret: Trump Rebuilds Ice Rink." *New York Times*, November 15. https://www.nytimes.com/1986/11/15/nyregion/about-new-york-pssst-here-s-a-secret-trump-rebuilds-ice-rink.html?searchResultPosition=6.

Geer, John G. 2006. *In Defense of Negativity: Attack Ads in Presidential Campaigns*. Chicago, IL: University of Chicago Press.

Gergen, David. 2000. *Eyewitness to Power: The Essence of Leadership*. New York: Simon & Schuster.

Gilbert, Joanne R. 2004. *Performing Marginality: Humor, Gender, and Cultural Critique*. Detroit, MI: Wayne State University Press.

Grill, Christiane. 2018. "What is Funny to Whom? Applying an Integrative Theoretical Framework to the Study of Political Humor Appreciation." In *Political Humor in a Changing Media Landscape*, eds. Jody C. Baumgartner and Amy B. Becker. Lanham, MD: Lexington.

Grynbaum, Michael M. 2019. "Fox News Welcomes Pete Buttigieg. Trump and 'Fox & Friends' Aren't Pleased." *New York Times*, May 20. https://www.nytimes.com/2019/05/20/business/media/fox-news-pete-buttigieg-chris-wallace.html?searchResultPosition=3.

Goodwin, Doris Kearns. 1994. *No Ordinary Time*. New York: Simon & Schuster.

Gould, Jack 1968. "Laugh-in Team Back with a Nixon Line." *New York Times*, September 17, p. 95.

Green, Joshua. 2017. *Devil's Bargain: Steve Bannon, Donald Trump and the Storming of the Presidency*. New York: Penguin.

Greenberg, Jonathan. 2018. "Trump Lied to Me about His Wealth to Get onto the Forbes 400. Here Are the Tapes." *Washington Post*, April 20. https://www.washingtonpost.com/outlook/trump-lied-to-me-about-his-wealth-to-get-onto-the-forbes-400-here-are-the-tapes/2018/04/20/ac762b08-4287-11e8-8569-26fda6b404c7_story.html?utm_term=.44a2d0cd1026.

Greene, Viceca. 2011. "Critique, Counternarratives, and Ironic Intervention in 'South Park' and Stephen Colbert." In *A Decade of Dark Humor: How Comedy, Irony, and Satire Shaped Post-9/11 America*, eds. Viveca Greene and Ted Gournelos. Jackson, MI: University of Mississippi Press.

Greene, Viceca and Ted Gournelos. 2011. "Popular Culture and Post-9/11 Politics." In *A Decade of Dark Humor: How Comedy, Irony, and Satire Shaped Post-9/11 America*, eds. Viveca Greene and Ted Gournelos. Jackson, MI: University of Mississippi Press.

Gurney, David. 2011. "Everything Changes Forever (Temporarily): Late Night Television Comedy after 9/11." In *A Decade of Dark Humor: How Comedy, Irony, and Satire Shaped*

*Post-9/11 America*, eds. Viveca Greene and Ted Gournelos. Jackson, MI: University of Mississippi Press.

Habermas, Jurgen. 1973. *Legitimation Crisis*. Translated by Thomas McCarthy. Boston, MA: Beacon Press.

Halbfinger, David M. 1997. "Death Penalty Will Stand, Court Rules." *New York Times*, December 23. https://www.nytimes.com/1997/12/23/nyregion/death-penalty-will-stand-court-rules.html?searchResultPosition=9.

Hartung, Adam. 2017. "Colbert Beat Fallon By Following Trends, Which Will Make CBS More Money." *Forbes*, September 28. https://www.forbes.com/sites/adamhartung/2017/09/28/colbert-beat-fallon-by-following-trends-which-will-make-cbs-more-money/#3a1464b926ef.

Hesse, Josiah. 2013. "Why Does Every 'Conservative Daily Show' Fail?" *Vulture*, December 2. https://www.vulture.com/2013/12/why-does-every-conservative-daily-show-fail.html.

Hetherington, Marc J., and Jonathan D. Weiler. 2009. *Authoritarianism and Polarization in American Politics*. Cambridge: Cambridge University Press.

Hibbing, John R., and Elizabeth Theiss-Morse. 1995. *Congress as Public Enemy: Public Attitudes towards American Political Institutions*. Cambridge, UK: Cambridge University Press.

Hoffman, Lindsay, and Tiffany Thomson. 2009. "The Effect of Television Viewing on Adolescents' Civic Participation: Political Efficacy as a Mediating Mechanism." *Journal of Broadcasting & Electronic Media* 53: 3–21.

Hopper, Jennifer R. 2017. *Presidential Framing in 21st Century News Media: The Politics of the Affordable Care Act*. New York: Routledge.

Hopper, Tristin. 2018. "The CIA Has Declassified a Bunch of Jokes. Here Are the Best Ones." *National Post*, September 20. https://nationalpost.com/news/the-cia-has-declassified-a-bunch-of-jokes-here-are-the-best-ones.

Huetteman, Emmarie and Yamiche Alcindor. 2017. "Betsy DeVos Confirmed as Education Secretary; Pence Breaks Tie." *New York Times*, February 7. https://www.nytimes.com/2017/02/07/us/politics/betsy-devos-education-secretary-confirmed.html.

Inglehart, Ronald. 1977. *The Silent Revolution*. Princeton, NJ: Princeton University Press.

Inglehart, Ronald. 1981. "Post-materialism in an Environment of Insecurity." *American Political Science Review* 75: 880–900.

Inglehart, Ronald. 1988. "The Renaissance of Political Culture." *American Political Science Review 82*: 1203–1230.

Inglehart, Ronald. 1990. *Culture Shift in Advanced Industrial Society*. Princeton, NJ: Princeton University Press.

Hardy, Bruce W., Jeffrey A. Gottfried, Kenneth M. Winneg, and Kathleen Hall Jamieson. 2014. "Stephen Colbert's Civics Lesson: How the Colbert SuperPAC Taught Viewers about Campaign Finance." *Mass Communication and Society* 17(3): 329–353.

Higgins, Andrew. 2019. "Ukraine Election: Comedian Dismissed by President Is Favored to Get Last Laugh." *New York Times*, April 20. https://www.nytimes.com/2019/04/20/world/europe/ukraine-election.html?searchResultPosition=1.

Higgins, Andrew, and Iuliia Mendel. 2019. "Ukraine Election: Volodymyr Zelensky, TV Comedian, Trounces President." *New York Times*, April 21. https://www.nytimes.com/2019/04/21/world/europe/Volodymyr-Zelensky-ukraine-elections.html?searchResultPosition=2.

Hurt, Harry, III. 1993. *Lost Tycoon: The Many Lives of Donald J. Trump*. New York: Norton.

Inside Edition. 2015. "Watch the Donald Trump Sketch That Was Mysteriously Deleted from 2004 SNL Episode." *Inside Edition*, October 15. https://www.insideedition.com/headlines/12399-watch-the-donald-trump-sketch-that-was-mysteriously-deleted-from-2004-snl-episode\.

Isikoff, Michael. 2000. *Uncovering Clinton: A Reporter's Story*. New York: Three Rivers Press.

Itzkoff, Dave. 2017. "Jimmy Fallon Was on Top of the World. Then Came Trump." *New York Times*, May 17. https://www.nytimes.com/2017/05/17/arts/television/jimmy-fallon-tonight-show-interview-trump.html.

Itzkoff, Dave. 2018. "Trump Slings Twitter Insults with Alec Baldwin, His *SNL* Impersonator." *New York Times*, March 2. https://www.nytimes.com/2018/03/02/arts/television/trump-alec-baldwin-snl.html.

Iyengar, Shanto, and Kyu S. Hahn. 2009. "Red Media, Blue Media: Evidence of Ideological Selectivity in Media Use." *Journal of Communication* 59: 19–39.

James, George. 1986. "Trump Drops 5-year Effort to Evict Tenants." *New York Times*, March 5. https://www.nytimes.com/1986/03/05/nyregion/trump-drops-5-year-effort-to-evict-tenants.html?searchResultPosition=88.

Kaczynski, Andrew, and Nathan McDermott. 2016. "Donald Trump Said a Lot of Gross Things About Women on 'Howard Stern'." *Buzzfeed*, February 24. https://www.buzzfeednews.com/article/andrewkaczynski/donald-trump-said-a-lot-of-gross-things-about-women-on-howar.

Kerr, Peter. 1984. "TV Notes: 2 New Cable Networks Being Planned." *New York Times*, January 30. https://www.nytimes.com/1984/01/30/movies/tv-notes-2-new-cable-networks-being-planned.html?searchResultPosition=2.

Kinsley, Michael. 1992. "Ask a Silly Question." *New Republic*, July 6.

Klemesrud, Judy. 1976. "Donald Trump, Real Estate Promoter, Builds Image as He Buys Buildings." *New York Times*, November 1. https://www.nytimes.com/1976/11/01/archives/donald-trump-real-estate-promoter-builds-image-as-he-buys-buildings.html?searchResultPosition=14.

Kolbert, Elizabeth. 1992. "The 1992 Campaign: Media; Whistle-stops a la 1992: Arsenio, Larry and Phil." *New York Times*, June 5. http://www.nytimes.com/1992/06/05/us/the-1992-campaign-media-whistle-stops-a-la-1992-arsenio-larry-and-phil.html.

Kolbin, John. 2017. "A Sharp Decline for Jimmy Fallon's *Tonight Show*." *New York Times*, November 28. https://www.nytimes.com/2017/11/28/business/media/jimmy-fallon-tonight-show-ratings-colbert-kimmel-decline.html.

Kruse, Kevin M., and Julian Zelizer. 2019. "Why Billionaires with Big Egos Now Dream of Being President." *Washington Post*, January 29. https://www.washingtonpost.com/outlook/2019/01/29/why-billionaires-with-big-egos-now-dream-being-president/?utm_term=.ff402cf20d87.

*Last Week Tonight*. 2016a. "Donald Trump." YouTube Video, 21:53. February 28. https://www.youtube.com/watch?v=DnpO_RTSNmQ.

*Last Week Tonight*. 2016b. "Border Wall." YouTube Video, 18:32, March 20. https://www.youtube.com/watch?v=vU8dCYocuyI.

*Last Week Tonight*. 2016c. "Republican National Convention." YouTube Video, 11:31, July 24. https://www.youtube.com/watch?v=zNdkrtfZP8I.

*Last Week Tonight*. 2016d. "Campaign Songs." YouTube Video, 7:25, July 24. https://www.youtube.com/watch?v=32n4h0kn-88.

*Last Week Tonight*. 2016e. "Democratic National Convention." YouTube Video, 18:09, July 31. https://www.youtube.com/watch?v=BUCnjlTfXDw.

*Last Week Tonight*. 2016f. "Scandals." YouTube Video, 21:15, September 25. https://www.youtube.com/watch?v=h1Lfd1aB9YI.

*Last Week Tonight*. 2016g. "President-Elect Trump." YouTube Video, 29:00. November 13. https://www.youtube.com/watch?v=-rSDUsMwakI.

*Last Week Tonight*. 2016h. "Trump University." YouTube Video, 12:37, November 29. https://www.youtube.com/watch?v=cBUeipXFisQ.

*Last Week Tonight*. 2017a. "Trump vs. Truth." YouTube Video, 23:49, February 12. https://www.youtube.com/watch?v=xecEV4dSAXE.

*Last Week Tonight*. 2017b. "American Health Care Act." YouTube Video, 18:30. March 12. https://www.youtube.com/watch?v=Ifi9M7DRazI.

*Last Week Tonight*. 2017c. "Federal Budget." YouTube Video, 12:04. March 19. https://www.youtube.com/watch?v=ySTQk6updjQ.

*Last Week Tonight*. 2017d. "Stupid Watergate." YouTube Video, 24:05. May 21. https://www.youtube.com/watch?v=FVFdsl29s_Q.

*Last Week Tonight*. 2017e. "Paris Agreement." YouTube Video, 20:57. June 4. https://www.youtube.com/watch?v=5scez5dqtAc.

*Last Week Tonight*. 2017f. "Coal." YouTube Video, 24:20. June 18. https://www.youtube.com/watch?v=aw6RsUhw1Q8.

*Last Week Tonight*. 2017g. "Alex Jones." YouTube Video, 22:21. July 30. https://www.youtube.com/watch?v=WyGq6cjcc3Q.

*Last Week Tonight*. 2017h. "North Korea." YouTube Video, 26:59. August 13. https://www.youtube.com/watch?v=TrS0uNBuG9c.

*Last Week Tonight*. 2017i. "The Trump Presidency." YouTube Video, 23:50. November 12. https://www.youtube.com/watch?v=1ZAPwfrtAFY.

Lee, Jasmine C., and Kevin Quealy. 2019. "The 567 People, Places and Things Donald Trump Has Insulted on Twitter: A Complete List." *New York Times*, February 20. https://www.nytimes.com/interactive/2016/01/28/upshot/donald-trump-twitter-insults.html.

Leonnig, Carol D. Adam Entous, Devlin Barrett, and Matt Zapotosky. 2017. "Michael Flynn Pleads Guilty to Lying to FBI on Contacts with Russian Ambassador." *Washington Post*, December 1. https://www.washingtonpost.com/politics/michael-flynn-charged-with-making-false-statement-to-the-fbi/2017/12/01/e03a6c48-d6a2-11e7-9461-ba77d604373d_story.html?utm_term=.4e8a11b25dce.

Lichter, S. Robert, Jody C. Baumgartner, and Jonathan S. Morris. 2015. *Politics is a Joke! How TV Comedians are Remaking Political Life*. Boulder, CO: Westview.

Lichter, S. Robert, and Stephen J. Farnsworth. (Forthcoming). "Late Night TV Humor and the Culture of Ridicule." In *The Routledge Handbook of Character Assassination and Reputation Management*, eds. Sergei A. Samoilenko, Martijn Icks, Jennifer Keohane, Eric B. Shiraev. London: Routledge.

Lichter, S. Robert, Stephen J. Farnsworth, and Deanne Canieso. 2016. "Late Night Tells 3 Times as Many Jokes About 2016 Republicans as Democrats." *Washington Post*, March 8. https://www.washingtonpost.com/news/the-fix/wp/2016/03/08/late-night-tells-3-times-as-many-jokes-about-2016-republicans-as-democrats/.

Liebovich, Louis W. 2001. *The Press and the Modern Presidency: Myths and Mindsets from Kennedy to Election 2000*. Westport, CT: Praeger.

MacWilliams, Matthew C. 2016. "Who Decides When the Party Doesn't? Authoritarian Voters and the Rise of Donald Trump." *PS: Political Science & Politics* 49: 716–721.

Manjoo, Farhad. 2017. "Can Facebook Fix Its Own Worst Bug?" *New York Times*, April 25. https://www.nytimes.com/2017/04/25/magazine/can-facebook-fix-its-own-worst-bug.html.

Mann, Thomas E., and Norman J. Ornstein. 2012. *It's Even Worse Than It Looks: How the American Constitutional System Collided with the New Politics of Extremism*. New York: Basic Books.

Martin, Jonathan. 2019. "'You Don't Have to Be in Des Moines.' Democrats Expand Primary Map, Spurred by Social Media." *New York Times*, June 1. https://www.nytimes.com/2019/06/01/us/politics/2020-democratic-primaries.html?searchResultPosition=1.

Martin, Rod A. 2007. *The Psychology of Humor: An Integrative Approach*. Burlington, MA: Elsevier Academic Press.

Marchese, David. 2019. "Stephen Colbert on the Political Targets of Satire." *New York Times Magazine*, June 2. https://www.nytimes.com/interactive/2019/06/03/magazine/stephen-colbert-politics-religion.html?searchResultPosition=1.

Martinelli, Marissa. 2016. "Obama Burns Trump, Sings Rihanna as He Slow Jams the News with Jimmy Fallon." *Slate*, June 10. http://www.slate.com/blogs/browbeat/2016/06/10/barack_obama_slow_jams_the_news_with_jimmy_fallon_slams_trump_video.html.

Mayer, Kenneth R., and David T. Canon. 1999. *The Dysfunctional Congress? The Individual Roots of an Institutional Dilemma*. Boulder, CO: Westview.

McClennen, Sophia A. 2018. "The Joke is on You: Satire and Blowback." In *Political Humor in a Changing Media Landscape*, eds. Jody C. Baumgartner and Amy B. Becker. Lanham, MD: Lexington.

McKain, Aaron. 2005. "Not Necessarily the News: Gatekeeping, Remediation and *The Daily Show*." *Journal of American Culture* 28(4): 415–430.

Media Monitor. 1991. Washington, DC: Center for Media and Public Affairs, November.

Merry, Stephanie. 2016. "No One Should Have Expected Jimmy Fallon to Go Tough on Trump. That was Letterman's Job." *Washington Post*, September 16. https://www.washingtonpost.com/news/arts-and-entertainment/wp/2016/09/16/no-one-should-have-expected-jimmy-fallon-to-go-tough-on-trump-that-was-lettermans-job/?utm_term=.ed2ca76e6e81.

Miller, Zeke, and Deb Riechmann. 2019. "Seeking Affirmation: Trump Has Aides Vouch He's 'Very Calm'." *Associated Press*, May 24. https://www.washingtonpost.com/politics/congress/iso-affirmation-trump-has-aides-vouch-that-hes-very-calm/2019/05/23/2d47af30-7dc5-11e9-b1f3-b233fe5811ef_story.html?utm_term=.b3baaeeadd07.

Mitchell, Amy, Jeffrey Gottfried, Jocelyn Kiley, and Katerina Eva Matsa. 2014. "Political Polarization and Media Habits." Pew Research Center. http://www.journalism.org/2014/10/21/political-polarization-media-habits/.

Morris, Jonathan S. 2009. "*The Daily Show* and Audience Attitude Change During the 2004 Party Conventions." *Political Behavior* 31: 79–102.

Morris, Jonathan S. 2018. "The Context for Comedy: Presidential Candidates and Comedy Television." In *Political Humor in a Changing Media Landscape*, eds. Jody C. Baumgartner and Amy B. Becker. Lanham, MD: Lexington.

Morris, Jonathan S. and Jody C. Baumgartner. 2008. "*The Daily Show* and Attitudes Toward the News Media." In *Laughing Matters: Humor and American Politics in the Media Age*, eds., Jody C. Baumgartner and Jonathan S. Morris. New York: Routledge.

Morrison, Oliver. 2015. "Waiting for the Conservative Jon Stewart: A Unified Theory of Why Political Satire Is Biased Toward, and Talk Radio Is Biased Against, Liberals in America." *The Atlantic*, February 14. https://www.theatlantic.com/entertainment/archive/2015/02/why-theres-no-conservative-jon-stewart/385480/.

Moy, Patricia, Michael Xenos, and Verena Hess. 2005. "Communication and Citizenship: Mapping the Political Effects of Infotainment." *Mass Communication & Society* 8: 111–131.

Nagourney, Adam. 1999. "A Question Trails Trump: Is He Really a Candidate?" *New York Times*, December 10. https://www.nytimes.com/1999/12/10/us/a-question-trails-trump-is-he-really-a-candidate.html?searchResultPosition=4.

Nagourney, Adam. 2000. "Reform Bid Said to Be a No-Go For Trump." *New York Times*, February 14. https://www.nytimes.com/2000/02/14/us/reform-bid-said-to-be-a-no-go-for-trump.html?searchResultPosition=1.

Nazaryan, Alexander. 2017. "Jimmy Kimmel Is Killing the Health Care Bill, and Delighting His Viewers in the Process." *Newsweek*, September 22. http://www.newsweek.com/jimmy-kimmel-bill-cassidy-obamacare-republicans-repeal-replace-669309.

Neustadt, Richard. 1990. *Presidential Power*. New York: Free Press.

Newport, Frank. 2016. "As Debate Looms, Voters Still Distrust Clinton and Trump." Gallup, release dated September 23. http://www.gallup.com/poll/195755/debate-looms-voters-distrust-clinton-trump.aspx?g_source=Obama+honest+and+trustworthy&g_medium=search&g_campaign=tiles.

Newport, Frank. 2017a. "U.S. Energy Concerns Continue to Diminish; Near Record Lows." Gallup, release dated March 10. https://news.gallup.com/poll/205754/energy-concerns-continue-diminish-near-record-low.aspx?utm_source=link_newsv9&utm_campaign=item_206681&utm_medium=copy.

Newport, Frank. 2017b. "Trump Disapproval Rooted in Character Concerns." Gallup, release dated July 13. http://www.gallup.com/poll/214091/trump-disapproval-rooted-character-concerns.aspx.

Niven, David, S. Robert Lichter, and Daniel Amundson. 2003. "The Political Content of Late-Night Comedy." *Harvard International Journal of Press/Politics* 8: 118–133.

O'Brien, David M. 1988. "The Reagan Judges: His Most Enduring Legacy?" In *The Reagan Legacy: Promise and Performance*, ed. Charles O. Jones. Chatham, NJ: Chatham House, pp. 60–101.

Owen, Diana. 2017. "Twitter Rants, Press Bashing, and Fake News: The Shameful Legacy of Media in the 2016 Election." In *Trumped: The 2016 Election That Broke All the Rules*, eds. Larry J. Sabato, Kyle Kondik, and Geoffrey Skelly. Lanham, MD: Rowman & Littlefield.

Pagliary, Jose. 2016. "Donald Trump Was a Nightmare Landlord in the 1980s." *CNN*, March 28. https://money.cnn.com/2016/03/28/news/trump-apartment-tenants/index.html.

Palmer, Jerry. 1988. *The Logic of the Absurd: On Film and Television Comedy*. London: British Film Institute.

Parker, Ashley. 2010. "The Whole Truthiness and Nothing But." *New York Times*, September 24. https://thecaucus.blogs.nytimes.com/2010/09/24/the-whole-truthiness-and-nothing-but/?searchResultPosition=2.

Parker, Ashley. 2016. "Covering Donald Trump, and Witnessing the Danger Up Close." *New York Times*, March 12. https://www.nytimes.com/2016/03/13/us/politics/covering-donald-trump-and-witnessing-the-danger-up-close.html.

Parker, Ashley. 2018. "Real or 'Fake News'? Either Way, Allegations of Lewd Tape Pose Challenge for Trump." *Washington Post*, April 13. https://www.washingtonpost.com/politics/real-or-fake-news-either-way-lewd-tape-allegations-pose-a-challenge-for-trump/2018/04/13/098cdedc-3f2b-11e8-8d53-eba0ed2371cc_story.html?utm_term=.3f963d0513da.

Parker, Ashley, and Philip Rucker. 2019. "The 10 Personas of Donald Trump in a Single Speech." *Washington Post*, March 9. https://www.washingtonpost.com/news/national/

wp/2019/03/09/feature/the-10-personas-of-donald-trump-in-a-single-speech/?utm_term=.874211e813db.

Parkin, Michael. 2018. "The Context for Comedy: Presidential Candidates and Comedy Television." In *Still good for a laugh? Political Humor in a Changing Media Landscape*, eds. Jody Baumgartner and Amy Becker. Lanham, MD: Lexington Books.

Patterson, Thomas E. 1994. *Out of Order*. New York: Vintage.

Patterson, Thomas E. 2013. *Informing the News*. New York: Vintage.

Patterson, Thomas E. 2016. "News Coverage of the 2016 General Election: How the Press Failed the Voters." Shorenstein Center on Media, Politics and Public Policy, Kennedy School, Harvard University. Report dated December 7. https://shorensteincenter.org/news-coverage-2016-general-election/.

Petty, Richard E., and John T. Cacioppo. 1986. *Communication and Persuasion: Central and Peripheral Routes to Attitude Change*. New York: Springer-Verlag.

Pew Research Center. 2007. "Today's Journalists Less Prominent." Report dated March 8. http://www.people-press.org/2007/03/08/todays-journalists-less-prominent/.

Pew Research Center. 2014. "Political Polarization and Media Habits." Report dated October 21. http://www.journalism.org/2014/10/21/political-polarization-media-habits/.

Pew Research Center. 2016a. "The 2016 Presidential Campaign – a News Event That's Hard to Miss." Report dated February 4. http://www.journalism.org/2016/02/04/the-2016-presidential-campaign-a-news-event-thats-hard-to-miss/http://www.journalism.org/2016/02/04/the-2016-presidential-campaign-a-news-event-thats-hard-to-miss/.

Pew Research Center. 2016b. "Many Americans Believe Fake News Is Sowing Confusion." Report dated December 15. http://www.journalism.org/2016/12/15/many-americans-believe-fake-news-is-sowing-confusion/.

Pew Research Center. 2017. "Trump, Clinton Voters Divided in Their Main Source for Election News." http://www.journalism.org/2017/01/18/trump-clinton-voters-divided-in-their-main-source-for-election-news/.

Pogrebin, Robin. 1996. "52-Story Comeback Is So Very Trump;Columbus Circle Tower Proclaims That Modesty Is an Overrated Virtue." *New York Times*, April 25. https://www.nytimes.com/1996/04/25/nyregion/52-story-comeback-so-very-trump-columbus-circle-tower-proclaims-that-modesty.html?searchResultPosition=35.

Poniewozik, James. 2017. "Colbert Rides a Trump Wave, While Fallon Treads Water." *New York Times*, February 22. https://www.nytimes.com/2017/02/22/arts/television/colbert-fallon-trump-late-night.html.

Postman, Neil. 1985. *Amusing Ourselves to Death*. New York: Penguin.

Povoledo, Elisabetta. 2019. "Italy's Fading Five Star Movement Puts Its Leader on the Block." *New York Times*, May 30. https://www.nytimes.com/2019/05/30/world/europe/italy-five-star-di-maio-confidence-vote.html?searchResultPosition=1.

Prior, Markus. 2003. "Any Good News in Soft News? The Impact of Soft News Preferences on Political Knowledge." *Political Communication* 20: 149–171.

Prior, Markus. 2005. "News vs. Entertainment: How Increasing Media Choices Widen Gaps in Political Knowledge and Turnout." *American Journal of Political Science* 20: 149–171.

Purdum, Todd S. 1993. "Trump Pledge: In This Plaza, I Thee Wed." *New York Times*, December 18. https://www.nytimes.com/1993/12/18/nyregion/trump-pledge-in-this-plaza-i-thee-wed.html?searchResultPosition=16.

Putnam, Robert D. 2000. *Bowling Alone: The Collapse and Revival of American Community*. New York: Simon & Schuster.

Rosenwald, Michael S. 2018. "'Wouldn't Be Prudent': George H.W. Bush's Unlikely friendship with Dana Carvey." *Washington Post*, December 2. https://www.washingtonpost.com/news/retropolis/wp/2018/12/01/wouldnt-be-prudent-george-h-w-bushs-unlikely-friendship-with-dana-carvey/?utm_term=.52f754e7e80b.

Russonello, Giovanni. 2017. "Jimmy Kimmel Accuses Bill Cassidy, G.O.P. Senator Behind Health Bill, of Lying." *New York Times*, September 20. https://www.nytimes.com/2017/09/20/arts/television/jimmy-kimmel-test-bill-cassidy-health-care.html?searchResultPosition=2.

Russonello, Giovanni. 2019a. "Jimmy Kimmel Fires Back After Trump Attacks Late-Night Shows." *New York Times*, March 14. https://www.nytimes.com/2019/03/14/arts/television/jimmy-kimmel-trump-jay-leno.html?searchResultPosition=8.

Russonello, Giovanni. 2019b. "Jimmy Kimmel Slams Trump's Immigration Proposal." *New York Times*, May 17. https://www.nytimes.com/2019/05/17/arts/television/jimmy-kimmel-trump-immigration-proposal.html?searchResultPosition=2.

Rutenberg, Jim. 2017. "Colbert, Kimmel and the Politics of Late Night." *New York Times*, September 24. https://www.nytimes.com/2017/09/24/business/colbert-kimmel-and-the-politics-of-late-night.html.

Sabato, Larry J. 1993. *Feeding Frenzy: How Attack Journalism Has Transformed American Politics*. New York: Free Press.

Sabato, Larry J. 2017. "The 2016 Election That Broke All, or at Least Most, of the Rules." In *Trumped: The 2016 Election That Broke All the Rules*, eds. Larry J. Sabato, Kyle Kondik, and Geoffrey Skelly. Lanham, MD: Rowman & Littlefield.

Sabato, Larry J., Mark Stencel, and S. Robert Lichter. 2000. *Peepshow: Media and Politics in an Age of Scandal*. Lanham, MD: Rowman & Littlefield.

Sanford, Bruce. 1999. *Don't Shoot the Messenger: How Our Growing Hatred of the Media Threatens Free Speech for All of Us*. New York: Free Press.

*Saturday Night Live*. 2016a. "Palin Endorsement Cold Open." YouTube Video, 5:09. January 24. https://www.youtube.com/watch?v=0pinZNYxQeo.

*Saturday Night Live*. 2016b. "Voters for Trump Ad." YouTube Video, 1:25. March 6. https://www.youtube.com/watch?v=Qg0pO9VG1J8.

*Saturday Night Live*. 2016c. "At This Hour Cold Open." YouTube Video, 5:13. April 3. https://www.youtube.com/watch?v=r4q1L_JtMiI.

*Saturday Night Live*. 2016d. "Trumpémon GO." YouTube Video, 2:13. July 20. https://www.youtube.com/watch?v=y_7uw0LoZqs.

*Saturday Night Live*. 2016e. "Donald Trump vs. Hillary Clinton Debate Cold Open." YouTube Video, 9:45. October 1. https://www.youtube.com/watch?v=-nQGBZQrtT0.

*Saturday Night Live*. 2016f. "Donald Trump vs. Hillary Clinton Town Hall Debate Cold Open." YouTube Video, 8:26. October 16. https://www.youtube.com/watch?v=qVMW_1aZXRk.

*Saturday Night Live*. 2016g. "Donald Trump Prepares Cold Open." YouTube Video, 6:08. November 20. https://www.youtube.com/watch?v=JUWSLlz0Fdo.

*Saturday Night Live*. 2016h. "Donald Trump Christmas Cold Open." YouTube Video, 5:55, December 18. https://www.youtube.com/watch?v=3Ar80sFzViw.

*Saturday Night Live*. 2017a. "Vladimir Putin Cold Open." YouTube Video, 4:05. January 22. https://www.youtube.com/watch?v=LNK430YOiT4.

*Saturday Night Live*. 2017b. "Sean Spicer Press Conference (Melissa McCarthy)." YouTube Video, 8:06. February 5. https://www.youtube.com/watch?v=UWuc18xISwI.

*Saturday Night Live*. 2017c. "Weekend Update on Donald Trump's Executive Orders." YouTube Video, 5:12. February 5. https://www.youtube.com/watch?v=RD9hzW3_xE8.

*Saturday Night Live*. 2017d. "Trump People's Court." YouTube Video, 4:53. February 12. https://www.youtube.com/watch?v=dLYfwprjtog.

*Saturday Night Live*. 2017e. "Weekend Update on the Ninth Circuit Court's Ruling." YouTube Video, 7:38. February 12. https://www.youtube.com/watch?v=Q-iX_G-nosc.

*Saturday Night Live*. 2017f. "Through Donald's Eyes." YouTube Video, 2:13. February 25. https://www.youtube.com/watch?v=rJ6WuWeBoY8.

*Saturday Night Live*. "2017g. "Weekend Update on Trumpcare." YouTube Video, 4:26. March 12. https://www.youtube.com/watch?v=gGtOWYAjZWY.

*Saturday Night Live*. 2017h. "Weekend Update on Donald Trump's Syria Missile Strike." YouTube Video, 4:55. April 9. https://www.youtube.com/watch?v=ttAbFhnIVog.

*Saturday Night Live*. 2017i. "Weekend Update on Failed North Korean Missile Launch." YouTube Video, 5:49. April 15. https://www.youtube.com/watch?v=2MFIRoHHg3g.

*Saturday Night Live*. 2017j. "Weekend Update on Comey's Investigation into Trump." YouTube Video, 5:47. May 20. https://www.youtube.com/watch?v=Rdskdey9uns.

*Saturday Night Live*. 2017k. "Kellywise." YouTube Video, 3:59. October 14. https://www.youtube.com/watch?v=Hlt3rA-oDao.

*Saturday Night Live*. 2017l. "Paul Manafort's House Cold Open." YouTube Video, 5:19. November 4. https://www.youtube.com/watch?v=spkflpPmPgs.

Scacco, Joshua, and Kevin Coe. 2016. "The Ubiquitous Presidency: Toward a New Paradigm for Studying Presidential Communication." *International Journal of Communication* 10: 2014–2037.

Schier, Steven E., and Todd E. Eberly. 2017. *The Trump Presidency: Outsider in the Oval Office*. Lanham, MD: Rowman & Littlefield.

Schwartz, Alex F. 2014. *Housing Policy in the United States*. New York: Routledge. Third Edition.

Schwartz, John. 2011. "Will Rogers, Populist Cowboy." *New York Times*, March 25. https://www.nytimes.com/2011/03/27/books/review/book-review-will-rogers-a-political-life-by-richard-d-white-jr.html.

Segal, David. 2004. "His Casino Business May Be Down, But Donald Trump Is on a Roll." *Washington Post*, September 9. https://www.washingtonpost.com/politics/his-casino-business-may-be-down-but-donald-trump-is-on-a-roll/2016/08/01/522c07ec-5811-11e6-9aee-8075993d73a2_story.html?utm_term=.65a28053df9f.

Shales, Tom. 1987a. "Che-e-e-e-ers Johnny!" *Washington Post*, October 1. https://www.washingtonpost.com/archive/lifestyle/1987/10/01/che-e-e-e-e-rs-johnny/62a6581a-244b-4e2c-80ff-c88534ae431e/?utm_term=.e34268697539.

Shales, Tom. 1987b. "The Bork Turnoff." *Washington Post*, October 9. https://www.washingtonpost.com/archive/lifestyle/1987/10/09/the-bork-turnoff/5342ccb1-404c-4540-92af-7f5a4b6b9b82/?utm_term=.3a5373369b73.

Skocpol, Theda. 1997. *Boomerang: Health Care Reform and the Turn Against Government*. New York: Norton.

Skocpol, Theda, and Vanessa Williamson. 2012. *The Tea Party and the Remaking of Republican Conservatism*. Oxford: Oxford University Press.

Sinderbrand, Rebecca. 2017. "How Kellyanne Conway Ushered in the Era of 'Alternative Facts'." *Washington Post*, January 22. https://www.washingtonpost.com/news/the-fix/

wp/2017/01/22/how-kellyanne-conway-ushered-in-the-era-of-alternative-facts/?utm_term=.389b286aa787.

Sniderman, Paul M. 1981. *A Question of Loyalty*. Berkeley, CA: University of California Press.

Stanley, Alessandra. 2004. "No Jokes or Spin. It's Time (Gasp) to Talk." *New York Times*, October 20. https://www.nytimes.com/2004/10/20/arts/television/no-jokes-or-spin-its-time-gasp-to-talk.html.

Stelter, Brian. 2010. "Final Tallies for 'Sanity' Rally." *New York Times*, November 1. https://thecaucus.blogs.nytimes.com/2010/11/01/final-tallies-for-sanity-rally/?searchResultPosition=6.

Stetler, Brian. 2012. "Colbert for President: A Run or a Comedy Riff?" *New York Times*, January 12. https://www.nytimes.com/2012/01/13/us/politics/stephen-colbert-to-explore-or-pretend-to-run-for-president.html?searchResultPosition=4.

Stelter, Brian. 2019. "Welcome to the Stephen Colbert Primary." *CNN*, January 14. https://www.cnn.com/2019/01/14/media/stephen-colbert-primary/index.html.

Stewart, Patrick A., Reagan G. Dye, and Austin D. Eubanks. 2018. "The Political Ethology of Debate Humor and Audience Laughter: Understanding Donald Trump, Hillary Clinton and Their Audiences." In *Political Humor in a Changing Media Landscape*, eds. Jody C. Baumgartner and Amy B. Becker. Lanham, MD: Lexington.

Stromer-Galley, Jennifer. 2014. *Presidential Campaigning in the Internet Age*. Oxford: Oxford University Press.

Stroud, Natalie J. 2008. "Media Use and Political Predispositions: Revisiting the Concept of Selective Exposure." *Political Behavior* 30(3): 341–366.

Sullivan, Margaret. 2019. "Trump Won't Stop Coining Nasty Nicknames for His Foes — But the Media Must Stop Amplifying Them." *Washington Post*, May 16. https://www.washingtonpost.com/lifestyle/style/trump-wont-stop-coining-nasty-nicknames-for-his-foes–but-the-media-must-stop-amplifying-them/2019/05/15/fa49cb52-7727-11e9-b3f5-5673edf2d127_story.html?utm_term=.0883ca48f7be.

Swanson, Ana. 2016. "The Myth and the Reality of Donald Trump's Business Empire." *Washington Post*, February 29. www.washingtonpost.com/news/wonk/wp/2016/02/29/the-myth-and-the-reality-of-donald-trumps-business-empire/?utm_term=.16baf08342dc.

Taber, Charles S., and Milton Lodge. 2006. "Motivated Scepticism in the Evaluation of Political Beliefs." *American Journal of Political Science* 50: 755–769.

Toto, Christian. 2014. "Goodnight, Jay. Leno Last Fair, Balanced Late Night Host." *Breitbart.com*, February 6. http://www.breitbart.com/big-hollywood/2014/02/06/leno-last-fair-balanced-late-night/.

Traub, James. 2004. "Trumpologies." *New York Times*, September 12. https://www.nytimes.com/2004/09/12/magazine/trumpologies.html?searchResultPosition=40.

Tropiano, Stephen. 2013. *Saturday Night Live FAQ: Everything Left to Know About Television's Longest-Running Comedy*. Montclair, NJ: Applause.

Trump, Donald J., with Charles Leerhsen. 1990. *Trump: Surviving at the Top*. New York: Random House.

Trump, Donald J., with Kate Bohner. 1997. *Trump: The Art of the Comeback*. New York: Times Books.

Trump, Donald J., with Tony Schwartz. 2004. [originally 1987]. *Trump: The Art of the Deal*. New York: Grand Central Publishing.

Tyler, Tom R. 1988. "What is Procedural Justice?" *Law & Society Review* 22(1): 103–135.

Tyler, Tom R., and Kenneth A. Rasinksi. 1991. "Procedural Justice, Institutional Legitimacy and the Acceptance of unpopular U.S. Supreme Court Decisions: A Reply to Gibson." *Law & Society Review* 25(3): 621–630.

Tynan, Kenneth. 1978. "Fifteen Years of the Salto Mortale." *The New Yorker*, February 20.

Unger, David. 2013. "Europe's Social Contract, Lying in Pieces." *New York Times*, June 8. https://www.nytimes.com/2013/06/09/opinion/sunday/europes-social-contract-lying-in-pieces.html?searchResultPosition=9.

Van Luling, Todd. 2017. "This Aggressive Ad for Trump's '90s Game Show Seems Just Like His Campaign." *HuffPost*, March 10. https://www.huffpost.com/entry/trump-card-gameshow_n_58c06960e4b054a0ea67787e.

Warner, Jamie. 2007. "Political Culture Jamming: The Dissident Humor of *The Daily Show with Jon Stewart*." *Popular Communication* 5: 17–36.

Waisanen, Don J. 2018. "The Rise of Advocacy Satire." In *Still Good for a Laugh? Political Humor in a Changing Media Landscape*, eds. Jody Baumgartner and Amy Becker. Lanham, MD: Lexington Books, pp. 11–27.

Walder, Joyce. 1999. "A Model as First Lady? Think Traditional." *New York Times*, December 1. https://www.nytimes.com/1999/12/01/nyregion/public-lives-a-model-as-first-lady-think-traditional.html?searchResultPosition=32.

Walsh, Katherine Cramer. 2012. "Putting Inequality in Its Place: Rural Consciousness and the Power of Perspective." *American Political Science Review* 106(3): 517–532.

Wayne, Stephen. J. 2000. "Presidential Personality and the Clinton Legacy." In *The Clinton Scandals and the Future of American Government*, eds. Mark J. Rozell and Clyde Wilcox. Washington, DC: Georgetown University Press, pp. 211–224.

Weber, Bruce. 1997. "Donald and Marla Are Headed for Divestiture." *New York Times*, May 3. https://www.nytimes.com/1997/05/03/nyregion/donald-and-marla-are-headed-for-divestiture.html?searchResultPosition=27.

Weinraub, Bernard. 1992. "Fade Out for Johnny Carson, His Dignity and Privacy Intact." *New York Times*, May 23. https://www.nytimes.com/1992/05/23/arts/fade-out-for-johnny-carson-his-dignity-and-privacy-intact.html.

Williamson, Vanessa, Theda Skocpol, and John Coggin. 2011. "The Tea Party and the Remaking of Republican Conservatism." *Perspectives on Politics* 9(1): 25–43.

Wilson, Michael. 2002. "Trump Draws Criticism for Ad He Ran After Jogger Attack." *New York Times*, October 23. https://www.nytimes.com/2002/10/23/nyregion/trump-draws-criticism-for-ad-he-ran-after-jogger-attack.html?searchResultPosition=13.

Winter, Aaron. 2011. "Laughing Doves: U.S. Anti-war Satire from Niagara to Fallujah." In *A Decade of Dark Humor: How Comedy, Irony, and Satire Shaped Post-9/11 America*, eds. Viveca Greene and Ted Gournelos. Jackson, MI: University of Mississippi Press.

Wootson, Cleve R., Jr. 2017. "Donald Trump Was Proud of His 1990 Playboy Cover. Hugh Hefner, Not So Much." *Washington Post*, September 28. https://www.washingtonpost.com/news/arts-and-entertainment/wp/2017/09/28/donald-trump-was-proud-of-his-1990-playboy-cover-hugh-hefner-not-so-much/?utm_term=.3670b61f1ebf.

Xenos, Michael, and Amy Becker. 2009. "Moments of Zen: Effects of *The Daily Show* on Information Seeking and Political Learning." *Political Communication* 26: 317–332.

Yahr, Emily. 2017a. "Jimmy Kimmel Gets Heated About Health-Care Bill, Says Sen. Bill Cassidy 'Lied Right to My Face'." *Washington Post*, September 20. https://www.washingtonpost.com/news/arts-and-entertainment/wp/2017/09/19/jimmy-kimmel-gets-heated-about-health-care-bill-says-bill-cassidy-lied-right-to-my-face/?utm_term=.d10135d96e9b.

Yahr, Emily. 2017b. "Jimmy Kimmel doubles down, slams Sen. Bill Cassidy, Trump and 'Fox & Friends' Over Health-care Bill." *Washington Post*, September 21. https://www.washingtonpost.com/news/arts-and-entertainment/wp/2017/09/21/jimmy-kimmel-doubles-down-slams-sen-bill-cassidy-trump-and-fox-friends-over-health-care-bill/?utm_term=.03aa8d70b369.

Young, Dannagal. 2004. "Late-night Comedy in Election 2000: Its Influence on Candidate Trait Ratings and the Moderating Effects of Political Knowledge and Partisanship." *Journal of Broadcasting & Electronic Media* 48(1): 1–22.

Young, Dannagal. 2006. "Late-night Comedy and the Salience of the Candidates Caricatured Traits in the 2000 Election." *Mass Communication and Society* 9: 339–366.

Young, Dannagal. 2013. "Laughter, Learning or Enlightenment? Viewing and Avoidance Motivations Behind *The Daily Show* and *The Colbert Report*." *Journal of Broadcasting & Electronic Media* 57(2): 153–169.

Young, Dannagal, Benjamin Bogozzi, Abigail Goldrin, Shannon Paulsen, and Erin Drouin. 2019. "Psychology, Political Identity, and Humor Appreciation: Why is Satire So Liberal?" *Psychology of Popular Media Culture* 8(2): 134–147.

# INDEX

Note: Information in tables is indicated by page numbers in **bold.**